C-4827   CAREER EXAMINATION SERIES

This is your
PASSBOOK for...

HVAC Technician

Test Preparation Study Guide
Questions & Answers

NATIONAL LEARNING CORPORATION®

COPYRIGHT NOTICE

This book is SOLELY intended for, is sold ONLY to, and its use is RESTRICTED to individual, bona fide applicants or candidates who qualify by virtue of having seriously filed applications for appropriate license, certificate, professional and/or promotional advancement, higher school matriculation, scholarship, or other legitimate requirements of education and/or governmental authorities.

This book is NOT intended for use, class instruction, tutoring, training, duplication, copying, reprinting, excerption, or adaptation, etc., by:

1) Other publishers
2) Proprietors and/or Instructors of "Coaching" and/or Preparatory Courses
3) Personnel and/or Training Divisions of commercial, industrial, and governmental organizations
4) Schools, colleges, or universities and/or their departments and staffs, including teachers and other personnel
5) Testing Agencies or Bureaus
6) Study groups which seek by the purchase of a single volume to copy and/or duplicate and/or adapt this material for use by the group as a whole without having purchased individual volumes for each of the members of the group
7) Et al.

Such persons would be in violation of appropriate Federal and State statutes.

PROVISION OF LICENSING AGREEMENTS – Recognized educational, commercial, industrial, and governmental institutions and organizations, and others legitimately engaged in educational pursuits, including training, testing, and measurement activities, may address request for a licensing agreement to the copyright owners, who will determine whether, and under what conditions, including fees and charges, the materials in this book may be used them. In other words, a licensing facility exists for the legitimate use of the material in this book on other than an individual basis. However, it is asseverated and affirmed here that the material in this book CANNOT be used without the receipt of the express permission of such a licensing agreement from the Publishers. Inquiries re licensing should be addressed to the company, attention rights and permissions department.

All rights reserved, including the right of reproduction in whole or in part, in any form or by any means, electronic or mechanical, including photocopying, recording, or by any information storage and retrieval system, without permission in writing from the Publisher.

Copyright © 2024 by
National Learning Corporation

212 Michael Drive, Syosset, NY 11791
(516) 921-8888 • www.passbooks.com
E-mail: info@passbooks.com

PUBLISHED IN THE UNITED STATES OF AMERICA

PASSBOOK® SERIES

THE *PASSBOOK® SERIES* has been created to prepare applicants and candidates for the ultimate academic battlefield – the examination room.

At some time in our lives, each and every one of us may be required to take an examination – for validation, matriculation, admission, qualification, registration, certification, or licensure.

Based on the assumption that every applicant or candidate has met the basic formal educational standards, has taken the required number of courses, and read the necessary texts, the *PASSBOOK® SERIES* furnishes the one special preparation which may assure passing with confidence, instead of failing with insecurity. Examination questions – together with answers – are furnished as the basic vehicle for study so that the mysteries of the examination and its compounding difficulties may be eliminated or diminished by a sure method.

This book is meant to help you pass your examination provided that you qualify and are serious in your objective.

The entire field is reviewed through the huge store of content information which is succinctly presented through a provocative and challenging approach – the question-and-answer method.

A climate of success is established by furnishing the correct answers at the end of each test.

You soon learn to recognize types of questions, forms of questions, and patterns of questioning. You may even begin to anticipate expected outcomes.

You perceive that many questions are repeated or adapted so that you can gain acute insights, which may enable you to score many sure points.

You learn how to confront new questions, or types of questions, and to attack them confidently and work out the correct answers.

You note objectives and emphases, and recognize pitfalls and dangers, so that you may make positive educational adjustments.

Moreover, you are kept fully informed in relation to new concepts, methods, practices, and directions in the field.

You discover that you are actually taking the examination all the time: you are preparing for the examination by "taking" an examination, not by reading extraneous and/or supererogatory textbooks.

In short, this PASSBOOK®, used directedly, should be an important factor in helping you to pass your test.

HVAC TECHNICIAN

DUTIES:
This work involves responsibility, on an assigned shift, for the operation of computerized energy systems and the maintenance and repair of automatic temperature control systems, absorption chillers, compressors, cooling towers, refrigeration equipment and mechanical heating, ventilating, air conditioning, and refrigeration (HVAC) equipment, or any other related systems and equipment. Work is performed under general supervision and supervision may be exercised over assigned personnel. Works in cooperation with and assists other departmental staff as needs dictate. Incumbent does related work as required.

SUBJECT OF THE EXAMINATION:
The written test is designed to evaluate knowledge, skills, and/or abilities in the following areas:

1. **Operation, Maintenance, and Repair of Pumps, Motors, Valves, Mechanical and Electrical Equipment** - These questions test for knowledge of the principles and practices involved in the operation, maintenance, and upkeep of various types of mechanical and electrical equipment, including pumps, valves, electric motors, and similar types of equipment.
2. **Reading and Interpretation of Plans and Specifications** - These questions test for the ability to read and interpret typical plans, layouts, diagrams, and technical specifications related to mechanical or electrical equipment and systems.
3. **Principles and Practices of Air Conditioning and Refrigeration** - These questions test for knowledge of the principles, practices, materials, and equipment involved in the operation, maintenance and upkeep of air-conditioning and refrigeration systems; and may include such areas as the operating processes and equipment involved in various types of air-conditioning and refrigeration systems; troubleshooting symptoms of problems in air-conditioning and refrigeration systems and determining proper remedial actions; and safe operating practices when working with air-conditioning and refrigeration systems.
4. **Principles and Practices of Heating and Ventilating Systems** - These questions test for knowledge of the principles, practices, materials and equipment involved in the operation, maintenance and upkeep of heating and ventilating systems; and may include such areas as the operating processes and equipment involved in various types of heating and ventilating systems; troubleshooting symptoms of problems in heating and ventilating systems and determining proper remedial actions; and safe operating practices when working with heating and ventilating systems.

HOW TO TAKE A TEST

I. YOU MUST PASS AN EXAMINATION

A. WHAT EVERY CANDIDATE SHOULD KNOW

Examination applicants often ask us for help in preparing for the written test. What can I study in advance? What kinds of questions will be asked? How will the test be given? How will the papers be graded?

As an applicant for a civil service examination, you may be wondering about some of these things. Our purpose here is to suggest effective methods of advance study and to describe civil service examinations.

Your chances for success on this examination can be increased if you know how to prepare. Those "pre-examination jitters" can be reduced if you know what to expect. You can even experience an adventure in good citizenship if you know why civil service exams are given.

B. WHY ARE CIVIL SERVICE EXAMINATIONS GIVEN?

Civil service examinations are important to you in two ways. As a citizen, you want public jobs filled by employees who know how to do their work. As a job seeker, you want a fair chance to compete for that job on an equal footing with other candidates. The best-known means of accomplishing this two-fold goal is the competitive examination.

Exams are widely publicized throughout the nation. They may be administered for jobs in federal, state, city, municipal, town or village governments or agencies.

Any citizen may apply, with some limitations, such as the age or residence of applicants. Your experience and education may be reviewed to see whether you meet the requirements for the particular examination. When these requirements exist, they are reasonable and applied consistently to all applicants. Thus, a competitive examination may cause you some uneasiness now, but it is your privilege and safeguard.

C. HOW ARE CIVIL SERVICE EXAMS DEVELOPED?

Examinations are carefully written by trained technicians who are specialists in the field known as "psychological measurement," in consultation with recognized authorities in the field of work that the test will cover. These experts recommend the subject matter areas or skills to be tested; only those knowledges or skills important to your success on the job are included. The most reliable books and source materials available are used as references. Together, the experts and technicians judge the difficulty level of the questions.

Test technicians know how to phrase questions so that the problem is clearly stated. Their ethics do not permit "trick" or "catch" questions. Questions may have been tried out on sample groups, or subjected to statistical analysis, to determine their usefulness.

Written tests are often used in combination with performance tests, ratings of training and experience, and oral interviews. All of these measures combine to form the best-known means of finding the right person for the right job.

II. HOW TO PASS THE WRITTEN TEST

A. NATURE OF THE EXAMINATION

To prepare intelligently for civil service examinations, you should know how they differ from school examinations you have taken. In school you were assigned certain definite pages to read or subjects to cover. The examination questions were quite detailed and usually emphasized memory. Civil service exams, on the other hand, try to discover your present ability to perform the duties of a position, plus your potentiality to learn these duties. In other words, a civil service exam attempts to predict how successful you will be. Questions cover such a broad area that they cannot be as minute and detailed as school exam questions.

In the public service similar kinds of work, or positions, are grouped together in one "class." This process is known as *position-classification*. All the positions in a class are paid according to the salary range for that class. One class title covers all of these positions, and they are all tested by the same examination.

B. FOUR BASIC STEPS

1) Study the announcement

How, then, can you know what subjects to study? Our best answer is: "Learn as much as possible about the class of positions for which you've applied." The exam will test the knowledge, skills and abilities needed to do the work.

Your most valuable source of information about the position you want is the official exam announcement. This announcement lists the training and experience qualifications. Check these standards and apply only if you come reasonably close to meeting them.

The brief description of the position in the examination announcement offers some clues to the subjects which will be tested. Think about the job itself. Review the duties in your mind. Can you perform them, or are there some in which you are rusty? Fill in the blank spots in your preparation.

Many jurisdictions preview the written test in the exam announcement by including a section called "Knowledge and Abilities Required," "Scope of the Examination," or some similar heading. Here you will find out specifically what fields will be tested.

2) Review your own background

Once you learn in general what the position is all about, and what you need to know to do the work, ask yourself which subjects you already know fairly well and which need improvement. You may wonder whether to concentrate on improving your strong areas or on building some background in your fields of weakness. When the announcement has specified "some knowledge" or "considerable knowledge," or has used adjectives like "beginning principles of..." or "advanced ... methods," you can get a clue as to the number and difficulty of questions to be asked in any given field. More questions, and hence broader coverage, would be included for those subjects which are more important in the work. Now weigh your strengths and weaknesses against the job requirements and prepare accordingly.

3) Determine the level of the position

Another way to tell how intensively you should prepare is to understand the level of the job for which you are applying. Is it the entering level? In other words, is this the position in which beginners in a field of work are hired? Or is it an intermediate or advanced level? Sometimes this is indicated by such words as "Junior" or "Senior" in the class title. Other jurisdictions use Roman numerals to designate the level – Clerk I, Clerk II, for example. The word "Supervisor" sometimes appears in the title. If the level is not indicated by the title, check the description of duties. Will you be working under very close supervision, or will you have responsibility for independent decisions in this work?

4) Choose appropriate study materials

Now that you know the subjects to be examined and the relative amount of each subject to be covered, you can choose suitable study materials. For beginning level jobs, or even advanced ones, if you have a pronounced weakness in some aspect of your training, read a modern, standard textbook in that field. Be sure it is up to date and has general coverage. Such books are normally available at your library, and the librarian will be glad to help you locate one. For entry-level positions, questions of appropriate difficulty are chosen – neither highly advanced questions, nor those too simple. Such questions require careful thought but not advanced training.

If the position for which you are applying is technical or advanced, you will read more advanced, specialized material. If you are already familiar with the basic principles of your field, elementary textbooks would waste your time. Concentrate on advanced textbooks and technical periodicals. Think through the concepts and review difficult problems in your field.

These are all general sources. You can get more ideas on your own initiative, following these leads. For example, training manuals and publications of the government agency which employs workers in your field can be useful, particularly for technical and professional positions. A letter or visit to the government department involved may result in more specific study suggestions, and certainly will provide you with a more definite idea of the exact nature of the position you are seeking.

III. KINDS OF TESTS

Tests are used for purposes other than measuring knowledge and ability to perform specified duties. For some positions, it is equally important to test ability to make adjustments to new situations or to profit from training. In others, basic mental abilities not dependent on information are essential. Questions which test these things may not appear as pertinent to the duties of the position as those which test for knowledge and information. Yet they are often highly important parts of a fair examination. For very general questions, it is almost impossible to help you direct your study efforts. What we can do is to point out some of the more common of these general abilities needed in public service positions and describe some typical questions.

1) General information

Broad, general information has been found useful for predicting job success in some kinds of work. This is tested in a variety of ways, from vocabulary lists to questions about current events. Basic background in some field of work, such as sociology or economics, may be sampled in a group of questions. Often these are principles which have become familiar to most persons through exposure rather than through formal training. It is difficult to advise you how to study for these questions; being alert to the world around you is our best suggestion.

2) Verbal ability

An example of an ability needed in many positions is verbal or language ability. Verbal ability is, in brief, the ability to use and understand words. Vocabulary and grammar tests are typical measures of this ability. Reading comprehension or paragraph interpretation questions are common in many kinds of civil service tests. You are given a paragraph of written material and asked to find its central meaning.

3) Numerical ability

Number skills can be tested by the familiar arithmetic problem, by checking paired lists of numbers to see which are alike and which are different, or by interpreting charts and graphs. In the latter test, a graph may be printed in the test booklet which you are asked to use as the basis for answering questions.

4) Observation

A popular test for law-enforcement positions is the observation test. A picture is shown to you for several minutes, then taken away. Questions about the picture test your ability to observe both details and larger elements.

5) Following directions

In many positions in the public service, the employee must be able to carry out written instructions dependably and accurately. You may be given a chart with several columns, each column listing a variety of information. The questions require you to carry out directions involving the information given in the chart.

6) Skills and aptitudes

Performance tests effectively measure some manual skills and aptitudes. When the skill is one in which you are trained, such as typing or shorthand, you can practice. These tests are often very much like those given in business school or high school courses. For many of the other skills and aptitudes, however, no short-time preparation can be made. Skills and abilities natural to you or that you have developed throughout your lifetime are being tested.

Many of the general questions just described provide all the data needed to answer the questions and ask you to use your reasoning ability to find the answers. Your best preparation for these tests, as well as for tests of facts and ideas, is to be at your physical and mental best. You, no doubt, have your own methods of getting into an exam-taking mood and keeping "in shape." The next section lists some ideas on this subject.

IV. KINDS OF QUESTIONS

Only rarely is the "essay" question, which you answer in narrative form, used in civil service tests. Civil service tests are usually of the short-answer type. Full instructions for answering these questions will be given to you at the examination. But in case this is your first experience with short-answer questions and separate answer sheets, here is what you need to know:

1) Multiple-choice Questions

Most popular of the short-answer questions is the "multiple choice" or "best answer" question. It can be used, for example, to test for factual knowledge, ability to solve problems or judgment in meeting situations found at work.

A multiple-choice question is normally one of three types—
- It can begin with an incomplete statement followed by several possible endings. You are to find the one ending which *best* completes the statement, although some of the others may not be entirely wrong.
- It can also be a complete statement in the form of a question which is answered by choosing one of the statements listed.

- It can be in the form of a problem – again you select the best answer.

Here is an example of a multiple-choice question with a discussion which should give you some clues as to the method for choosing the right answer:

When an employee has a complaint about his assignment, the action which will *best* help him overcome his difficulty is to
- A. discuss his difficulty with his coworkers
- B. take the problem to the head of the organization
- C. take the problem to the person who gave him the assignment
- D. say nothing to anyone about his complaint

In answering this question, you should study each of the choices to find which is best. Consider choice "A" – Certainly an employee may discuss his complaint with fellow employees, but no change or improvement can result, and the complaint remains unresolved. Choice "B" is a poor choice since the head of the organization probably does not know what assignment you have been given, and taking your problem to him is known as "going over the head" of the supervisor. The supervisor, or person who made the assignment, is the person who can clarify it or correct any injustice. Choice "C" is, therefore, correct. To say nothing, as in choice "D," is unwise. Supervisors have and interest in knowing the problems employees are facing, and the employee is seeking a solution to his problem.

2) True/False Questions

The "true/false" or "right/wrong" form of question is sometimes used. Here a complete statement is given. Your job is to decide whether the statement is right or wrong.

SAMPLE: A roaming cell-phone call to a nearby city costs less than a non-roaming call to a distant city.

This statement is wrong, or false, since roaming calls are more expensive.

This is not a complete list of all possible question forms, although most of the others are variations of these common types. You will always get complete directions for answering questions. Be sure you understand *how* to mark your answers – ask questions until you do.

V. RECORDING YOUR ANSWERS

Computer terminals are used more and more today for many different kinds of exams.

For an examination with very few applicants, you may be told to record your answers in the test booklet itself. Separate answer sheets are much more common. If this separate answer sheet is to be scored by machine – and this is often the case – it is highly important that you mark your answers correctly in order to get credit.

An electronic scoring machine is often used in civil service offices because of the speed with which papers can be scored. Machine-scored answer sheets must be marked with a pencil, which will be given to you. This pencil has a high graphite content which responds to the electronic scoring machine. As a matter of fact, stray dots may register as answers, so do not let your pencil rest on the answer sheet while you are pondering the correct answer. Also, if your pencil lead breaks or is otherwise defective, ask for another.

Since the answer sheet will be dropped in a slot in the scoring machine, be careful not to bend the corners or get the paper crumpled.

The answer sheet normally has five vertical columns of numbers, with 30 numbers to a column. These numbers correspond to the question numbers in your test booklet. After each number, going across the page are four or five pairs of dotted lines. These short dotted lines have small letters or numbers above them. The first two pairs may also have a "T" or "F" above the letters. This indicates that the first two pairs only are to be used if the questions are of the true-false type. If the questions are multiple choice, disregard the "T" and "F" and pay attention only to the small letters or numbers.

Answer your questions in the manner of the sample that follows:

32. The largest city in the United States is
    A. Washington, D.C.
    B. New York City
    C. Chicago
    D. Detroit
    E. San Francisco

1) Choose the answer you think is best. (New York City is the largest, so "B" is correct.)
2) Find the row of dotted lines numbered the same as the question you are answering. (Find row number 32)
3) Find the pair of dotted lines corresponding to the answer. (Find the pair of lines under the mark "B.")
4) Make a solid black mark between the dotted lines.

VI. BEFORE THE TEST

Common sense will help you find procedures to follow to get ready for an examination. Too many of us, however, overlook these sensible measures. Indeed, nervousness and fatigue have been found to be the most serious reasons why applicants fail to do their best on civil service tests. Here is a list of reminders:

- Begin your preparation early – Don't wait until the last minute to go scurrying around for books and materials or to find out what the position is all about.
- Prepare continuously – An hour a night for a week is better than an all-night cram session. This has been definitely established. What is more, a night a week for a month will return better dividends than crowding your study into a shorter period of time.
- Locate the place of the exam – You have been sent a notice telling you when and where to report for the examination. If the location is in a different town or otherwise unfamiliar to you, it would be well to inquire the best route and learn something about the building.
- Relax the night before the test – Allow your mind to rest. Do not study at all that night. Plan some mild recreation or diversion; then go to bed early and get a good night's sleep.
- Get up early enough to make a leisurely trip to the place for the test – This way unforeseen events, traffic snarls, unfamiliar buildings, etc. will not upset you.
- Dress comfortably – A written test is not a fashion show. You will be known by number and not by name, so wear something comfortable.

- Leave excess paraphernalia at home – Shopping bags and odd bundles will get in your way. You need bring only the items mentioned in the official notice you received; usually everything you need is provided. Do not bring reference books to the exam. They will only confuse those last minutes and be taken away from you when in the test room.
- Arrive somewhat ahead of time – If because of transportation schedules you must get there very early, bring a newspaper or magazine to take your mind off yourself while waiting.
- Locate the examination room – When you have found the proper room, you will be directed to the seat or part of the room where you will sit. Sometimes you are given a sheet of instructions to read while you are waiting. Do not fill out any forms until you are told to do so; just read them and be prepared.
- Relax and prepare to listen to the instructions
- If you have any physical problem that may keep you from doing your best, be sure to tell the test administrator. If you are sick or in poor health, you really cannot do your best on the exam. You can come back and take the test some other time.

VII. AT THE TEST

The day of the test is here and you have the test booklet in your hand. The temptation to get going is very strong. Caution! There is more to success than knowing the right answers. You must know how to identify your papers and understand variations in the type of short-answer question used in this particular examination. Follow these suggestions for maximum results from your efforts:

1) Cooperate with the monitor

The test administrator has a duty to create a situation in which you can be as much at ease as possible. He will give instructions, tell you when to begin, check to see that you are marking your answer sheet correctly, and so on. He is not there to guard you, although he will see that your competitors do not take unfair advantage. He wants to help you do your best.

2) Listen to all instructions

Don't jump the gun! Wait until you understand all directions. In most civil service tests you get more time than you need to answer the questions. So don't be in a hurry. Read each word of instructions until you clearly understand the meaning. Study the examples, listen to all announcements and follow directions. Ask questions if you do not understand what to do.

3) Identify your papers

Civil service exams are usually identified by number only. You will be assigned a number; you must not put your name on your test papers. Be sure to copy your number correctly. Since more than one exam may be given, copy your exact examination title.

4) Plan your time

Unless you are told that a test is a "speed" or "rate of work" test, speed itself is usually not important. Time enough to answer all the questions will be provided, but this does not mean that you have all day. An overall time limit has been set. Divide the total time (in minutes) by the number of questions to determine the approximate time you have for each question.

5) Do not linger over difficult questions

If you come across a difficult question, mark it with a paper clip (useful to have along) and come back to it when you have been through the booklet. One caution if you do this – be sure to skip a number on your answer sheet as well. Check often to be sure that you have not lost your place and that you are marking in the row numbered the same as the question you are answering.

6) Read the questions

Be sure you know what the question asks! Many capable people are unsuccessful because they failed to *read* the questions correctly.

7) Answer all questions

Unless you have been instructed that a penalty will be deducted for incorrect answers, it is better to guess than to omit a question.

8) Speed tests

It is often better NOT to guess on speed tests. It has been found that on timed tests people are tempted to spend the last few seconds before time is called in marking answers at random – without even reading them – in the hope of picking up a few extra points. To discourage this practice, the instructions may warn you that your score will be "corrected" for guessing. That is, a penalty will be applied. The incorrect answers will be deducted from the correct ones, or some other penalty formula will be used.

9) Review your answers

If you finish before time is called, go back to the questions you guessed or omitted to give them further thought. Review other answers if you have time.

10) Return your test materials

If you are ready to leave before others have finished or time is called, take ALL your materials to the monitor and leave quietly. Never take any test material with you. The monitor can discover whose papers are not complete, and taking a test booklet may be grounds for disqualification.

VIII. EXAMINATION TECHNIQUES

1) Read the general instructions carefully. These are usually printed on the first page of the exam booklet. As a rule, these instructions refer to the timing of the examination; the fact that you should not start work until the signal and must stop work at a signal, etc. If there are any *special* instructions, such as a choice of questions to be answered, make sure that you note this instruction carefully.

2) When you are ready to start work on the examination, that is as soon as the signal has been given, read the instructions to each question booklet, underline any key words or phrases, such as *least, best, outline, describe* and the like. In this way you will tend to answer as requested rather than discover on reviewing your paper that you *listed without describing*, that you selected the *worst* choice rather than the *best* choice, etc.

3) If the examination is of the objective or multiple-choice type – that is, each question will also give a series of possible answers: A, B, C or D, and you are called upon to select the best answer and write the letter next to that answer on your answer paper – it is advisable to start answering each question in turn. There may be anywhere from 50 to 100 such questions in the three or four hours allotted and you can see how much time would be taken if you read through all the questions before beginning to answer any. Furthermore, if you come across a question or group of questions which you know would be difficult to answer, it would undoubtedly affect your handling of all the other questions.

4) If the examination is of the essay type and contains but a few questions, it is a moot point as to whether you should read all the questions before starting to answer any one. Of course, if you are given a choice – say five out of seven and the like – then it is essential to read all the questions so you can eliminate the two that are most difficult. If, however, you are asked to answer all the questions, there may be danger in trying to answer the easiest one first because you may find that you will spend too much time on it. The best technique is to answer the first question, then proceed to the second, etc.

5) Time your answers. Before the exam begins, write down the time it started, then add the time allowed for the examination and write down the time it must be completed, then divide the time available somewhat as follows:
   - If 3-1/2 hours are allowed, that would be 210 minutes. If you have 80 objective-type questions, that would be an average of 2-1/2 minutes per question. Allow yourself no more than 2 minutes per question, or a total of 160 minutes, which will permit about 50 minutes to review.
   - If for the time allotment of 210 minutes there are 7 essay questions to answer, that would average about 30 minutes a question. Give yourself only 25 minutes per question so that you have about 35 minutes to review.

6) The most important instruction is to *read each question* and make sure you know what is wanted. The second most important instruction is to *time yourself properly* so that you answer every question. The third most important instruction is to *answer every question*. Guess if you have to but include something for each question. Remember that you will receive no credit for a blank and will probably receive some credit if you write something in answer to an essay question. If you guess a letter – say "B" for a multiple-choice question – you may have guessed right. If you leave a blank as an answer to a multiple-choice question, the examiners may respect your feelings but it will not add a point to your score. Some exams may penalize you for wrong answers, so in such cases *only*, you may not want to guess unless you have some basis for your answer.

7) Suggestions
   a. Objective-type questions
      1. Examine the question booklet for proper sequence of pages and questions
      2. Read all instructions carefully
      3. Skip any question which seems too difficult; return to it after all other questions have been answered
      4. Apportion your time properly; do not spend too much time on any single question or group of questions

5. Note and underline key words – *all, most, fewest, least, best, worst, same, opposite,* etc.
6. Pay particular attention to negatives
7. Note unusual option, e.g., unduly long, short, complex, different or similar in content to the body of the question
8. Observe the use of "hedging" words – *probably, may, most likely,* etc.
9. Make sure that your answer is put next to the same number as the question
10. Do not second-guess unless you have good reason to believe the second answer is definitely more correct
11. Cross out original answer if you decide another answer is more accurate; do not erase until you are ready to hand your paper in
12. Answer all questions; guess unless instructed otherwise
13. Leave time for review

b. Essay questions
1. Read each question carefully
2. Determine exactly what is wanted. Underline key words or phrases.
3. Decide on outline or paragraph answer
4. Include many different points and elements unless asked to develop any one or two points or elements
5. Show impartiality by giving pros and cons unless directed to select one side only
6. Make and write down any assumptions you find necessary to answer the questions
7. Watch your English, grammar, punctuation and choice of words
8. Time your answers; don't crowd material

8) Answering the essay question

Most essay questions can be answered by framing the specific response around several key words or ideas. Here are a few such key words or ideas:

M's: manpower, materials, methods, money, management
P's: purpose, program, policy, plan, procedure, practice, problems, pitfalls, personnel, public relations

   a. Six basic steps in handling problems:
1. Preliminary plan and background development
2. Collect information, data and facts
3. Analyze and interpret information, data and facts
4. Analyze and develop solutions as well as make recommendations
5. Prepare report and sell recommendations
6. Install recommendations and follow up effectiveness

   b. Pitfalls to avoid
1. *Taking things for granted* – A statement of the situation does not necessarily imply that each of the elements is necessarily true; for example, a complaint may be invalid and biased so that all that can be taken for granted is that a complaint has been registered

2. *Considering only one side of a situation* – Wherever possible, indicate several alternatives and then point out the reasons you selected the best one
3. *Failing to indicate follow up* – Whenever your answer indicates action on your part, make certain that you will take proper follow-up action to see how successful your recommendations, procedures or actions turn out to be
4. *Taking too long in answering any single question* – Remember to time your answers properly

IX. AFTER THE TEST

Scoring procedures differ in detail among civil service jurisdictions although the general principles are the same. Whether the papers are hand-scored or graded by machine we have described, they are nearly always graded by number. That is, the person who marks the paper knows only the number – never the name – of the applicant. Not until all the papers have been graded will they be matched with names. If other tests, such as training and experience or oral interview ratings have been given, scores will be combined. Different parts of the examination usually have different weights. For example, the written test might count 60 percent of the final grade, and a rating of training and experience 40 percent. In many jurisdictions, veterans will have a certain number of points added to their grades.

After the final grade has been determined, the names are placed in grade order and an eligible list is established. There are various methods for resolving ties between those who get the same final grade – probably the most common is to place first the name of the person whose application was received first. Job offers are made from the eligible list in the order the names appear on it. You will be notified of your grade and your rank as soon as all these computations have been made. This will be done as rapidly as possible.

People who are found to meet the requirements in the announcement are called "eligibles." Their names are put on a list of eligible candidates. An eligible's chances of getting a job depend on how high he stands on this list and how fast agencies are filling jobs from the list.

When a job is to be filled from a list of eligibles, the agency asks for the names of people on the list of eligibles for that job. When the civil service commission receives this request, it sends to the agency the names of the three people highest on this list. Or, if the job to be filled has specialized requirements, the office sends the agency the names of the top three persons who meet these requirements from the general list.

The appointing officer makes a choice from among the three people whose names were sent to him. If the selected person accepts the appointment, the names of the others are put back on the list to be considered for future openings.

That is the rule in hiring from all kinds of eligible lists, whether they are for typist, carpenter, chemist, or something else. For every vacancy, the appointing officer has his choice of any one of the top three eligibles on the list. This explains why the person whose name is on top of the list sometimes does not get an appointment when some of the persons lower on the list do. If the appointing officer chooses the second or third eligible, the No. 1 eligible does not get a job at once, but stays on the list until he is appointed or the list is terminated.

X. HOW TO PASS THE INTERVIEW TEST

The examination for which you applied requires an oral interview test. You have already taken the written test and you are now being called for the interview test – the final part of the formal examination.

You may think that it is not possible to prepare for an interview test and that there are no procedures to follow during an interview. Our purpose is to point out some things you can do in advance that will help you and some good rules to follow and pitfalls to avoid while you are being interviewed.

What is an interview supposed to test?

The written examination is designed to test the technical knowledge and competence of the candidate; the oral is designed to evaluate intangible qualities, not readily measured otherwise, and to establish a list showing the relative fitness of each candidate – as measured against his competitors – for the position sought. Scoring is not on the basis of "right" and "wrong," but on a sliding scale of values ranging from "not passable" to "outstanding." As a matter of fact, it is possible to achieve a relatively low score without a single "incorrect" answer because of evident weakness in the qualities being measured.

Occasionally, an examination may consist entirely of an oral test – either an individual or a group oral. In such cases, information is sought concerning the technical knowledges and abilities of the candidate, since there has been no written examination for this purpose. More commonly, however, an oral test is used to supplement a written examination.

Who conducts interviews?

The composition of oral boards varies among different jurisdictions. In nearly all, a representative of the personnel department serves as chairman. One of the members of the board may be a representative of the department in which the candidate would work. In some cases, "outside experts" are used, and, frequently, a businessman or some other representative of the general public is asked to serve. Labor and management or other special groups may be represented. The aim is to secure the services of experts in the appropriate field.

However the board is composed, it is a good idea (and not at all improper or unethical) to ascertain in advance of the interview who the members are and what groups they represent. When you are introduced to them, you will have some idea of their backgrounds and interests, and at least you will not stutter and stammer over their names.

What should be done before the interview?

While knowledge about the board members is useful and takes some of the surprise element out of the interview, there is other preparation which is more substantive. It *is* possible to prepare for an oral interview – in several ways:

1) Keep a copy of your application and review it carefully before the interview

This may be the only document before the oral board, and the starting point of the interview. Know what education and experience you have listed there, and the sequence and dates of all of it. Sometimes the board will ask you to review the highlights of your experience for them; you should not have to hem and haw doing it.

2) Study the class specification and the examination announcement

Usually, the oral board has one or both of these to guide them. The qualities, characteristics or knowledges required by the position sought are stated in these documents. They offer valuable clues as to the nature of the oral interview. For example, if the job involves supervisory responsibilities, the announcement will usually indicate that knowledge of modern supervisory methods and the qualifications of the candidate as a supervisor will be tested. If so, you can expect such questions, frequently in the form of a hypothetical situation which you are expected to solve. NEVER go into an oral without knowledge of the duties and responsibilities of the job you seek.

3) Think through each qualification required

Try to visualize the kind of questions you would ask if you were a board member. How well could you answer them? Try especially to appraise your own knowledge and background in each area, *measured against the job sought*, and identify any areas in which you are weak. Be critical and realistic – do not flatter yourself.

4) Do some general reading in areas in which you feel you may be weak

For example, if the job involves supervision and your past experience has NOT, some general reading in supervisory methods and practices, particularly in the field of human relations, might be useful. Do NOT study agency procedures or detailed manuals. The oral board will be testing your understanding and capacity, not your memory.

5) Get a good night's sleep and watch your general health and mental attitude

You will want a clear head at the interview. Take care of a cold or any other minor ailment, and of course, no hangovers.

What should be done on the day of the interview?

Now comes the day of the interview itself. Give yourself plenty of time to get there. Plan to arrive somewhat ahead of the scheduled time, particularly if your appointment is in the fore part of the day. If a previous candidate fails to appear, the board might be ready for you a bit early. By early afternoon an oral board is almost invariably behind schedule if there are many candidates, and you may have to wait. Take along a book or magazine to read, or your application to review, but leave any extraneous material in the waiting room when you go in for your interview. In any event, relax and compose yourself.

The matter of dress is important. The board is forming impressions about you – from your experience, your manners, your attitude, and your appearance. Give your personal appearance careful attention. Dress your best, but not your flashiest. Choose conservative, appropriate clothing, and be sure it is immaculate. This is a business interview, and your appearance should indicate that you regard it as such. Besides, being well groomed and properly dressed will help boost your confidence.

Sooner or later, someone will call your name and escort you into the interview room. *This is it.* From here on you are on your own. It is too late for any more preparation. But remember, you asked for this opportunity to prove your fitness, and you are here because your request was granted.

What happens when you go in?

The usual sequence of events will be as follows: The clerk (who is often the board stenographer) will introduce you to the chairman of the oral board, who will introduce you to the other members of the board. Acknowledge the introductions before you sit down. Do not be surprised if you find a microphone facing you or a stenotypist sitting by. Oral interviews are usually recorded in the event of an appeal or other review.

Usually the chairman of the board will open the interview by reviewing the highlights of your education and work experience from your application – primarily for the benefit of the other members of the board, as well as to get the material into the record. Do not interrupt or comment unless there is an error or significant misinterpretation; if that is the case, do not hesitate. But do not quibble about insignificant matters. Also, he will usually ask you some question about your education, experience or your present job – partly to get you to start talking and to establish the interviewing "rapport." He may start the actual questioning, or turn it over to one of the other members. Frequently, each member undertakes the questioning on a particular area, one in which he is perhaps most competent, so you can expect each member to participate in the examination. Because time is limited, you may also expect some rather abrupt switches in the direction the questioning takes, so do not be upset by it. Normally, a board member will not pursue a single line of questioning unless he discovers a particular strength or weakness.

After each member has participated, the chairman will usually ask whether any member has any further questions, then will ask you if you have anything you wish to add. Unless you are expecting this question, it may floor you. Worse, it may start you off on an extended, extemporaneous speech. The board is not usually seeking more information. The question is principally to offer you a last opportunity to present further qualifications or to indicate that you have nothing to add. So, if you feel that a significant qualification or characteristic has been overlooked, it is proper to point it out in a sentence or so. Do not compliment the board on the thoroughness of their examination – they have been sketchy, and you know it. If you wish, merely say, "No thank you, I have nothing further to add." This is a point where you can "talk yourself out" of a good impression or fail to present an important bit of information. Remember, *you close the interview yourself*.

The chairman will then say, "That is all, Mr. _____, thank you." Do not be startled; the interview is over, and quicker than you think. Thank him, gather your belongings and take your leave. Save your sigh of relief for the other side of the door.

How to put your best foot forward
Throughout this entire process, you may feel that the board individually and collectively is trying to pierce your defenses, seek out your hidden weaknesses and embarrass and confuse you. Actually, this is not true. They are obliged to make an appraisal of your qualifications for the job you are seeking, and they want to see you in your best light. Remember, they must interview all candidates and a non-cooperative candidate may become a failure in spite of their best efforts to bring out his qualifications. Here are 15 suggestions that will help you:

1) Be natural – Keep your attitude confident, not cocky
If you are not confident that you can do the job, do not expect the board to be. Do not apologize for your weaknesses, try to bring out your strong points. The board is interested in a positive, not negative, presentation. Cockiness will antagonize any board member and make him wonder if you are covering up a weakness by a false show of strength.

2) Get comfortable, but don't lounge or sprawl
Sit erectly but not stiffly. A careless posture may lead the board to conclude that you are careless in other things, or at least that you are not impressed by the importance of the occasion. Either conclusion is natural, even if incorrect. Do not fuss with your clothing, a pencil or an ashtray. Your hands may occasionally be useful to emphasize a point; do not let them become a point of distraction.

3) Do not wisecrack or make small talk
This is a serious situation, and your attitude should show that you consider it as such. Further, the time of the board is limited – they do not want to waste it, and neither should you.

4) Do not exaggerate your experience or abilities

In the first place, from information in the application or other interviews and sources, the board may know more about you than you think. Secondly, you probably will not get away with it. An experienced board is rather adept at spotting such a situation, so do not take the chance.

5) If you know a board member, do not make a point of it, yet do not hide it

Certainly you are not fooling him, and probably not the other members of the board. Do not try to take advantage of your acquaintanceship – it will probably do you little good.

6) Do not dominate the interview

Let the board do that. They will give you the clues – do not assume that you have to do all the talking. Realize that the board has a number of questions to ask you, and do not try to take up all the interview time by showing off your extensive knowledge of the answer to the first one.

7) Be attentive

You only have 20 minutes or so, and you should keep your attention at its sharpest throughout. When a member is addressing a problem or question to you, give him your undivided attention. Address your reply principally to him, but do not exclude the other board members.

8) Do not interrupt

A board member may be stating a problem for you to analyze. He will ask you a question when the time comes. Let him state the problem, and wait for the question.

9) Make sure you understand the question

Do not try to answer until you are sure what the question is. If it is not clear, restate it in your own words or ask the board member to clarify it for you. However, do not haggle about minor elements.

10) Reply promptly but not hastily

A common entry on oral board rating sheets is "candidate responded readily," or "candidate hesitated in replies." Respond as promptly and quickly as you can, but do not jump to a hasty, ill-considered answer.

11) Do not be peremptory in your answers

A brief answer is proper – but do not fire your answer back. That is a losing game from your point of view. The board member can probably ask questions much faster than you can answer them.

12) Do not try to create the answer you think the board member wants

He is interested in what kind of mind you have and how it works – not in playing games. Furthermore, he can usually spot this practice and will actually grade you down on it.

13) Do not switch sides in your reply merely to agree with a board member

Frequently, a member will take a contrary position merely to draw you out and to see if you are willing and able to defend your point of view. Do not start a debate, yet do not surrender a good position. If a position is worth taking, it is worth defending.

14) Do not be afraid to admit an error in judgment if you are shown to be wrong

The board knows that you are forced to reply without any opportunity for careful consideration. Your answer may be demonstrably wrong. If so, admit it and get on with the interview.

15) Do not dwell at length on your present job

The opening question may relate to your present assignment. Answer the question but do not go into an extended discussion. You are being examined for a *new* job, not your present one. As a matter of fact, try to phrase ALL your answers in terms of the job for which you are being examined.

Basis of Rating

Probably you will forget most of these "do's" and "don'ts" when you walk into the oral interview room. Even remembering them all will not ensure you a passing grade. Perhaps you did not have the qualifications in the first place. But remembering them will help you to put your best foot forward, without treading on the toes of the board members.

Rumor and popular opinion to the contrary notwithstanding, an oral board wants you to make the best appearance possible. They know you are under pressure – but they also want to see how you respond to it as a guide to what your reaction would be under the pressures of the job you seek. They will be influenced by the degree of poise you display, the personal traits you show and the manner in which you respond.

ABOUT THIS BOOK

This book contains tests divided into Examination Sections. Go through each test, answering every question in the margin. We have also attached a sample answer sheet at the back of the book that can be removed and used. At the end of each test look at the answer key and check your answers. On the ones you got wrong, look at the right answer choice and learn. Do not fill in the answers first. Do not memorize the questions and answers, but understand the answer and principles involved. On your test, the questions will likely be different from the samples. Questions are changed and new ones added. If you understand these past questions you should have success with any changes that arise. Tests may consist of several types of questions. We have additional books on each subject should more study be advisable or necessary for you. Finally, the more you study, the better prepared you will be. This book is intended to be the last thing you study before you walk into the examination room. Prior study of relevant texts is also recommended. NLC publishes some of these in our Fundamental Series. Knowledge and good sense are important factors in passing your exam. Good luck also helps. So now study this Passbook, absorb the material contained within and take that knowledge into the examination. Then do your best to pass that exam.

EXAMINATION SECTION

EXAMINATION SECTION
TEST 1

DIRECTIONS: Each question or incomplete statement is followed by several suggested answers or completions. Select the one that BEST answers the question or completes the statement. *PRINT THE LETTER OF THE CORRECT ANSWER IN THE SPACE AT THE RIGHT.*

1. In refrigerating work, the term *automatic* expansion valve refers to a

   A. thermostatic expansion valve
   B. high side float valve
   C. capillary tube used to produce a pressure drop
   D. constant pressure expansion valve

2. In a given refrigerating system, the ratio of the heat absorbed in the evaporator to the heat equivalent of the energy supplied by the compressor is 4.5.
   The theoretical horsepower per ton of refrigeration is MOST NEARLY

   A. 0.69   B. 0.87   C. 1.04   D. 1.73

3. In an air-water vapor mixture, the temperature which is the measure of the total heat of the mixture is the

   A. dewpoint
   B. dry bulb
   C. sum of dry bulb and wet bulb
   D. wet bulb

4. In a refrigerating system, the

   A. refrigerating capacity of the machine is equal to the ice-making capacity of the plant
   B. standard ton is the abstraction of 12,000 Btu per hour
   C. rectifier of the absorption system is on the low pressure side
   D. cooling water temperature for a CO_2 system should be as high as possible

5. In a two-stage double-acting air compressor, the

   A. unloaders operate on head and crank end of both cylinders simultaneously
   B. intercooler pressure is the arithmetic average of inlet and discharge pressures
   C. unloaders act on the inlet valves
   D. unloaders commonly unload the high pressure cylinder first

6. Air passing through a spray chamber in which the spray water is recirculated but not heated or cooled will

   A. be humidified at approximately constant wet bulb temperature
   B. always leave in a saturated condition
   C. be de-humidified
   D. leave the spray chamber at the same water vapor pressure

7. When the solid absorbent silica-gel is used in an air conditioning system, the air passing over it

   A. will be humidified
   B. has its dry bulb temperature increased
   C. will have its wet bulb temperature decreased
   D. will reach a higher water vapor pressure

8. In the process of heating atmospheric air in an air conditioning apparatus, the

   A. absolute or specific humidity increases
   B. relative humidity remains constant
   C. absolute or specific humidity does not change
   D. water vapor pressure decreases

9. 100 pounds per minute of outside air at 90° F. dry bulb and 200 pounds per minute of recirculated air at 72° F. dry bulb are mixed in an air conditioning system.
   The resulting dry bulb temperature will be, in °F., MOST NEARLY

   A. 84   B. 78   C. 88   D. 81

10. In a compression refrigerating system, the principal useful refrigerating effect is obtained in the

    A. condenser
    B. evaporator
    C. expansion valve
    D. compressor

11. Recirculation of conditioned air in an air conditioned building is done MAINLY to

    A. reduce refrigeration tonnage required
    B. increase room entropy
    C. increase air specific humidity
    D. reduce room temperature below the dewpoint

12. *Sweating* of cold water pipes in a room is due to the

    A. surface of the pipe being below the wet bulb temperature of the room air
    B. surface of the pipe being below the dew point temperature of the room air
    C. air in the room exceeding 100% relative humidity
    D. specific humidity exceeding the relative humidity

13. In a two-stage air compressor, the intercooler is placed between the

    A. compressor and air receiver
    B. compressor and intake pipe
    C. after cooler and air receiver
    D. intake of the second stage and the discharge of the first stage

14. The quantity of heat required to change the stage (e.g., liquid to vapor, or solid to liquid) of a body within a change in temperature is USUALLY called

    A. specific heat
    B. enthalpy
    C. latent heat
    D. entropy

15. When a refrigeration machine is in operation under normal load, the refrigerant leaving the compressor is in a state of

    A. low pressure vapor   B. hot liquid
    C. high pressure vapor   D. cold liquid

16. In a commercial ammonia refrigerating system, the ammonia that has just passed through the expansion valve

    A. is partially vaporized
    B. has become highly superheated
    C. has a greater enthalpy than it had before entering the expansion valve
    D. is all in a liquid state

17. An ice making machine freezes 50 lbs. of water at 45° F. to ice at 25° F. (under atmospheric conditions) in one hour.
    The cooling load, in tons, of refrigeration is MOST NEARLY

    A. 0.7   B. 1.4   C. 6.8   D. 13.6

18. The pressure drop through a ventilating duct is 3.8 inches of water when the air velocity is 32 feet per second.
    The pressure drop, in inches of water, when the air velocity is reduced to 24 feet per second will be MOST NEARLY

    A. 6.8   B. 3.8   C. 3.0   D. 2.1

19. The three methods in common use in the design and sizing of air duct systems are known as

    A. abrupt enlargement, dynamic loss, maximum velocity
    B. turbulent loss, equal friction, static regain
    C. velocity reduction, equal friction, static regain
    D. velocity reduction, maximum velocity, dynamic loss

20. The actual amount of water vapor which atmospheric air can hold is governed by the

    A. pressure   B. temperature
    C. relative humidity   D. specific volume

21. A pitot tube inserted in a ventilating duct is USUALLY used to determine the _____ in the duct.

    A. velocity pressure
    B. total pressure
    C. barometric pressure
    D. static pressure in p.s.i. absolute

22. Wetness forming inside frame building walls is often due to water vapor migration into the wall. The vapor movement is usually from the warm air side to the cool air side.
    The vapor USUALLY moves in this direction because the

    A. relative humidity of cool air is lower than the relative humidity of warm air
    B. partial pressure of the vapor is lower on the cool side than on the warm air side of the wall

C. warm air has a lower dewpoint temperature
D. specific humidity or humidity ratio is so much lower for the warm air than for the cool air

23. Of the following, the dividing point between the high pressure and low pressure side of a refrigeration system is the

    A. evaporator
    B. receiver
    C. condenser
    D. expansion valve

24. In operating a closed water circulating system, it is good practice to

    A. treat the water chemically for corrosion control
    B. drain and flush the system regularly to control corrosion
    C. leave the system undisturbed because it is sealed and needs no maintenance
    D. replace the pump shaft seals every three months

25. The function of an unloader on an electric motor-driven air compressor is to

    A. release the pressure in the cylinders in order to reduce the starting load
    B. reduce the speed of the motor when the maximum pressure is reached
    C. prevent excess pressure in the receiver
    D. drain the condensate from the cylinder head

26. The MOST highly toxic of the following refrigerants is

    A. sulphur dioxide
    B. ammonia
    C. methyl chloride
    D. freon 12

27. Of the following piping materials, the one which is NOT generally used for pneumatic temperature control systems is

    A. copper
    B. plastic
    C. steel
    D. galvanized iron

28. In accordance with recommended maintenance practice, thermostats used in a pneumatic temperature control system should be checked

    A. weekly
    B. bi-monthly
    C. monthly
    D. once a year

29. Of the following, the BEST method to use to determine the moisture level in a refrigeration system is to

    A. weigh the drier after it has been in the system for a period of time
    B. visually check the sight glass for particles of corrosion
    C. use a moisture indicator
    D. test a sample of lubricating oil with phosphorus pentoxide

30. A full-flow drier is USUALLY recommended to be used in a hermetic refrigeration compressor system to keep the system dry and to

    A. prevent the products of decomposition from getting into the evaporator in the event of a motor burn-out
    B. condense out liquid refrigerant during compressor off cycles and compressor start-up

C. prevent the compressor unit from decreasing in capacity
D. prevent the liquid from dumping into the compressor crankcase

31. The rating of a unit ventilator is USUALLY determined by a(n)   31._____

   A. anemometer
   B. hydrometer
   C. psychrometer
   D. ammeter

32. The STANDARD capacity rating conditions for any refrigeration compressor is _____ for   32._____
   the suction and _____ for the discharge.

   A. 5° F., 19.6 psig; 86° F., 154.5 psig
   B. 5° F., 9.6 psig; 96° F., 154.5 psig
   C. 10° F., 9.6 psig; 96° F., 144.5 psig
   D. 10° F., 19.6 psig; 96° F., 134.5 psig

33. Of the following, the MAIN purpose of a subcooler in a refrigerant piping system for a   33._____
   two-stage system is to

   A. reduce the total power requirements and total heat rejection to the second stage
   B. reduce total power requirements and return oil to the compressor
   C. improve the flow of evaporator gas per ton and increase the temperature
   D. increase the heat rejection per ton and avoid system shutdown

34. In large refrigeration systems, the USUAL location for charging the refrigeration system   34._____
   is into the

   A. suction line
   B. liquid line between the receiver shut-off valve and the expansion valve
   C. line between the condenser and the compressor
   D. line between the high pressure cut-off switch and the expansion valve

35. Assume that one of your assistants was near the Freon 11 refrigeration system when a   35._____
   liquid Freon line ruptured. Some of the liquid Freon 11 has gotten into your assis-tant's
   right eye.
   Of the following actions, the one which you should NOT take is to

   A. immediately call for an eye specialist (medical doctor)
   B. gently and quickly rub the Freon 11 out of the eye
   C. use a boric-acid solution to clean out the Freon 11 from his eye
   D. wash the eye by gently blowing the Freon 11 out of his eye with air

KEY (CORRECT ANSWERS)

1.	D	16.	A
2.	C	17.	A
3.	D	18.	D
4.	B	19.	C
5.	C	20.	B
6.	A	21.	A
7.	B	22.	B
8.	C	23.	D
9.	B	24.	A
10.	B	25.	A
11.	A	26.	A
12.	B	27.	C
13.	D	28.	D
14.	C	29.	C
15.	C	30.	A

31. A
32. A
33. A
34. B
35. B

EXAMINATION SECTION
TEST 1

DIRECTIONS: Each question or incomplete statement is followed by several suggested answers or completions. Select the one that BEST answers the question or completes the statement. *PRINT THE LETTER OF THE CORRECT ANSWER IN THE SPACE AT THE RIGHT.*

1. *Separates from the lubricating oil in operating with oil floating on top of the liquid refrigerant..*
   To which refrigerant does this statement apply? 1.____

   A. Freon-12
   B. Freon-22
   C. Ammonia
   D. Carbon dioxide

2. Refrigerants withdrawn from refrigerating systems shall be 2.____

   A. placed in Interstate Commerce Commission containers only
   B. discharged to the sewer
   C. slowly discharged into the atmosphere
   D. placed in containers meeting the requirements of Local Law 373 only

3. If an operator carelessly used a paraffin oil in an ammonia refrigeration system, the probability is that the 3.____

   A. compressor discharge valves would foul
   B. expansion valve would freeze
   C. evaporator would foul up with wax
   D. oil would flash at compressor discharge temperature

4. In order for an electric induction motor to operate satisfactorily and deliver its full horsepower, the motor should operate MOST NEARLY at 4.____

   A. no more than 10% variation above its rated voltage and no greater than 20% variation below its rated frequency
   B. its rated voltage and at least 20% slip
   C. its rated voltage and a 20% frequency variation
   D. its rated frequency and at not more than 10% above or below its rated voltage

5. In a comparison of the absorption system with the vapor compression system, the one of the following statements which is INCORRECT is that the 5.____

   A. expansion valves of both systems are similar
   B. absorption system requires heat and power and the compression system only requires power
   C. absorption system alone requires an analyzer
   D. compressors of both systems are similar

6. A system using silica gel that has picked up moisture may be reactivated by heating it for a period of four hours or more at a temperature of APPROXIMATELY _____ °F. 6.____

   A. 200 B. 450 C. 700 D. 850

7. A two stage compression system is often used when it is desired to

   A. conserve lubricating oil
   B. use ammonia rather than Freon
   C. work evaporator at very low temperature
   D. get more work from a single stage compressor

8. The force exerted on a cylinder 6" in diameter at 100 psig is

   A. 3600#   B. 2800#   C. 1600#   D. 600#

9. The boiling temperature of Freon 22, compared with Freon 12, is

   A. 20° lower   B. 10° lower
   C. 25° higher   D. 15° higher

10. In the absorption system, the absorber absorbs

    A. any foreign matter in the system
    B. the heat directly from the brine coil or direct coil
    C. the suction gas into the weak liquid
    D. the weak liquid into the brine

11. Freon 12 systems shall have parts that will not cause corrosion of materials. PROHIBITED materials include _____ alloys.

    A. brass   B. copper
    C. extra heavy steel   D. magnesium

12. A spray type of dehumidifier is to be used to air condition and give the best results to a set dew point of 54° F. The temperature of the return chilled water would be _____ ° F.

    A. 35.5   B. 48.0   C. 52.0   D. 46.5

13. With reference to a synchronous motor, it is NOT correct that

    A. it is a constant speed motor
    B. it can be run using 220, 440, or 2300 volts
    C. these motors are excited by direct current
    D. these motors are usually run with a lagging field current

14. In a calcium chloride brine tank of 1000 cubic feet, how many pounds of dichromate would you use in the INITIAL charge?

    A. 20   B. 40   C. 100   D. 200

15. In a refrigeration plant that is equipped with an automatic condenser water regulating valve, the line for actuating this valve should be tapped into the

    A. condenser water supply ahead of the valve
    B. condenser water waste line from the condenser
    C. refrigerant high pressure side of the system
    D. refrigerant low pressure side of the system

16. How many water boxes are on a shell and tube, vertical condenser? 16.____

    A. One on top
    B. Two on top
    C. One on top and bottom
    D. Two on bottom

17. If Nessler's solution is added to a sample of salt brine, in the event of there being a trace 17.____
    of ammonia present in the brine, the color of the solution will turn

    A. blue   B. red   C. pink   D. yellow

18. The refrigerant enters the condenser as a _____ and leaves as a _____. 18.____

    A. high pressure gas; low pressure liquid
    B. superheated gas; low pressure liquid
    C. high pressure liquid; low pressure liquid
    D. superheated gas; superheated gas

19. To remove water from an industrial ammonia system, you would 19.____

    A. use a regenerator
    B. drain from the low suction
    C. drain from the high side
    D. drain the entire system

20. Which of the following is an indication that the reciprocating type of compression system 20.____
    is short of refrigerant?

    A. High head pressure and low suction pressure
    B. Low suction pressure and low head pressure
    C. High suction and low discharge pressure
    D. Both pressures are always normal

21. In a refrigerating unit having a high side float, if the float is punctured and sinks, the result 21.____
    will be that the

    A. compressor will overload
    B. high side will fluctuate
    C. low side will go down
    D. expansion valve will frost

22. A sign on the wall of a motor room contains various pertinent information. 22.____
    Which of the following can be omitted?

    A. Number of condensers   B. Pounds of refrigerant
    C. Name of installers   D. Horsepower of prime mover

23. When withdrawing refrigerant from a system into containers, they cannot, in any case, 23.____
    be filled more than _____%.

    A. 70   B. 75   C. 80   D. 85

24. If a system contains 400 pounds of Group 2 refrigerant, the number of breathing service 24.____
    masks required is

    A. one   B. two   C. three   D. none

25. Where would you place an accumulator in the system?   25._____
    A. On the suction side of the compressor
    B. Just before the condenser on the discharge side of the system
    C. On the high side of the liquid line
    D. Before the king valve

KEY (CORRECT ANSWERS)

1. D   11. C
2. A   12. C
3. C   13. B
4. D   14. C
5. D   15. C

6. B   16. A
7. C   17. D
8. B   18. B
9. A   19. A
10. C   20. A

21. C
22. A
23. B
24. A
25. A

TEST 2

DIRECTIONS: Each question or incomplete statement is followed by several suggested answers or completions. Select the one that BEST answers the question or completes the statement. *PRINT THE LETTER OF THE CORRECT ANSWER IN THE SPACE AT THE RIGHT.*

1. The quantity of water flowing through an automatically controlled condenser will INCREASE as the

    A. head pressure decreases
    B. suction pressure decreases
    C. load increases
    D. head pressure increases

2. An indication that the refrigeration system is in need of purging of foul gases is _____ head pressure with _____.

    A. high; high suction pressure
    B. high; a little water on the condenser
    C. high; plenty of water on the condenser
    D. low; a hot receiver

3. In testing condenser water for carbon dioxide leaks, you would use

    A. Nessler's reagent in a sample of brine
    B. brom-thymol-blue in a sample of water
    C. a halide torch on a brine sample
    D. litmus paper in a sample of brine

4. The number of baffles in a three pass shell and tube brine cooler is

    A. one   B. two   C. three   D. four

5. In testing for ammonia leaks in a plant, red litmus paper was used. If ammonia was present, the paper would turn

    A. green   B. dark red
    C. blue   D. none of the above

6. A substance that CANNOT be used to make a brine solution that is to be used at -25° F is

    A. calcium chloride   B. ethylene glycol
    C. sodium chloride   D. anti-freeze

7. In a spray pond similar to a condenser to kill algae in the water, you would use

    A. silica gel   B. chromite
    C. potassium permanganate   D. potash

8. The accumulator on a single stage double-acting ammonia compressor

    A. acts like an analyzer in the absorption system
    B. is tied in on high side
    C. removes liquid entrained in the suction line
    D. is tied in on low side

11

9. If a system contains 400 pounds of Group 2 refrigerant, the number of breathing service masks required is

   A. one B. two C. three D. none

10. In a compression system with a low side float, the ball in the float is punctured and sinks. What would MOST likely happen?
    The

    A. low side would be falling with compressor running
    B. compressor would stop and head pressure would rise
    C. head pressure would fall
    D. low side would be rising with compressor running

11. The capacity of a water cooled condenser is LEAST affected by

    A. water temperature
    B. amount of water
    C. refrigerant temperature
    D. ambient temperature

12. The brine in a shell and tube cooler

    A. is in the shell
    B. is in the tube
    C. alternates between the tube and shell
    D. is in the refrigerant in tubes

13. The suction gas pressure in a system is 15" Hg.
    If this is converted to absolute pressure, it will be MOST NEARLY

    A. 0 B. 15 C. 7 D. 23

14. Sulphur dioxide may be discharged into

    A. carbonated brine
    B. absorptive brine
    C. calcium chloride
    D. water

15. A vertical compressor has trunk type pistons and is single-acting. If the oil rings leaked very badly, it would cause

    A. pounding upon starting
    B. a decreased capacity
    C. a slow start which speeds up
    D. scored and scratched cylinder walls

16. Which one of the following has items that are NOT part of a belt driven compressor?

    A. Piston, cylinder, frame, and crankcase
    B. Stuffing box, suction valve, and frame
    C. Crankcase, discharge valve, and stuffing box
    D. Frame, crankcase, suction valve, valve rod, and piston

17. The LOWEST operating temperature you would recommend for sodium chloride is _____ °F.

    A. 0 B. 5 C. 10 D. 20

18. What is the LOWEST operating temperature you would recommend for calcium chloride?

   A. -45° F   B. -60° F   C. -20° F   D. 0° F

19. The one of the following dessicants that would change physically and/or chemically under the absorption process of water is

   A. silica gel
   B. activated alumina
   C. calcium chloride
   D. activated bauxite

20. Which of the following refrigerants sublimates?

   A. CO_2 B. NH_3 C. R-12   D. R-502

21. Carbon dioxide has a critical point of 87° F.
    This means that, regardless of how high the pressure is raised, it will NOT

   A. evaporate
   B. condense
   C. become saturated
   D. gain sensible heat

22. You would NOT use muntz metal with

   A. carbon dioxide
   B. Freon 12
   C. ammonia
   D. methyl chloride

23. One ton of refrigeration is equal to _____ BTU per _____.

   A. 144; minute
   B. 200; hour
   C. 288,000; hour
   D. 12,000; hour

24. There are several test cocks on a Freon receiver-condenser, one at the end about one quarter of the way up from the bottom.
    This test cock is used for

   A. purging non-condensable gases or air from the system
   B. testing the liquid level in the receiver
   C. an auxiliary charging connection
   D. pumping down purposes

25. A 200 ton air conditioning plant is set up with Freon compressors.
    Assuming that neither of the compressors is equipped with bypass solenoids, in order to be able to get AT LEAST four steps of capacity with these two machines, they should be driven by _____ motors.

   A. synchronous
   B. repulsion and induction
   C. capacitor type
   D. wound rotor induction

KEY (CORRECT ANSWERS)

1. D
2. C
3. B
4. B
5. A

6. C
7. C
8. C
9. A
10. D

11. D
12. D
13. C
14. B
15. D

16. D
17. A
18. A
19. C
20. A

21. B
22. C
23. D
24. B
25. D

TEST 3

DIRECTIONS: Each question or incomplete statement is followed by several suggested answers or completions. Select the one that BEST answers the question or completes the statement. *PRINT THE LETTER OF THE CORRECT ANSWER IN THE SPACE AT THE RIGHT.*

1. In order to determine the actual operating capacity of a chilled water cooler, it is essential that an operator know the specific heat of the water as well as the poundage of water flow per unit of time. With respect to the specific heat of water, in the normal liquid temperature range, it can be properly said that the specific heat of water is

    A. the same at all temperatures from 32° F to 212° F
    B. high at low temperatures and low at high temperatures
    C. high at low temperatures and high at high temperatures
    D. low at low temperatures and high at high temperatures

    1._____

2. A Freon refrigerating plant is being used in an air conditioning system to remove sensible heat from the air in a two stage after cooler to a silica gel air dehydrating unit. If the outside surface of the coils in the after cooler operate wet, the probability is that the

    A. suction pressure is too high
    B. refrigerant is wet
    C. coils in the after cooler are not properly vented
    D. none of the above

    2._____

3. The use of screwed joints in refrigeration systems for refrigerant pressures above 250 psi is permitted, provided that the nominal size of the pipe is NOT more than _____ inches.

    A. 1 1/4   B. 1 3/4   C. 2 1/4   D. 3

    3._____

4. Refrigerant 718 is

    A. propane   B. ammonia   C. water   D. air

    4._____

5. Thirty gallons of water per minute are to be reduced from 80° F to 40° F. How many tons of refrigeration are required to do this?

    A. 10   B. 30   C. 50   D. 70

    5._____

6. A plant refrigerating unit has 600 pounds of refrigerant in it. The CFM from the blower should be

    A. 1275   B. 1450   C. 1100   D. 600

    6._____

7. If an absorption system was to be placed in operation and the low and high sides were to be 16# and 150# of steam, _____ # would be required per ton of refrigeration.

    A. 70   B. 20   C. 200   D. 10

    7._____

8. It is NOT correct that a synchronous motor

    A. is a constant speed motor
    B. can be run using 220, 440, or 2300 volts
    C. is usually run with a lagging field current
    D. is excited by direct current

    8._____

15

9. The concentration of a brine which is used in an indirect system is determined by

   A. an Orsat meter
   B. Nessler's reagent
   C. a manometer
   D. a hydrometer

10. In the ammonia and Freon compression systems, the working pressure

    A. is the same for both ammonia and Freon
    B. is not comparable
    C. of Freon is higher
    D. of ammonia is higher

11. If the high pressure side of a compression system was reading considerably *higher* than normal, you would

    A. reduce compressor speed
    B. open the expansion valve
    C. increase the oil pressure
    D. send more water to the condenser

12. In the manufacturing of ice, air is piped into water cans to

    A. make clear ice
    B. speed up freezing time
    C. prevent ice from becoming brittle
    D. increase the brine velocity

13. How much liquid ammonia passes the expansion valve for 100 tons?

    A. 100#   B. 20#   C. 200#   D. 50#

14. One of the DISADVANTAGES of using carbon dioxide is that it has a lower critical point than usual, close to _____ °F.

    A. 67   B. 144   C. 39   D. 87

15. Upon noticing the discharge pressure gauge of a system that reads 980#, you would assume that the refrigerant was

    A. methyl chloride
    B. carbon dioxide
    C. ammonia
    D. Freon

16. The MAXIMUM permissible number of pounds of a Group 2 refrigerant for an indirect system in a commercial building having a Class T machinery room is

    A. 300   B. 500   C. 1000   D. unlimited

17. Upon increasing the supply of water to the condenser, the head pressure still remains the same.
    The NEXT thing you should do is

    A. speed up the compressor
    B. purge the receiver of refrigerant
    C. purge the system of non-condensable gases
    D. purge the system of gummy oil

18. With reference to specific minimum requirements for refrigerant pipe and tubing, the one of the following that is MOST NEARLY correct is:

    A. Standard soft annealed copper tubing used for refrigerant piping shall not be used in sizes larger than a half inch
    B. Joints in copper tubing systems containing Group 2 refrigerant should be soldered
    C. Standard I.P.S. copper and brass pipe and tubing shall not be less than 80% copper
    D. Standard wall steel or wrought iron pipe may be used for refrigeration liquid lines for one and a quarter inches or smaller

19. _____ gallons of water can fit in a pipe 14" in diameter and 110' long.

    A. 360   B. 880   C. 1090   D. 1276.4

20. The color of the lubricating oil in a CO_2 refrigerating plant manufacturing dry ice is

    A. lemon yellow   B. pale lemon
    C. lily or water white D. pale orange

21. In a compression cycle, a multi-cylinder, single-acting compressor operates automatically on room temperature (the *on and off cycle*). Upon starting, it pounds for a while. The MOST likely reason for this would be

    A. a worn wrist-pin bushing
    B. oil pumping due to overcharge of oil
    C. piston slap
    D. worn crankcase bearing

22. What design of valve would you use for an expansion valve? A _____ valve.

    A. globe   B. needle
    C. gate   D. V-notched globe

23. Synchronous motors that are used for industrial refrigeration have

    A. AC and DC supplied to them
    B. constant speed
    C. ability to correct the power factor
    D. all of the above

24. An absorption system uses 100 pounds of steam per day.
    This is a _____ ton plant.

    A. five   B. one   C. ten   D. fifty

25. The characteristics of ammonia include

    A. colorless gas   B. sharp odor
    C. lighter than air   D. all of the above

KEY (CORRECT ANSWERS)

1.	A	11.	D
2.	C	12.	A
3.	D	13.	D
4.	C	14.	D
5.	C	15.	B
6.	B	16.	A
7.	B	17.	C
8.	B	18.	C
9.	D	19.	B
10.	D	20.	C

21. B
22. B
23. D
24. A
25. D

TEST 4

DIRECTIONS: Each question or incomplete statement is followed by several suggested answers or completions. Select the one that BEST answers the question or completes the statement. *PRINT THE LETTER OF THE CORRECT ANSWER IN THE SPACE AT THE RIGHT.*

1. The use of screwed joints in piping systems for refrigerant pressures of 250 psi or less is permitted provided that the nominal size of the pipe is NOT more than _____ inches. 1.____

    A. 3 B. 4 C. 4 1/2 D. 2

2. The strong liquor in the absorption system is formed in the 2.____

    A. generator B. evaporator
    C. condenser D. absorber

3. An indicator card was taken on a horizontal double-acting single cylinder compressor, and the compression stroke was considerably left of its normal position. This would indicate that 3.____

    A. there was liquid in the cylinder
    B. the discharge valve was not seated properly
    C. the suction valve was not seated properly
    D. the suction gas was superheated

4. Assuming that all other factors remain the same, 4.____

    A. as the load on the evaporator decreases, the low side pressure decreases
    B. if the suction pressure increases, the capacity decreases
    C. if the head pressure increases, the capacity increases
    D. in refrigeration the coefficient of ammonia is lower than that of Freon 12

5. In a spray pond similar to a condenser, to kill algae in the water you would use 5.____

    A. silica gel B. chromite
    C. potassium permanganate D. potash

6. Regarding centrifugal compressors, it is TRUE that 6.____

    A. refrigerant leaks into the coiling system are common
    B. only the main bearing and thrust need to be oiled
    C. they have no auxiliary oil pump
    D. the auxiliary oil pump is hand-operated

7. Sweat joints in copper tubing for Group 1 refrigerant shall be 7.____

    A. threaded with 75% pitch
    B. brazed
    C. brazed or soldered
    D. gas free and using 50% glycerine and 50% litharge

8. The result of a Freon compressor not having properly seated magnetic bypass valves is 8.____

    A. reduced capacity B. loss of oil
    C. loss of refrigerant D. increased capacity

19

9. The area of a piston 16" in diameter is _____ square inches.

   A. 148.9   B. 200   C. 154   D. 162

10. With a broken sight glass, what devices are used for safety and loss of refrigerant on a receiver?

    A. Automatic safety valves, piped to outside
    B. Metal guards about glass
    C. Manual hand valves
    D. Automatic shut-off valves and metal guards about glass

11. The strong liquor in the absorber will become WEAKER when the

    A. expansion valve is closed
    B. evaporator load increases
    C. evaporator load decreases
    D. condenser pressure decreases

12. If the liquid line becomes partly clogged between the receiver and the expansion valve, the line

    A. between restriction and receiver will become hot
    B. between restriction and receiver will have 2" of frost
    C. above restriction will become hot
    D. above restriction will become frosted

13. When withdrawing refrigerant from a system into containers, the containers CANNOT be filled more than _____ %.

    A. 20   B. 50   C. 75   D. 85

14. The oil pressure in a reciprocating compressor should be _____ # above the _____ pressure.

    A. 40 to 60; suction   B. 40 to 60; discharge
    C. 10 to 30; suction   D. 10 to 30; discharge

15. The one of the following Freons that has the MOST refrigeration effect per pound is F-

    A. 11   B. 12   C. 113   D. 114

16. What effect will moisture have on a Freon system?

    A. Frozen king valve   B. Frozen compressor
    C. No effect   D. Frozen expansion valve

17. An absorption system is to be placed into operation under standard ton conditions, a suction of 19.5#, and discharge of 156#. The steam gauge reads 5 psig. What is the consumption of steam per ton hour of refrigerant?

    A. 20   B. 41   C. 51   D. 61

18. The balance in an absorption system is maintained by the

    A. governor on the ammonia pump
    B. steam pressure to the generator

C. liquid regulator valve in weak liquid line to absorber
D. temperature on the exchanger

19. Methyl chloride refrigerant is classified in group   19.____

    A. 4   B. 3   C. 2   D. 1

20. The term *viscosity* in a refrigeration oil means   20.____

    A. ability to mix   B. corrosive action
    C. internal friction   D. cold

21. A refrigerant that will break down into phosgene and other compounds when exposed to   21.____
    a hot gas flame such as cooking gas is

    A. ammonia anhydrous   B. carbon dioxide
    C. aqua ammonia   D. Freon 11

22. In some NH_3 plants, a unit is used which cools the gases being purged before they are   22.____
    passed over to the water bottle.
    This cooling is done in order to

    A. increase the rate of purging
    B. cool the gases before passing to the water bottle
    C. save the operator from manually purging the system
    D. recover ammonia which is still with the gas

23. *Carron oil* is used for ammonia burns and is made up of equal parts of linseed oil and   23.____

    A. nitric acid   B. lime water
    C. water   D. vinegar

24. The refrigerant that usually operates with a condenser pressure above 1050# is   24.____

    A. ammonia   B. sulphur dioxide
    C. carbon dioxide   D. F-114

25. The FIRST indication that a shipping drum of refrigerant used to charge a refrigeration   25.____
    system is EMPTYING is

    A. the appearance of frost on the drum
    B. a gurgling noise
    C. the appearance of a fog in the vicinity of the drum
    D. a hissing noise

KEY (CORRECT ANSWERS)

1.	A	11.	C
2.	B	12.	D
3.	D	13.	C
4.	A	14.	C
5.	C	15.	A
6.	B	16.	D
7.	C	17.	A
8.	A	18.	C
9.	B	19.	C
10.	D	20.	C

21. D
22. D
23. B
24. C
25. A

EXAMINATION SECTION
TEST 1

DIRECTIONS: Each question or incomplete statement is followed by several suggested answers or completions. Select the one that BEST answers the question or completes the statement. *PRINT THE LETTER OF THE CORRECT ANSWER IN THE SPACE AT THE RIGHT.*

1. What type of condenser would you install to conserve water?　　　　　　1.____

    A. Shell and tube　　　　　　　　B. Evaporative
    C. Atmospheric　　　　　　　　　D. Double pipe

2. The engine room first aid kit should contain _____ acid.　　　　　　　2.____

    A. hydrochloric　　　　　　　　　B. nitric
    C. sulphuric　　　　　　　　　　　D. picric

3. The steam jet refrigeration system is used for　　　　　　　　　　　　3.____

    A. deep freezing work　　　　　　B. air conditioning work
    C. cold storage　　　　　　　　　 D. the noon whistle

4. A flooded evaporator USUALLY has a(n) _____ metering device.　　　　4.____

    A. high side float
    B. low side float
    C. automatic expansion valve
    D. thermostatic expansion valve

5. Refrigerant enters the condenser as a _____ and leaves as a _____.　　5.____

    A. high pressure gas; high pressure liquid
    B. high pressure gas; low pressure liquid
    C. high pressure liquid; low pressure liquid
    D. superheated gas; superheated gas

6. When a high side float is punctured and sinks, it results in　　　　　　　6.____

    A. starved evaporator　　　　　　 B. flooded evaporator
    C. frozen valve　　　　　　　　　 D. high head pressure

7. A compound gauge registers　　　　　　　　　　　　　　　　　　　　　　7.____

    A. inches of pressure present
    B. pounds of pressure below atmospheric pressure
    C. inches of water above atmosphere and inches of air below
    D. pounds of pressure above atmosphere and inches of vacuum below

8. An air conditioning Freon compressor is equipped with a unit shell and coil condenser-　　8.____
   receiver slung under the base of the compressor.
   If the system is overcharged with refrigerant, the PROBABILITY is that

    A. only head pressure would go up
    B. both head pressure and suction pressure would go up
    C. capacity of the compressor would go up
    D. system would continue to operate without change

9. In relation to compressors, which statement is MOST correct?

   A. Valve lift for low speed reciprocating compressors is less.
   B. The HP per ton decreases as the suction decreases.
   C. The refrigerating effect per pound of refrigerant decreases as the suction pressure increases.
   D. The valve lift for high speed reciprocating compressors should be less than required for low speed compressors.

10. What type of constant speed motor is generally used in large refrigerating plants?

    A. Slip ring
    B. Synchronous
    C. Squirrel gauge
    D. Double wound squirrel gauge

11. The capacity of an evaporative condenser will INCREASE if the

    A. wet bulb reading is high
    B. wet bulb reading is low
    C. capacity does not change
    D. amount of water used is less

12. One ton of refrigeration is equal to how many BTUs?

    A. 1,200 per minute
    B. 200 per hour
    C. 12,000 per hour
    D. 288,000 per hour

13. A(n) _____ condenser could be used in winter without water.

    A. submerged
    B. shell and tube
    C. shell and coil
    D. atmospheric with drip

14. The evaporative coils in a cooler are along the ceiling, and one of these coils has insulating baffles.
    The baffles are there to

    A. catch the dripping when the coils are defrosting
    B. supply gravity air to circulate in the cooler
    C. see that gravity air circulates over the coils
    D. none of the above

15. In methyl chloride systems, a dryer would PROBABLY be placed in the _____ near the _____.

    A. discharge; compressor
    B. liquid line; expansion valve
    C. suction line; compressor
    D. suction line; evaporator

16. A Freon 12 compressor used in an air conditioning system has a magnetic bypass to   16.____

    A. equalize pressure in the cylinder
    B. relieve pressure when it becomes high
    C. regulate compressor capacity
    D. relieve oil from the cylinder to the crankcase

17. The formula $C = 0.8P_1D^2$ is used for determining the capacity of a   17.____

    A. fusible plug   B. stop valve
    C. safety valve   D. venturi

18. A scale trap is placed in the suction line of a compression system to remove foreign matter. It would be MOST effective when the plant is   18.____

    A. new
    B. shut down for a long time
    C. old
    D. none of the above

19. In a small ammonia plant using brine as a cooling agent, due to a leak, the brine became saturated with ammonia. After fixing the leak, you, as an operator, would   19.____

    A. dump the brine and make up a new batch
    B. recirculate the brine through the system; if no leaks, reuse it
    C. treat the brine with Nessler's solution and reuse it
    D. treat the brine with sulphur and reuse it

20. When starting a large air conditioning system of the reciprocating type on a day when the latent heat load is high, one of the FIRST things an engineer should do is   20.____

    A. open the bypass valve to lighten the load
    B. set the thermostat a few degrees higher
    C. install larger fuses to take the starting load
    D. turn on the cooling water and start the air blower

21. Which of the following statements is CORRECT?
    A(n)   21.____

    A. enclosed cooling tower has a forced draft effect
    B. spray pond works exactly like an evaporative condenser
    C. evaporative condenser depends upon the evaporation of some water for its economical operation
    D. evaporative condenser has no refrigerant coil in it

22. The symbol for refrigeration shown at the right represents   22.____

    A. high side float   B. low side float
    C. water valve   D. oil trap

23. The one of the following types of condensers in which eliminator plates are USUALLY found is the _____ type   23.____

    A. shell and coil   B. shell and tube
    C. evaporative   D. double tube

24. There are several test cocks on a Freon receiver condenser. The one at the end, about one quarter of the way up from the bottom. This test cock is used for   24.____

    A. purging non-condensable gases or air from the system
    B. testing the liquid level in the receiver
    C. an auxiliary charging connection
    D. pumping down purposes

25. The FASTEST way to remove the frost from direct expansion coils in a cold storage room is to   25.____

    A. spray water over them
    B. shut the coils off and let the frost melt off
    C. chop or scrape the frost off
    D. run a hot gas line to the coils

KEY (CORRECT ANSWERS)

1. B		11. B	
2. D		12. C	
3. B		13. D	
4. B		14. C	
5. A		15. B	
6. A		16. C	
7. D		17. A	
8. B		18. A	
9. D		19. A	
10. B		20. D	

21. C
22. A
23. C
24. B
25. D

TEST 2

DIRECTIONS: Each question or incomplete statement is followed by several suggested answers or completions. Select the one that BEST answers the question or completes the statement. *PRINT THE LETTER OF THE CORRECT ANSWER IN THE SPACE AT THE RIGHT.*

1. In a shell and tube brine cooler with an electric float valve, if the gas equalizer line is clogged,

    A. it operates normally
    B. liquid in the tank goes up and down
    C. liquid in the tank does not correspond with the level in the float
    D. there is no change

    1._____

2. The weak liquor heat exchanger or an ammonia absorption system is used to pre-

    A. heat weak liquor
    B. heat strong liquor
    C. cool strong liquor
    D. cool suction gas

    2._____

3. The subcooling of liquid refrigerant, immediately before the liquid passes through the expansion valve, would MOST likely result in an increase

    A. of 50% in the horsepower per ton factor
    B. in head pressure
    C. in compressor speed
    D. in the net available refrigerating effect

    3._____

4. A Freon compressor was V-belt driven when installed, but the belts were too tight. After the unit has been running for a while, this will

    A. increase the speed of the compressor
    B. decrease the speed of the motor and the compressor
    C. increase the speed of the motor
    D. cause the motor to run hot

    4._____

5. In a room, there is a cylinder half-filled with ammonia at 50° F. The pressure inside the tank will be _____ pounds.

    A. 40   B. 125   C. 75   D. 250

    5._____

6. What percentage of oil travels with refrigerant in a system?

    A. 10%   B. 125%   C. 30%   D. 50%

    6._____

7. When attempting to read the high side pressure gauge on an operating ammonia compressor, it is noted that the pointer *hunts,* or has a wide and relatively slow back and forth movement. This would MOST likely indicate that the compressor

    A. is overloaded
    B. valve action is sluggish
    C. suction valves are stuck
    D. is operating normally

    7._____

8. One DISADVANTAGE of using carbon dioxide is that it has a lower critical point than usual, close to _____ ° F.

    A. 67   B. 144   C. 39.4   D. 87

    8._____

27

9. If a Freon 12 single-acting compressor had oil foaming in the crankcase, this would be caused by

    A. addition of liquid Freon
    B. sudden drop in oil temperature
    C. addition of oil to the crankcase
    D. sudden drop in crankcase pressure

10. The refrigerant that separates from the lubricating oil in an operating evaporator with oil floating on top of the liquid refrigerant is

    A. Freon 12   B. Freon 22
    C. ammonia   D. carbon dioxide

11. In a system using a silica gel drier that has picked up moisture, it may be reactivated by heating it for a period of four hours or more, at a temperature of APPROXIMATELY _____ °F.

    A. 200   B. 700   C. 450   D. 850

12. In a large plant, there are several squirrel gauge motors and three or four synchronous motors.
One purpose of the synchronous motor is

    A. to correct the power factor
    B. to correct the plant power demand
    C. to allow for more than one speed
    D. its high speed

13. Of the different types of solenoid valves used in refrigeration, the one which, when energized, tends to close the port is the _____ type.

    A. closed   B. normally open
    C. fluctuating   D. partially closed

14. A Freon 12 compressor used for air conditioning has a low temperature cooling coil of 45° (no superheat).
The low temperature gas coming back to the compressor would be

    A. 20#   B. 40#   C. 60#   D. 80#

15. In a given temperature of air, the ratio of vapor pressure to humidity is called

    A. absolute humidity   B. relative humidity
    C. pressure   D. partial pressure

16. A compressor that has two compression strokes and two suction strokes per cylinder per revolution of the crankshaft is a

    A. single-acting compressor
    B. double-acting compressor
    C. two stage compressor
    D. compressor in duplex

17. In the lubrication of a Freon refrigeration compressor,

    A. vegetable oil is preferred for best results
    B. Freon has the same degree of miscibility with oils as does ammonia
    C. a chemical action between the Freon and lubricating oil occurs
    D. the refrigerant mixes with the lubricating oil

18. The refrigerant stored in a machinery room shall NOT be more than _____% of the normal charge or more than _____ pounds of refrigerant in addition to the charge in the system.

    A. 20; 300   B. 30; 300   C. 35; 350   D. 25; 325

19. A motor has a protection device to prevent burning out or damage called a

    A. fusetron   B. dual fuse
    C. circuit breaker   D. thermal protector

20. For a pressure testing of newly installed R-12 systems, it is BEST to use

    A. dry carbon dioxide with a trace of R-12 in it
    B. water in a hydrostatic test
    C. dry hydrogen with a trace of R-12 in it
    D. anhydrous ammonia

21. A dehydrator should be used in a(n) _____ system.

    A. sulphur dioxide   B. Freon 12
    C. ammonia   D. carbon dioxide

22. In the absorption system, the flow of ammonia gas in relation to the strong liquor in the analyzer is _____ flow.

    A. cross   B. counter   C. parallel   D. diagonal

23. A volume of water of 10,000 cubic inches weighs _____ pounds.

    A. 144   B. 970   C. 361   D. 231

24. The refrigerant known as *Refrigerant 40* is

    A. propane   B. sulphur dioxide
    C. methyl chloride   D. ammonia

25. What design of valve would you use for an expansion valve?
    A _____ valve.

    A. globe   B. needle
    C. gate   D. V-notched globe

KEY (CORRECT ANSWERS)

1. C
2. B
3. D
4. D
5. C

6. A
7. B
8. D
9. D
10. D

11. C
12. A
13. B
14. B
15. B

16. B
17. D
18. A
19. D
20. A

21. B
22. B
23. C
24. C
25. B

TEST 3

DIRECTIONS: Each question or incomplete statement is followed by several suggested answers or completions. Select the one that BEST answers the question or completes the statement. *PRINT THE LETTER OF THE CORRECT ANSWER IN THE SPACE AT THE RIGHT.*

1. In comparing the absorption system with the compression system, the steam coil in the generator is equivalent to the   1.____

    A. hot discharge refrigerant vapor
    B. electric motor
    C. hot discharge valve assembly
    D. compressor

2. On a horizontal compressor having a gravity feed oil system from a tank above the compressor, the pressure inside the tank is   2.____

    A. zero psig   B. 14.7 gauge
    C. 20 pounds   D. 10 pounds above suction

3. Which of the following would cause frost to form on the outer surface of an evaporator coil?   3.____

    A. Water in the refrigerant
    B. Water in the liquid line
    C. Moisture in the refrigerant
    D. Moisture in the air within the cooler

4. The material used for the packing of an ammonia stuffing box would MOST likely be   4.____

    A. steel
    B. solid lead
    C. bellows and spring arrangement
    D. graphite, hemp, and lead

5. It is CORRECT to state that   5.____

    A. copper cannot be used with R-12
    B. aluminum cannot be used with methyl chloride
    C. black iron cannot be used with R-22
    D. magnesium can be used with Freon

6. What color does blue litmus paper turn when ammonia is present?   6.____

    A. Red   B. White
    C. Green   D. None of the above

7. In the absorption system, the condenser, receiver, expansion valve, and the evaporator can be designed   7.____

    A. similar to the compression equipment
    B. as an open type design

31

C. the same as the compression equipment, only zinc coated
D. of copper only

8. You would NOT use muntz metal with

   A. carbon dioxide
   B. Freon 12
   C. ammonia
   D. methyl chloride

9. A ten-ton refrigeration unit has the capacity of _____ BTU per minute.

   A. 2,000   B. 20,000   C. 12,000   D. 288,000

10. The oil gauge pressure on an ammonia vertical compressor should be

    A. zero pounds when the suction pressure is zero per inch
    B. forty pounds
    C. 30 psig when the suction pressure is 10 psig
    D. 50 pounds fluctuating with the discharge pressure

11. The MINIMUM required rated discharge capacity of a pressure relief device or fusible plug for a refrigerant-containing vessel, shall be determined by the formula C = Fdl. C is equal to

    A. feet per second
    B. feet per hour
    C. refrigerant per ton
    D. air in # per minute

12. What percentage of oil is mixed with the refrigerant in the compression cycle?

    A. 10%   B. 20%   C. 30%   D. 40%

13. If the liquid line were *warmer* than usual, it would indicate

    A. excessive refrigerant
    B. shortage of refrigerant
    C. receiver full of liquid
    D. high head pressure

14. A spare rupture member can be substituted for a relief valve in a(n) _____ system.

    A. aqua ammonia
    B. sulphur dioxide
    C. carbon dioxide
    D. ammonia

15. What kind of piping would you NOT choose for anhydrous ammonia or aqua ammonia?

    A. Black steel
    B. Stainless steel
    C. Galvanized steel
    D. Wrought iron

16. In an absorption system, if the heat exchanger were removed, the result would be to

    A. more steam added to the generator to get results
    B. stop the liquid pump from the absorber
    C. stop the weak liquor pump from the generator
    D. pipe the cold gas from the evaporator directly to the generator

17. What produces the LOWER reading of the wet bulb?

    A. The thermometer is calibrated that way
    B. Cooling by evaporation
    C. The cloth and water form a cooling solution
    D. It does not read lower

18. The color of the lubricating oil in a carbon dioxide refrigerating plant manufacturing dry ice is

    A. lemon yellow
    B. pale lemon
    C. lily or water white
    D. pale orange

19. In a packaged air conditioning unit, the refrigeration unit was overcharged.
    The result would be

    A. increased head pressure and suction pressure
    B. decreased head pressure
    C. low suction pressure
    D. low head and low suction pressure

20. The GREATEST operating capacity can be maintained by a MAXIMUM

    A. suction and discharge superheat
    B. discharge pressure
    C. suction pressure
    D. constant water flow to the system

21. An ammonia type compression system uses sea water as found in the New York Harbor for condensing service.
    In order to test for the presence of ammonia in this water, one should use _____ solution.

    A. Carrene
    B. sulphur
    C. Nessler's
    D. halide

22. A vertical single-acting compressor has pistons with suction valves. In this arrangement, only the top of the cylinder is water jacketed.
    The BEST reason for this is

    A. lower cost of the casting
    B. less water is used
    C. the lower part of the cylinder would be cooler than the jacket water
    D. only the discharge valves need cooling

23. In order to prevent rust or corrosion in a salt brine used to manufacture ice, an operator would add

    A. sodium dichromate
    B. aluminum sulphate
    C. Nessler's solution
    D. universal indicator solution

24. The brine in an icemaking plant will PROBABLY be between

    A. 0° and 11° C
    B. 0° and 11° F
    C. 25° and 29° C
    D. 14° and 22° F

25. In a reciprocating compressor, the pistons are of double trunk type. The ADVANTAGE of this is   25.____

    A. oil will not mix with refrigerant
    B. lighter piston
    C. more piston rings can be used
    D. shorter connecting rods

KEY (CORRECT ANSWERS)

1.	D	11.	D
2.	A	12.	A
3.	D	13.	B
4.	D	14.	C
5.	B	15.	C
6.	D	16.	A
7.	A	17.	B
8.	C	18.	C
9.	A	19.	A
10.	C	20.	C

21. C
22. C
23. A
24. B
25. A

EXAMINATION SECTION
TEST 1

DIRECTIONS: Each question or incomplete statement is followed by several suggested answers or completions. Select the one that BEST answers the question or completes the statement. *PRINT THE LETTER OF THE CORRECT ANSWER IN THE SPACE AT THE RIGHT.*

1. A plant refrigerating unit has 600 pounds of refrigerant in it. The CFM from the exhaust blower should be

    A. 1275 B. 1450 C. 1100 D. 600

2. A rupture member can be substituted for a relief valve in a(n) _____ system.

    A. aqua ammonia   B. sulphur dioxide
    C. carbon dioxide   D. ammonia

3. Which of the following groups of refrigerants is in Group 3?

    A. CO_2
       F-12
       F-22
       Propane

    B. F-11
       F-113
       Ammonia
       Butane

    C. Ethane
       Butane
       F-12
       Carbon dioxide

    D. Butane
       Ethane
       Propane
       Ethylene

4. When withdrawing refrigerant from a system into containers, they cannot be filled more than _____%.

    A. 70 B. 75 C. 80 D. 85

5. When field testing Refrigerant 12, the high and low sides should be tested to _____ #.

    A. 300-150 B. 235-140 C. 95-50 D. 1500-1000

6. In a refrigerating system with a gauge where the dial points to 100 psi, under normal operating conditions, the LAST number of the gauge should read

    A. 105 B. 110 C. 115 D. 120

7. The MAXIMUM pounds in a direct system, per 1,000 cubic feet of occupied space, for Refrigerant 12 is

    A. 31 B. 41 C. 51 D. 61

8. The metallic mixtures of alloys used to make a gas tight soldered joint should melt at _____ °F.

    A. 600   B. 800° F and above 300
    C. 935   D. 1000° F and above 400

9. A specification calls for the installation of a unit air conditioning system in the lobby of a building. This is to contain 30# Freon 12.
   In keeping with the rules, this system may

   A. be installed
   B. be installed, if the system is reduced to 20#
   C. not be installed; no unit can be placed in the lobby
   D. not be installed, as it contains a group 2 refrigerant

10. The minimum required rated discharge capacity of the pressure relief device or fusible plug for a refrigerant containing vessel shall be determined by the formula C = Fdl.
    What is C equal to?

    A. Feet per hour
    B. Refrigerant per minute
    C. Air in pounds per minute
    D. Amount of second

11. To pack tongue and groove, flanges on ammonia lines should be made of

    A. rubber   B. asbestos sheet
    C. tin   D. sheet lead

12. How many kinds of lubricants are used in a horizontal double-acting compressor?

    A. One   B. Two   C. Three   D. Four

13. Flash gas would be found in the

    A. receiver   B. condenser
    C. king valve   D. evaporator

14. The accepted method to test oil for moisture content is the dielectric test. This test imposes high voltage electric pressure on electrodes immersed in an oil sample. If any current flows, there is moisture present.
    The electrodes are spaced _____ inch(es), _____ volts.

    A. 1/2 to 1; 40,000   B. 1 to 2; 25,000
    C. 2 to 3; 22,000   D. 1 1/2 to 4; 33,000

15. Heat transfer takes place by
    I. evaporation
    II. convection
    III. conduction
    IV. radiation
    The CORRECT answer is:

    A. I, II   B. II, III, IV
    C. I, II, III   D. III, IV

16. A pan of an evaporative condenser 8 feet long, 4 feet wide, and 9 inches deep contains _____ gallons of water.

    A. 120   B. 180   C. 280   D. 204.5

17. A hermetically sealed unit is a unit with the

    A. motor and compressor, *both* enclosed in a sealed casing
    B. motor *only* sealed in a casing
    C. compressor *only* sealed in a casing
    D. carrier absorption system

18. Regarding centrifugal compressors, it is TRUE that

    A. only the main bearing and thrust need to be oiled
    B. refrigerant leaks into the oiling system are common
    C. they have no auxiliary oil pump
    D. the auxiliary oil pump is hand-operated

19. There are dummy tubes or a *Tell Tale* welded to the shell of a large accumulator in an industrial ammonia plant. The pipe extends through the insulation.
Its purpose is to

    A. increase the capacity of the system
    B. facilitate taking ammonia samples
    C. check and mark the refrigerant level in the vessel
    D. make the accumulator physically stronger

20. Synchronous motors that are used for industrial refrigeration have

    A. AC and DC supplied to them
    B. constant speed
    C. ability to correct the power factor
    D. all of the above

21. An absorption system uses 100 pounds of steam per day.
This is a _____ -ton plant.

    A. five   B. one   C. ten   D. fifty

22. The characteristics of ammonia include

    A. colorless gas   B. sharp odor
    C. lighter than air   D. all of the above

23. Where would you place an accumulator in the system?

    A. On the suction side of the compressor
    B. Just before the condenser on the discharge side of the system
    C. On the high side of the liquid line
    D. Before the king valve

24. Methyl chloride refrigerant is classified in Group

    A. 4   B. 3   C. 2   D. 1

25. A rotary booster compressor has _____ bearing(s).

    A. one   B. two   C. three   D. four

KEY (CORRECT ANSWERS)

1. B
2. C
3. D
4. B
5. B

6. D
7. A
8. D
9. A
10. C

11. D
12. B
13. D
14. B
15. B

16. A
17. A
18. A
19. C
20. D

21. A
22. D
23. A
24. C
25. B

TEST 2

DIRECTIONS: Each question or incomplete statement is followed by several suggested answers or completions. Select the one that BEST answers the question or completes the statement. *PRINT THE LETTER OF THE CORRECT ANSWER IN THE SPACE AT THE RIGHT.*

1. How many BTU's are removed to cool 2,000 bars of butter from 70° F to 36° F if the specific heat of butter is .87 and each bar weighs 1.5 pounds?   1.____

    A. 74,130   B. 51,000   C. 88,500   D. 104,731

2. A system with one compressor is using two evaporators of different temperatures, one with 35° F and the other with 20° F.   2.____
The back pressure valve would be located on the

    A. common suction line
    B. common liquid line
    C. suction line nearer to the lower temperature cooler
    D. suction line of the high temperature cooler

3. There are several refrigerants in the Freon group that are in common use. In connection with Freon 11, it can be stated that this refrigerant is widely used in air conditioning systems that have a _____ compressor.   3.____

    A. small reciprocating   B. large reciprocating
    C. rotary   D. large centrifugal

4. With the same compressor displacement, the refrigerant that will give the MOST refrigerating effect per pound circulated is   4.____

    A. Freon 12   B. ammonia   C. butane   D. Freon 11

5. The term *anhydrous* is used with a refrigerant to indicate the   5.____

    A. presence of ammonia   B. presence of water
    C. absence of Freon   D. absence of water

6. A *swirl* is a device used in a(n) _____ condenser.   6.____

    A. shell and coil   B. closed shell and tube
    C. open shell and tube   D. atmospheric

7. Carbon dioxide is in refrigerant Group   7.____

    A. 1   B. 2   C. 3   D. 6

8. In many direct refrigerant systems, thermal expansion valves with equalizer lines may be installed.   8.____
If the equalizer line became plugged, the effect on the cooling coil with a full load would be

    A. a starved coil   B. a flooded coil
    C. 4% superheat   D. 7% superheat

39

9. In a Freon 12 air conditioning system, the finned evaporator coil is wet. It can be CORRECTLY stated that

   A. the system is not operating efficiently
   B. there is a shortage of refrigerant
   C. there is an oversized expansion valve
   D. the system is operating efficiently

10. In absorption systems, the ammonia pump transfers _____ from the _____.

    A. strong liquor; absorber to the generator
    B. ammonia gas; generator to the condenser
    C. weak liquor; generator to the absorber
    D. liquid ammonia; condenser to the receiver

11. In an automatic Freon 12 system for air conditioning, you, as the original installer, have to make a tight pipe joint.
    You would use a

    A. serrated flange without a leak gasket
    B. threaded *streamline fitting* and white lead
    C. combination of solder, litharge, glycerine, and white lead
    D. *streamline fitting* and solder to copper piping

12. The chemical in a dehydrator for a Freon or methyl chloride system is

    A. sawdust   B. silica gel
    C. aluminum   D. dichromate

13. A brine cooler in a refrigeration cycle is between the

    A. evaporator and the compressor
    B. compressor and the receiver
    C. compressor and the condenser
    D. expansion valve and the compressor

14. A piston design for a compressor without a cross-head is

    A. box   B. balanced   C. trunk   D. telescopic

15. In an automatic Freon unit with a low pressure control (off and on type), upon starting, there is a pounding condition.
    This is due to

    A. a worn piston pin
    B. a slapping piston pin
    C. excessive oil in the compressor
    D. a worn crank bearing

16. When the crosshead is properly aligned, the piston rod of a horizontal ammonia compressor is MOST likely to wear

    A. at the crosshead end   B. at the piston end
    C. at the middle of the rod   D. on the side

17. In a carbon dioxide system, the condenser cooling water rises to 87° F. Could some of the refrigeration be used to cool the cooling water so that the gas could condense at a savings?
    The BEST response is:

    A. It is impractical because the water would freeze
    B. In general, it would be a very economical set-up
    C. Refrigeration loss would be greater, but the total would gain
    D. The cooling refrigeration gains, but the plant total would lose

18. Upon testing for ammonia leaks with red litmus paper, if ammonia is present, the color changes to

    A. green   B. blue   C. red   D. yellow

19. A horizontal shell and tube cooler is equipped with eliminators. The PRIMARY function of the eliminators is to

    A. prevent the carry-over of liquid refrigerant
    B. protect the tubes in the event of a freeze-up
    C. absorb noises and vibration impulses
    D. prevent oil from being carried into the cooler

20. A large cooler is equipped with ceiling-hung brine cooling coils. The insulated baffles are properly arranged along one side and underneath the cooling coils. These baffles are PRIMARILY used

    A. as drip pans when defrosting
    B. to get proper gravity circulation of air through the coils
    C. to help support the weight of the coils when they frost up
    D. to collect the brine in case of a leak in the coils

21. Anhydrous ammonia is MOST like water in

    A. odor
    B. color
    C. saturates at atmospheric pressure
    D. sublimes like water at 212° F and 14.69 pounds absolute

22. Carron oil (a liniment used for ammonia burns) is made up of equal parts of

    A. linseed oil and lime water
    B. vaseline and picric acid
    C. lanolin and vinegar
    D. sulphur dioxide and water

23. In an absorption type refrigerating plant, the weak liquor is very often used to

    A. precool the condenser water   B. precool the liquid ammonia
    C. preheat the strong liquor   D. preheat the steam

24. The degree of solubility in reference to a refrigerating oil is usually the LOWEST when using

    A. genetron 141
    B. methyl chloride
    C. Freon 12
    D. carbon dioxide

25. In a large plant, there is a synchronous motor. It could be said that

    A. the speed will vary
    B. in a weak field, current will be leading
    C. a strong field will make up for the lagging
    D. excitation will cause current to lag

KEY (CORRECT ANSWERS)

1. B	11. D
2. D	12. B
3. D	13. D
4. B	14. C
5. D	15. C
6. C	16. C
7. A	17. D
8. B	18. B
9. D	19. A
10. A	20. B

21. B
22. A
23. C
24. D
25. B

TEST 3

DIRECTIONS: Each question or incomplete statement is followed by several suggested answers or completions. Select the one that BEST answers the question or completes the statement. *PRINT THE LETTER OF THE CORRECT ANSWER IN THE SPACE AT THE RIGHT.*

1. In a given temperature of air, the ratio of vapor pressure to humidity is called   1._____

    A. absolute humidity
    B. relative humidity
    C. pressure
    D. partial pressure

2. A compressor that has two compression strokes and two suction strokes per cylinder per revolution of the crankshaft is a   2._____

    A. single-acting compressor
    B. double-acting compressor
    C. two stage compressor
    D. compressor in duplex

3. In the lubrication of a Freon refrigeration compressor,   3._____

    A. vegetable oil is preferred for best results
    B. Freon has the same degree of miscibility with oils as does ammonia
    C. a chemical action between the Freon and lubricating oil occurs
    D. the refrigerant mixes with the lubricating oil

4. A Freon refrigeration plant is being used in an air conditioning system to remove the sensible heat from the air in a two stage after cooler to a silica gel air dehydrating unit. If the outside surface of the coils in the after cooler were to operate wet, the probability is that the   4._____

    A. suction pressure is too high
    B. refrigerant is wet
    C. coils of the after cooler are not properly vented
    D. none of the above

5. The speed, in revolutions per minute, of a six pole synchronous motor rated at 80 HP, 400 volts, and 60 cycles is   5._____

    A. 480   B. 900   C. 1200   D. 1800

6. The capacity of an evaporative condenser INCREASES as _____ bulb temperature _____.   6._____

    A. wet; decreases
    B. wet; increases
    C. wet and dry; increases
    D. dry; increases

7. For a pressure testing of newly installed R-12 systems, it is BEST to use   7._____

    A. dry carbon dioxide with a trace of R-12 in it
    B. water in a hydrostatic test
    C. dry hydrogen with a trace of R-12 in it
    D. anhydrous ammonia

8. A dehydrator should be used in a(n) _____ system.

   A. sulphur dioxide B. Freon 12
   C. ammonia D. carbon dioxide

9. In the absorption system, the flow of ammonia gas in relation to the strong liquor in the analyzer is called _____ flow.

   A. cross B. parallel C. counter D. diagonal

10. In an ice plant, the agitation air is precooled because it

    A. lessens the load on the ice field
    B. increases air pressure capacity
    C. prevents freezing of air lines
    D. decreases air pressure capacity

11. The one of the following that can be used to make up a threaded joint (NH_3) is

    A. red lead and shellac B. Red Indian shellac
    C. white lead D. litharge and glycerine

12. If Nessler's solution is added to a sample of brine, in the event of ammonia being present, the color of the solution in the brine will turn

    A. blue B. red C. yellow D. pink

13. An ammonia system was working with 8" vacuum on the return line. The absolute pressure would be CLOSE to _____#.

    A. 7 B. 22 C. 25 D. 10

14. A thermostatic expansion valve in a refrigeration system regulates the

    A. pressure of the evaporator
    B. pressure of the compressor
    C. flow of refrigerant to the precooler
    D. flow of refrigerant to the evaporator

15. In testing condenser water for carbon dioxide leaks, you would use

    A. Nessler's solution B. bromthymol blue
    C. a halide torch D. litmus paper

16. The purpose of the halide torch is

    A. to heat copper fitting for soldering
    B. a safety light
    C. to find carbon dioxide leaks
    D. to find Freon leaks

17. An oil lantern is used in the stuffing box

    A. to hold the seat tight and rigid
    B. as a guiding light
    C. as a seal
    D. as a space to hold oil

18. One of the effects of the presence of non-condensable gases in a refrigerating system is _____ pressure.

    A. high condensing
    B. low suction
    C. high suction
    D. low condensing

19. It is true that the greater the temperature differential between the water and the refrigerant gas, the more effective the condenser is.
    An operator, keeping this in mind, would

    A. raise the condenser pressure
    B. cut back on the inlet water
    C. raise the temperature of the incoming water
    D. reduce the power to the compressor (unit)

20. At a cost of .04 cents per KWH, what would be the cost per hour for a 100 HP motor running at 80% efficiency?

    A. $3.20   B. $3.70   C. $4.20   D. $4.90

21. In an air conditioning system having ducts, the evaporator coil has moisture on it during most days of the summer.
    This is due to

    A. not enough liquid refrigerant
    B. excessive liquid refrigerant
    C. the feeler bulb which requires movement to make frost
    D. generally a condition that is normal

22. Ammonia operates at higher pressures than Freon 12, but the higher temperatures and pressures required are offset by _____ volumetric displacement per ton.

    A. better
    B. worse
    C. the same
    D. none of the above

23. An oil interceptor placed in an ammonia plant of 300 tons is found

    A. so that it returns oil to the pump
    B. on the discharge line between the compressor and condenser
    C. lower than the compressor base
    D. before the pump and is used as an oil strainer

24. One ton of refrigeration equals

    A. 12,000 BTU per minute
    B. 1,200 BTU for 6 minutes
    C. 288,000 BTU per hour
    D. 144 BTU per minute

25. How many tons of ice would a 15 ton refrigeration unit make per day?

    A. 30   B. 15   C. 8   D. 5

KEY (CORRECT ANSWERS)

1.	B	11.	D
2.	B	12.	C
3.	D	13.	D
4.	C	14.	D
5.	B	15.	B
6.	D	16.	D
7.	A	17.	D
8.	B	18.	A
9.	C	19.	B
10.	B	20.	B

21. D
22. A
23. B
24. B
25. C

———

TEST 4

DIRECTIONS: Each question or incomplete statement is followed by several suggested answers or completions. Select the one that BEST answers the question or completes the statement. *PRINT THE LETTER OF THE CORRECT ANSWER IN THE SPACE AT THE RIGHT.*

1. In the absorption system, the weak liquid cooler is sometimes used to cool the

    A. liquid ammonia going to the evaporator
    B. strong liquid before it goes to the analyzer
    C. aqua ammonia before it goes to the condenser
    D. weak liquid before it goes to the absorber

    1.____

2. In an ammonia flooded coil system, it is noticed that the evaporator tubes are dry and warm at the bottom and the upper coils are frosted. The reason for this is

    A. the evaporator is overloaded
    B. the evaporator is oil-logged
    C. the evaporator is underloaded
    D. this is normal operation for such a system

    2.____

3. A thermostatic expansion valve has an external equalizer line. If the line became clogged while the system was operating, the evaporator would

    A. become flooded
    B. operate at 9 of superheat
    C. operate at full capacity
    D. starve

    3.____

4. If the specific gravity of water is 1, then for a brine, it would be

    A. the same   B. greater   C. less   D. 1.44

    4.____

5. In a large ammonia plant, the power factor reading on the panel board reads 90% or 90. This indicates that the power factor is

    A. good   B. bad   C. constant   D. irregular

    5.____

6. _____ CANNOT be used with ammonia.

    A. Lead   B. Copper   C. Steel   D. Iron

    6.____

7. A means to detect a carbon dioxide leak is a _____ test.

    A. white litmus paper   B. red litmus paper
    C. blue litmus paper   D. soapy water

    7.____

8. The BEST evaporator to overcome flash gas is

    A. a direct expansion with a thermal expansion valve
    B. a coil with a bypass valve
    C. the flooded evaporator type
    D. one with a constant pressure valve

    8.____

9. The _____ pump is the only moving part in the absorption system.

   A. steam
   B. water
   C. aqua ammonia
   D. compressed air

10. A system having less than 50# of refrigerant in it is usually stopped before purging of non-condensable gases. The reason for this is that

    A. it prevents the loss of large amounts of refrigerant
    B. the operator is present
    C. it saves time in the long run
    D. it is better because it takes longer

11. In a cold storage plant of 21 rooms with expansion coils in each, EVERY coil should have

    A. a strainer
    B. a common header
    C. an oil accumulator
    D. its own expansion valve

12. In a low temperature Freon 12 system, you would expect to find the booster compressor

    A. on the low pressure side of the system
    B. on the high side of the plant
    C. in a special room
    D. separate

13. With the same compressor displacement and the same suction pressure, which will give the MOST effective refrigeration per pound pumped?

    A. Freon 12
    B. Carrene
    C. Ammonia
    D. Carbon dioxide

14. If the liquid line becomes partly clogged between the receiver and the expansion valve, the result may be that the line

    A. between restriction and receiver will become hot
    B. between restriction and receiver will have 2" of frost
    C. above restriction will become hot
    D. above restriction will become frosted

15. Methyl chloride belongs to refrigerant group

    A. 1   B. 2   C. 3   D. 4

16. Assuming that all other conditions in a refrigeration system remain constant, the horsepower per ton of refrigeration will MOST likely _____ as the _____.

    A. increase; suction pressure increases
    B. increase; head pressure decreases
    C. increase; head pressure increases
    D. decrease; suction pressure decreases

17. The pump in the absorption system should PREFERABLY handle

    A. 50% gas and 50% liquid
    B. 100% liquid
    C. 100% gas
    D. none of the above

18. An employee received an ammonia burn near his eyes. You should apply _____ solution.

   A. 10% sulphuric acid
   B. 1% hydrochloric
   C. 2% boric acid
   D. 6% muriatic

19. To test for a leak in a CO_2 plant,

   A. pump NH_3 into the system and use Nessler's solution
   B. pump methyl chloride in and use litmus paper
   C. leave the CO_2 plant in operation and use a soapy water solution
   D. pump Freon into the system and use litmus paper

20. The CORRECT sequence of flow of refrigerant in the NH_3 compression system is

   A. compressor, scale trap, condenser, expansion valve, and evaporator
   B. compressor, oil trap, condenser, king valve, expansion valve, evaporator, and scale trap
   C. generator, condenser, expansion valve, evaporator, and absorber
   D. expansion valve, evaporator, condenser, oil trap, and condenser

21. Lithium bromide absorption systems, for use in air conditioning, have the LOWEST possible water temperature of _____ °F.

   A. 31   B. 33   C. 35   D. 38

22. The one of the following that could NOT be used in dehumidifying and cooling air in a modern air conditioning system is

   A. silica gel
   B. solution of calcium chloride
   C. zeolite method
   D. direct expansion refrigerating coil

23. To INCREASE the capacity of an absorption system, you would

   A. increase the steam pressure on the generator and pump
   B. increase the water in the condenser
   C. decrease the water in the absorber
   D. close the expansion valve

24. In changing a plant from Freon 12 to another refrigerant, which of the following would require the LEAST change in machinery?

   A. Ammonia
   B. Methyl chloride
   C. Carrene
   D. Carbon dioxide

25. In a calcium chloride brine tank of 1000 cubic feet, how many pounds of sodium dichromate would you use?

   A. 20   B. 40   C. 100   D. 200

KEY (CORRECT ANSWERS)

1. D
2. B
3. A
4. B
5. A

6. B
7. D
8. C
9. C
10. A

11. D
12. A
13. C
14. B
15. B

16. C
17. B
18. C
19. C
20. B

21. D
22. C
23. A
24. B
25. C

EXAMINATION SECTION
TEST 1

DIRECTIONS: Each question or incomplete statement is followed by several suggested answers or completions. Select the one that BEST answers the question or completes the statement. *PRINT THE LETTER OF THE CORRECT ANSWER IN THE SPACE AT THE RIGHT.*

1. A thermostatic expansion valve in a refrigeration system is used to regulate the 1._____

    A. pressure of the evaporator
    B. pressure of the compressor
    C. flow of the refrigerant to the precooler
    D. flow of refrigerant to the evaporator

2. The refrigerant is liquified in the compression system in the 2._____

    A. compressor   B. evaporator
    C. receiver   D. condenser

3. A compressor that has two compression strokes and two suction strokes per cylinder per revolution of the crank is a(n) _____ compressor. 3._____

    A. single-acting   B. double-acting
    C. two stage   D. in duplex

4. The MAIN bearings on the exciter in a large cold storage plant are 4._____

    A. ball bearings in a race
    B. barrel bearings in a race
    C. split babbitt bearings
    D. bronze sleeve bearings

5. Upon inspecting a rotary type booster system, you would expect to find the intercooler 5._____

    A. between the booster compressor and main compressor suction
    B. before the condenser of the main plant
    C. before the booster compressor on the suction line of the system
    D. between the booster compressor and the condenser

6. In a compression system driven by an induction motor, the compressor can USUALLY be run at _____ speed(s). 6._____

    A. one   B. two   C. three   D. four

7. How would you test for a carbon dioxide leak? 7._____

    A. Make a hydrostatic test
    B. Drain the system and use a trace of F-12
    C. Use a soapy water solution
    D. Pour hot water on the expansion coils

8. When a bypass valve is used, its object is for the purpose of 8._____

    A. starting the compressor   B. pumping down the compressor
    C. using a synchronous motor   D. increasing the compression

9. In the absorption system, the flow of ammonia gas in relation to the strong liquor in the analyzer is called _____ flow.

   A. A. cross B. counter C. parallel D. diagonal

10. A horizontal shell and tube cooler is equipped with eliminators. The PRIMARY function of the eliminators is to

   A. prevent the carry-over of liquid refrigerant
   B. protect the tubes in the event of a freeze-up
   C. absorb noises and vibration impulses
   D. prevent oil from being carried into the cooler

11. A Freon 12 system is operating with a discharge of 93.34 psi and a suction of 11.75 psig. Accordingly, the condenser is at 86F. What is the compression ratio?

   A. 8 to 1 B. 5.6 to 1 C. 4.1 to 1 D. 2.5 to 1

12. A solenoid valve has a closed port when energized. This is normally referred to as a(n)_____ type valve.

   A. open B. closed C. dual D. multi

13. How many BTU's must be removed to cool twenty gallons of water from 80° F to 40° F?

   A. 2.000 B. 6,666 C. 5.550 D. 7.777

14. A system using 80 lbs. of Group 1 refrigerant with two liquid receivers and two compressors requires _____ stop valves.

   A. 3 B. 4 C. 5 D. 6

15. The adjustable bypass in a Freon vertical compressor is to

   A. increase refrigeration
   B. help the engineer on watch
   C. regulate capacity
   D. regulate the oil level

16. In reference to an ammonia compression system, the number of cubic feet pumped per minute per ton is

   A. 8 B. 2 C. 3.8 D. 1.25

17. The LARGEST size *threaded* pipe allowed in an ammonia refrigeration system with a maximum of 250# pressure is _____ inches.

   A. 3 B. 3 1/2 C. 4 D. 4 1/2

18. One of the thermal properties of a refrigerant that is NOT recommended is

   A. convenient evaporating and condensing pressures
   B. a low critical and high freezing point
   C. a high latent heat of evaporation
   D. low viscosity and high film heat conductivity

19. In a Freon 12 compressor type plant, the liquid is cooled by the suction gas before the liquid passes to the evaporator. The PRIMARY reason for doing this is to   19._____

    A. dry the suction gas
    B. boil off any oil which may be present in the suction gas
    C. take advantage of a simpler piping arrangement
    D. increase the refrigerating effect per pound of refrigerant pumped

20. The face air velocity going through a dry filter at 425 cubic feet per minute had a filter media of 1.0. If it increased to 0.50, the velocity of the air going through would   20._____

    A. decrease and remain steady
    B. increase and remain steady
    C. decrease and fluctuate
    D. remain the same

21. How would you install a cartridge type of dehydrator in an F-12, F-22, or F-500 system? _____ in the liquid line with the flange on the _____.   21._____

    A. Vertical; bottom
    B. Vertical; top
    C. Horizontal and vertical; top
    D. Horizontal or vertical; bottom

22. The term *anhydrous* used in connection with refrigerants indicates the   22._____

    A. presence of ammonia   B. presence of water
    C. absence of Freon   D. absence of water

23. The MAXIMUM amount of refrigerant that could be stored in a machinery room is _____ pounds.   23._____

    A. 600   B. 500   C. 400   D. 300

24. The purpose of using eliminators at the top of an evaporative condenser is to   24._____

    A. eliminate gas noises and vibration
    B. eliminate oil carry-over
    C. control the gas flow
    D. eliminate moisture carry-over

25. Unless approved by the proper authority, a flammable refrigerant shall NOT be used in a refrigerating system in excess of _____ lbs.   25._____

    A. 1000   B. 1200   C. 1400   D. 1500

KEY (CORRECT ANSWERS)

1.	D	11.	A
2.	D	12.	A
3.	B	13.	B
4.	D	14.	D
5.	A	15.	C
6.	A	16.	C
7.	C	17.	A
8.	A	18.	B
9.	B	19.	D
10.	A	20.	A |//
21.	D		
22.	D		
23.	D		
24.	D		
25.	A		

TEST 2

DIRECTIONS: Each question or incomplete statement is followed by several suggested answers or completions. Select the one that BEST answers the question or completes the statement. *PRINT THE LETTER OF THE CORRECT ANSWER IN THE SPACE AT THE RIGHT.*

1. When attempting to read the high side pressure gauge on an operating ammonia compressor, it is noted that the pointer *hunts*, or has a wide and relatively slow back and forth movement. This would MOST likely indicate that the compressor

    A. suction valves are stuck open
    B. is overloaded
    C. valve action is sluggish
    D. is operating normally

    1.____

2. In a two cylinder vertical single stage compressor equipped with a gear type oil pump for pressure lubrication, for good performance, the oil discharge pressure should range APPROXIMATELY from _____ psig above _____ pressure.

    A. 10 to 30; suction
    B. 10 to 30; head
    C. 50 to 90; suction
    D. 50 to 90; head

    2.____

3. An air conditioning system has mechanical refrigeration equipment which consists of 3 compressors, each of which may be operated at 50% or 100% capacity. The MAXIMUM number of capacities that this set can operate at is

    A. 3   B. 4   C. 6   D. 8

    3.____

4. What determines the MAXIMUM output of an electric motor?

    A. Engineers' rating
    B. Temperature of the motor
    C. Name plate rating
    D. Power supply

    4.____

5. The cylinder of an H.D.A. compressor is running hot and under decreased capacity. The reason for this is

    A. the suction is coming to compressor saturated
    B. a high plant demand
    C. broken oil and leaking piston rings
    D. suction coming back at 35 superheated

    5.____

6. There is (are) _____ baffle(s) in a three pass shell and tube condenser.

    A. one   B. two   C. three   D. four

    6.____

7. A 200 ton air conditioning plant is set up with 2 Freon compressors. Assuming that neither of the compressors is equipped with bypass solenoids, in order to be able to get AT LEAST four steps of capacity, these machines would be driven by _____ motors.

    A. synchronous
    B. capacitor
    C. induction repulsion
    D. wound rotor induction

    7.____

8. The term *viscosity* in refrigeration oil means

    A. internal friction
    B. corrosive action
    C. weight value
    D. ability to mix

    8.____

9. Muntz metal CANNOT be used with

   A. ammonia
   B. Freon 12
   C. carbon dioxide
   D. methyl chloride

10. What color does red litmus paper turn when ammonia is present?

    A. Red   B. White   C. Blue   D. No change

11. Good chemical structure of a refrigerant is determined by

    A. viscosity
    B. refrigerant stability
    C. flammability
    D. a low critical point

12. _____ does NOT increase the capacity of a water cooled condenser.

    A. Refrigerant gas
    B. Ambient temperature
    C. Water temperature
    D. Quantity of water

13. If an equalizer line is placed immediately on the discharge side of the thermostatic expansion valve, it is installed

    A. incorrectly
    B. very well
    C. well, but not practically
    D. according to manufacturer's specifications

14. In a refrigerating system with a gauge, the dial points to 100 psig. Under normal operating conditions, the LAST number of the gauge should read

    A. 105   B. 110   C. 115   D. 120

15. Many Freons are used for air conditioning. Regarding F-11, it can be said that a _____ type compressor is needed.

    A. large centrifugal
    B. large rotary
    C. small rotary
    D. large reciprocating

16. The thermal expansion valve is rated by

    A. tons of refrigeration
    B. pounds of pressure per hour
    C. pounds of pressure per minute
    D. cubic inches per minute

17. For a given application, a particular compressor is found to have a volumetric efficiency of 72% when operating at its design speed of 300 rpm. If the speed is increased to 500 rpm, it is MOST likely that the volumetric efficiency will

    A. decrease
    B. increase and remain higher as long as it is run at the higher speed
    C. remain constant at 72%
    D. increase for the first 24 hours of operation at the higher speed and then decrease

18. A finned evaporator coil is equipped with a thermal expansion valve. The bulb of this valve is properly clamped to the suction line at the coil. In normal operation, the suction gas will leave this coil MOST NEARLY in a state of

   A. 5° F to 9° F of superheat
   B. 20° F to 30° F of superheat
   C. saturation
   D. 1° F to 2° F of superheat

18._____

19. Of the following types of water-cooled condensers, the one which consists of one or more assemblies of two tubes, one within the other, in which the refrigerant vapor is condensed in the annular space or in the inner tube, is known as the _____ condenser.

   A. atmospheric   B. shell and coil
   C. shell and U-tube   D. double pipe

19._____

20. How many gallons of water can an irregular-shaped container having a volume of 8085 cubic inches hold?

   A. 25   B. 30   C. 35   D. 40

20._____

21. The use of screwed joints in refrigeration systems for refrigerant pressures above 250 psi is permitted, provided that the nominal size of the pipe is NOT more than _____ inches.

   A. 1 1/4   B. 1 3/4   C. 2 1/4   D. 3

21._____

22. The capacity of a water-cooled condenser will increase whenever the temperature difference between the refrigerant gas and the water is increased. To INCREASE the capacity of a water-cooled condenser, an operator would

   A. increase the quantity of water
   B. raise the temperature of the entering water
   C. raise the condensing pressure
   D. decrease the power input to the compressor

22._____

23. In a large air conditioning installation consisting of three direct expansion conditioners and a single Freon compressor, a thermostat is installed on each conditioner. The compressor would be under the control of

   A. condenser water   B. any two thermostats
   C. any one thermostat   D. a low pressurestat

23._____

24. The volume of a cylinder with a 10" bore and a 12" stroke is _____ cubic inches.

   A. 502   B. 621   C. 892   D. 942

24._____

25. In an F-12 compression system used for an air conditioning installation operating at a suction pressure of 45 psi, the evaporating temperature would be _____ F.

   A. 60   B. 50   C. 40   D. 30

25._____

KEY (CORRECT ANSWERS)

1. C
2. A
3. C
4. B
5. B

6. B
7. D
8. A
9. A
10. C

11. B
12. B
13. A
14. D
15. A

16. A
17. A
18. A
19. D
20. C

21. D
22. A
23. D
24. D
25. B

TEST 3

DIRECTIONS: Each question or incomplete statement is followed by several suggested answers or completions. Select the one that BEST answers the question or completes the statement. *PRINT THE LETTER OF THE CORRECT ANSWER IN THE SPACE AT THE RIGHT.*

1. The percentage of oil circulated with the refrigerant in a well-designed refrigeration system should NOT be more than _____ %.

    A. 10   B. 20   C. 25   D. 30

    1._____

2. In an air conditioning plant equipped with an indirect low side using water as a brine, the sequence to follow for plant operation is to

    A. start the compressor
    B. test safety valves
    C. start fan and circulating pump first
    D. set expansion valve

    2._____

3. The strong liquor in the absorber will become WEAKER when the

    A. expansion valve is closed
    B. evaporator load increases
    C. evaporator load decreases
    D. condenser pressure decreases

    3._____

4. Copper and its alloys would NOT be used with

    A. ammonia   B. sulphur dioxide
    C. carbon dioxide   D. methyl chloride

    4._____

5. To detect a Freon 12 leak, the halide torch flame would

    A. go out   B. change color
    C. stay the same   D. give off white smoke

    5._____

6. A refrigerant unit used for air conditioning is pumped down and secured for the fall and winter. As an operator, you notice frost on the outlet side of the king valve. This would be caused by

    A. foul air or non-condensable gases in the receiver
    B. water in refrigerant
    C. valve seized in closed position
    D. leaky valve seat or plug

    6._____

7. What type fittings are used on an ammonia compression system?

    A. Flanged   B. Tongue and groove
    C. Male and female face   D. Serrated

    7._____

8. A ten ton refrigeration unit has the capacity of _____ BTU per minute.

    A. 2,000   B. 20,000   C. 12,000   D. 288,000

    8._____

9. A forced feed lubricator for a horizontal compressor uses refrigeration oil and has two lines leading to the

    A. cross head and seal
    B. stuffing box and crank pin
    C. wrist pin and cylinder
    D. stuffing box and cylinder

10. In the compression system with a low side float, the ball in the float is punctured and sinks. What would MOST likely happen? The

    A. low side would be falling with compressor running
    B. low side would be rising with compressor running
    C. head pressure would fall
    D. compressor would stop and head pressure would rise

11. In order to get long-term protection against rust action of brine in the ice field, you would use

    A. aluminum sulphate
    B. sodium dichromate
    C. Nessler's solution
    D. universal indicator solution

12. Of the following Freons, the one which has the HIGHEST refrigeration effect is F-

    A. 12   B. 114   C. 11   D. 113

13. Upon inspecting a TEV installation, you find that the thermal bulb is clamped to the pipe right after the expansion valve. The result is that

    A. the expansion valve would continually flood the coil
    B. the opening would continually freeze in a wide open position
    C. this is incorrect and would starve the cooling coil
    D. oil and moisture would be more likely to accumulate

14. The NEAREST boiling point for F-22 in degrees minus Fahrenheit is

    A. 40   B. 50   C. 30   D. 20

15. In a vertical single-acting compressor with an oil pump as part of the compressor, the suction pressure is 30#. The oil gauge should read APPROXIMATELY _____ pounds.

    A. 30   B. 20   C. 80   D. 50

16. A water-cooled condenser with a tube within a tube and the refrigerant in the outer tube is a(n) _____ condenser.

    A. shell and coil   B. double pipe
    C. shell and tube   D. atmospheric

17. In a carbon dioxide system, the oiling method is USUALLY

    A. splash system   B. low pressure oiling
    C. high pressure oiling   D. excess refrigerant receiver

18. When Freon 12 compressors are running in parallel, the reason for connecting the crankcases in parallel is to

   A. maintain steady suction pressure
   B. maintain the oil at the same level
   C. equalize the load
   D. obtain lower temperature

18._____

19. Refrigerant enters the condenser as a _____ gas and leaves as a _____.

   A. superheated; high temperature gas
   B. high pressure; low pressure liquid
   C. high pressure; high pressure liquid
   D. superheated; superheated gas

19._____

20. In a Freon air conditioning system that is used to cool the entire office, the ratio or horsepower in reference to tons of refrigeration is MOST NEARLY

   A. 1   B. 2   C. 2.50   D. 3.5

20._____

21. Of the following thermal properties of a refrigerant, the one that is NOT desirable is

   A. a convenient evaporator and condensing pressure
   B. high latent heat of evaporization and high vapor specific heat
   C. low critical and high freezing temperature
   D. low viscosity and high film heat conductivity

21._____

22. An accumulator is MOST commonly used with a

   A. condenser
   B. direct expansion evaporator
   C. flooded evaporator
   D. high pressure system

22._____

23. An absorption system is to be placed into operation under standard ton conditions, a suction of 19.5#, and discharge of 156#. The steam gauge reads 5 psig. What is the consumption of steam per ton hour of refrigeration?

   A. 10   B. 20   C. 50   D. 100

23._____

24. The MAXIMUM pounds in a direct system per 1,000 cubic foot of occupied space for Freon 12 is

   A. 31   B. 41   C. 51   D. 61

24._____

25. How many stop valves are required by the code in a system using 30# of Group 1 refrigerant and having two compressors and two receivers?

   A. Two   B. Four   C. Five   D. 'Six

25._____

KEY (CORRECT ANSWERS)

1.	A	11.	B
2.	B	12.	C
3.	C	13.	C
4.	A	14.	A
5.	B	15.	D
6.	D	16.	B
7.	C	17.	C
8.	A	18.	B
9.	D	19.	C
10.	B	20.	A

21. C
22. C
23. C
24. A
25. D

EXAMINATION SECTION
TEST 1

DIRECTIONS: Each question or incomplete statement is followed by several suggested answers or completions. Select the one that BEST answers the question or completes the statement. *PRINT THE LETTER OF THE CORRECT ANSWER IN THE SPACE AT THE RIGHT.*

1. The combustion efficiency of a boiler can be determined with a CO_2 indicator and the

    A. under fire draft
    B. boiler room humidity
    C. flue gas temperature
    D. outside air temperature

2. A quick, practical method of determining if the cast-iron waste pipe delivered to a job has been damaged in transit is to

    A. hydraulically test it
    B. "ring" each length with a hammer
    C. drop each length to see whether it breaks
    D. visually examine the pipe for cracks

3. An electrostatic precipitator is used to

    A. filter the air supply
    B. remove sludge from the fuel oil
    C. remove particles from the fuel gas
    D. supply samples for an Orsat analysis

4. The PRIMARY cause of cracking and spalling of refractory lining in the furnace of a steam generator is *most likely* due to

    A. continuous over-firing of boiler
    B. slag accumulation on furnace walls
    C. change in fuel from solid to liquid
    D. uneven heating and cooling within the refractory brick

5. The term "effective temperature" in air conditioning means

    A. the dry bulb temperature
    B. the average of the wet and dry bulb temperatures
    C. the square root of the product of wet and dry bulb temperatures
    D. an arbitrary index combining the effects of temperature, humidity, and movement

6. The piping in all buildings having dual water distribution systems should be identified by a color coding of _____ for potable water lines and _____ for non-potable water lines.

    A. green; red
    B. green; yellow
    C. yellow; green
    D. yellow; red

7. The breaking of a component of a machine subjected to excessive vibration is called

    A. tensile failure
    B. fatigue failure
    C. caustic embrittlement
    D. amplitude failure

8. The TWO MOST important factors to be considered in selecting fans for ventilating systems are

   A. noise and efficiency
   B. space available and weight
   C. first cost and dimensional bulk
   D. construction and arrangement of drive

9. In the modern power plant deaerator, air is removed from water to

   A. reduce heat losses in the heaters
   B. reduce corrosion of boiler steel due to the air
   C. reduce the load of the main condenser air pumps
   D. prevent pumps from becoming vapor bound

10. The abbreviations BOD, COD, and DO are associated with

    A. flue gas analysis
    B. air pollution control
    C. boiler water treatment
    D. water pollution control

11. The piping of a newly installed drainage system should be tested upon completion of the rough plumbing with a head of water of NOT LESS THAN _____ feet.

    A. 10   B. 15   C. 20   D. 25

12. Of the following statements concerning aquastats, the one which is CORRECT is:

    A. Aquastats may be obtained with either a narrow or wide range of settings
    B. Aquastats have a mercury tube switch which is controlled by the stack switch
    C. An aquastat is a device used to shut down the burner in the event of low water in the boiler
    D. An aquastat should be located about 4 inches above the normal water line of the boiler

13. The SAFEST way to protect the domestic water supply from contamination by sewage or non-potable water is to insert

    A. air gaps
    B. swing connections
    C. double check valves
    D. tanks with overhead discharge

14. The MAIN function of a back-pressure valve which is sometimes found in the connection between a water drain pipe and the sewer system is to

    A. equalize the pressure between the drain pipe and the sewer
    B. prevent sewer water from flowing into the drain pipe
    C. provide pressure to enable waste to reach the sewer
    D. make sure that there is not too much water pressure in the sewer line

15. Boiler water is neutral if its pH value is

    A. 0   B. 1   C. 7   D. 14

16. A domestic hot water mixing or tempering valve should be preceded in the hot water line by a

    A. strainer
    B. foot valve
    C. check valve
    D. steam trap

17. Between a steam boiler and its safety valve there should be

    A. no valve of any type
    B. a gate valve of the same size as the safety valve
    C. a swing check valve of at least the same size as the safety valve
    D. a cock having a clear opening equal in area to the pipe connecting the boiler and safety valve

18. A diagram of horizontal plumbing drainage lines should have cleanouts shown

    A. at least every 25 feet
    B. at least every 100 feet
    C. wherever a basin is located
    D. wherever a change in direction occurs

19. When a Bourdon gauge is used to measure steam pressures, some form of siphon or water seal must be maintained.
    The reason for this is to

    A. obtain "absolute" pressure readings
    B. prevent steam from entering the gage
    C. prevent condensate from entering the gage
    D. obtain readings below atmospheric pressure

20. In a closed heat exchanger, oil is cooled by condensate which is to be returned to a boiler. In order to avoid the possibility of contaminating the condensate with oil should a tube fail in the oil cooler, it would be good practice to

    A. cool the oil by air instead of water
    B. treat the condensate with an oil solvent
    C. keep the oil pressure in the exchanger higher than the water pressure
    D. keep the water pressure in the exchanger higher than the oil pressure

21. A radiator thermostatic trap is used on a vacuum return type of heating system to

    A. release the pocketed air only
    B. reduce the amount of condensate
    C. maintain a predetermined radiator water level
    D. prevent the return of live steam to the return line

22. According to the color coding of piping, fire protection piping should be painted

    A. green   B. yellow   C. purple   D. red

23. The MAIN purpose of a standpipe system is to

    A. supply the roof water tank
    B. provide water for firefighting

C. circulate water for the heating system
D. provide adequate pressure for the water supply

24. The name "Saybolt" is associated with the measurement of

   A. viscosity
   B. Btu content
   C. octane rating
   D. temperature

25. Recirculation of conditioned air in an air-conditioned building is done MAINLY to

   A. reduce refrigeration tonnage required
   B. increase room entrophy
   C. increase air specific humidity
   D. reduce room temperature below the dewpoint

26. In a plumbing installation, vent pipes are GENERALLY used to

   A. prevent the loss of water seal from traps by evaporation
   B. prevent the loss of water seal due to several causes other than evaporation
   C. act as an additional path for liquids to flow through during normal use of a plumbing fixture
   D. prevent the backflow of water in a cross-connection between a drinking water line and a sewage line

27. The designation "150 W" cast on the bonnet of a gate valve is an indication of the

   A. water working temperature
   B. water working pressure
   C. area of the opening in square inches
   D. weight of the valve in pounds

28. In the city, the size soil pipe necessary in a sewage drainage system is determined by the

   A. legal occupancy of the building
   B. vertical height of the soil line
   C. number of restrooms connected to the soil line
   D. number of "fixture units" connected to the soil line

29. Fins or other extended surfaces are used on heat exchanger tubes when

   A. the exchanger is a water-to-water exchanger
   B. water is on one side of the tube and condensing steam on the other side
   C. the surface coefficient of heat transfer on both sides of the tube is high
   D. the surface coefficient of heat transfer on one side of the tube is low compared to the coefficient on the other side of the tube

30. A fusible plug may be put in a fire tube boiler as an emergency device to indicate low water level. The fusible plug is installed so that under normal operating conditions,

   A. both sides are exposed to steam
   B. one side is exposed to water and the other side to steam
   C. one side is exposed to steam and the other side to hot gases
   D. one side is exposed to the water and the other side to hot gases

31. Extra strong wrought-iron pipe, as compared to standard wrought-iron pipe of the same nominal size, has

    A. the same outside diameter but a smaller inside diameter
    B. the same inside diameter but a larger outside diameter
    C. a larger outside diameter and a smaller inside diameter
    D. larger inside and outside diameters

32. Fans may be rated on a dynamic or a static efficiency basis. The dynamic efficiency would *probably* be

    A. lower in value because of the energy absorbed by the air velocity
    B. the same as the static in the case of centrifugal blowers running at various speeds
    C. the same as the static in the case of axial flow blowers running at various speeds
    D. higher in value than the static

33. The function of the stack relay in an oil burner installation is to

    A. regulate the draft over the fire
    B. regulate the flow of fuel oil to the burner
    C. stop the motor if the oil has not ignited
    D. stop the motor if the water or steam pressure is too high

34. The type of centrifugal pump which is inherently balanced for hydraulic thrust is the

    A. double suction impeller type
    B. single suction impeller type
    C. single stage type
    D. multistage type

35. The specifications for a job using sheet lead calls for "4-lb. sheet lead." This means that each sheet should weigh

    A. 4 lbs.
    B. 4 lbs. per square
    C. 4 lbs. per square foot
    D. 4 lbs. per cubic inch

36. The total cooling load design conditions for a building are divided for convenience into two components.
    These are:

    A. infiltration and radiation
    B. sensible heat and latent heat
    C. wet and dry bulb temperatures
    D. solar heat gain and moisture transfer

37. The function of a Hartford loop used on some steam boilers is to

    A. limit boiler steam pressure
    B. limit temperature of the steam
    C. prevent high water levels in the boiler
    D. prevent back flow of water from the boiler into the return main

38. Vibration from a ventilating blower can be prevented from being transmitted to the duct work by

   A. installing straighteners in the duct
   B. throttling the air supply to the blower
   C. bolting the blower tightly to the duct
   D. installing a canvas sleeve at the blower outlet

39. A specification states that access panels to suspended ceiling will be of metal. The MAIN reason for providing access panels is to

   A. improve the insulation of the ceiling
   B. improve the appearance of the ceiling
   C. make it easier to construct the building
   D. make it easier to maintain the building

40. A plumber on a job reports that the steamfitter has installed a 3" steam line in a location at which the plans show the house trap. On inspecting the job, you should

   A. tell the steamfitter to remove the steam line
   B. study the condition to see if the house trap can be relocated
   C. tell the plumber and steamfitter to work it out between themselves and then report to you
   D. tell the plumber to find another location for the trap because the steamfitter has already completed his work

41. In the installation of any heating system, the MOST important consideration is that

   A. all elements be made of a good grade of cast iron
   B. all radiators and connectors be mounted horizontally
   C. the smallest velocity of flow of heating medium be used
   D. there be proper clearance between hot surfaces and surrounding combustible material

42. Which one of the following is the PRIMARY object in drawing up a set of specifications for materials to be purchased?

   A. Control of quality
   B. Outline of intended use
   C. Establishment of standard sizes
   D. Location and method of inspection.

43. The drawing which should be used as a LEGAL reference when checking completed construction work is the _____ drawing.

   A. contract
   B. assembly
   C. working or shop
   D. preliminary

Questions 44-50.

DIRECTIONS: Questions 44 through 50 refer to the plumbing drawing shown below.

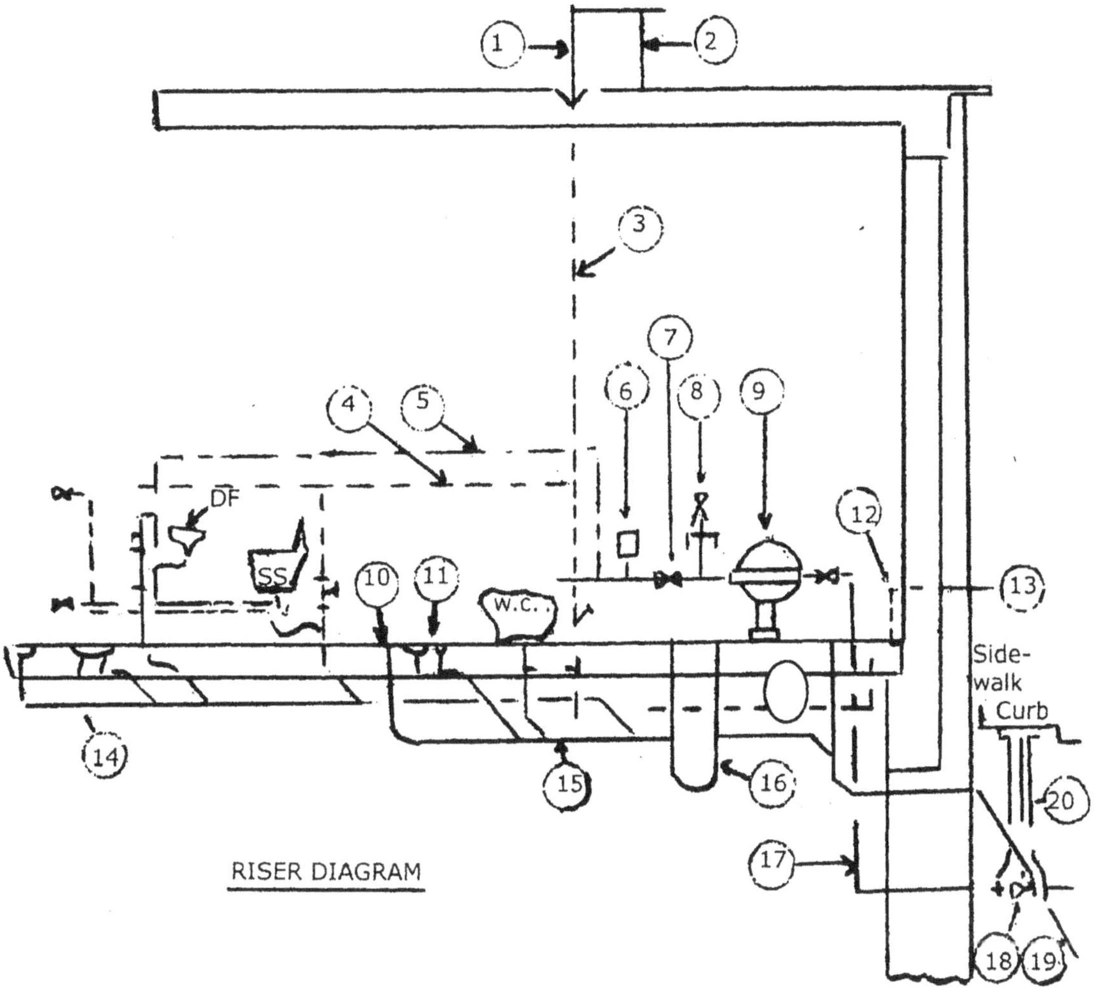

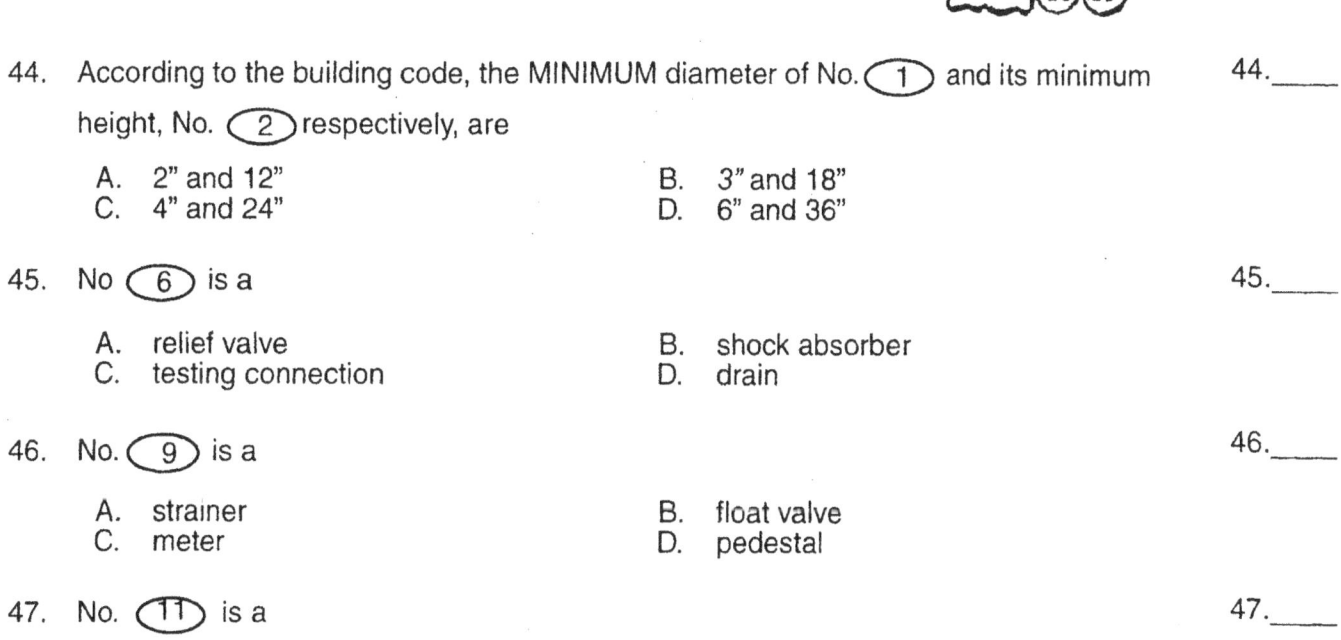

RISER DIAGRAM

44. According to the building code, the MINIMUM diameter of No. ① and its minimum height, No. ② respectively, are

    A. 2" and 12"
    B. 3" and 18"
    C. 4" and 24"
    D. 6" and 36"

44.____

45. No. ⑥ is a

    A. relief valve
    B. shock absorber
    C. testing connection
    D. drain

45.____

46. No. ⑨ is a

    A. strainer
    B. float valve
    C. meter
    D. pedestal

46.____

47. No. ⑪ is a

    A. floor drain
    B. cleanout
    C. trap
    D. vent connection

47.____

48. No. (13) is a

    A. standpipe
    B. air inlet
    C. sprinkler head
    D. cleanout

49. The size of No. (16) is

    A. 2" x 2"
    B. 2" x 3"
    C. 3" x 3"
    D. 4" x 4"

50. No. (18) is a

    A. pressure reducing valve
    B. butterfly valve
    C. curb cock
    D. sprinkler head

KEY (CORRECT ANSWERS)

1. C	11. A	21. D	31. A	41. D
2. B	12. C	22. D	32. D	42. A
3. C	13. A	23. B	33. C	43. A
4. D	14. B	24. A	34. A	44. C
5. D	15. C	25. A	35. C	45. B
6. B	16. A	26. B	36. B	46. C
7. B	17. A	27. B	37. D	47. A
8. A	18. D	28. D	38. D	48. B
9. B	19. B	29. D	39. D	49. D
10. D	20. D	30. D	40. B	50. C

EXAMINATION SECTION
TEST 1

DIRECTIONS: Each question or incomplete statement is followed by several suggested answers or completions. Select the one that BEST answers the question or completes the statement. *PRINT THE LETTER OF THE CORRECT ANSWER IN THE SPACE AT THE RIGHT.*

1. The one of the following gases which will NOT be found in the flue gases produced by the complete combustion of fuel oil is

   A. oxygen
   B. hydrogen
   C. nitrogen
   D. carbon dioxide

   1.____

2. The amount of CO_2 in a flue gas sample is USUALLY stated in

   A. parts per million
   B. pounds
   C. percent
   D. pounds per mol

   2.____

3. A change in the efficiency of combustion in a boiler can USUALLY be determined by comparing the previously recorded readings with the current readings of the

   A. stack temperature and CO_2
   B. Ringelman chart and CO_2
   C. stack temperature and CO
   D. over-the-fire draft and CO

   3.____

4. The tube-metal temperature is appreciably higher in a superheater tube than in a boiler tube when they are both subjected to the same temperatures because the superheater tube

   A. outside gas film conductivity is higher than that of the boiler tube
   B. outside gas film conductivity is lower than that of the boiler tube
   C. inside vapor film conductivity is lower than the water film conductivity in the boiler tube
   D. inside vapor film conductivity is higher than the water film conductivity in the boiler tube

   4.____

5. In a balanced draft furnace, the

   A. draft changes from positive to negative in the furnace
   B. breeching contains a barometric damper
   C. draft reading is negative at the furnace inlet
   D. draft reading is positive at the furnace outlet

   5.____

6. The heating of a #6 fuel oil in an oil burner to a temperature higher than necessary solely for proper atomization is

   A. *desirable* because it can increase the burner capacity by increasing the specific volume of the oil
   B. *desirable* because it can increase the flame stability when vaporization occurs intermittently in the supply line to the burner

   6.____

C. *undesirable* because it can decrease the burner capacity by decreasing the specific volume of the oil
D. *undesirable* because it can decrease the burner capacity by increasing the specific volume of the oil

7. In a cylindrical boiler drum, the ratio of the force tending to burst a longitudinal seam to the force tending to burst a circumferential seam is MOST NEARLY

    A. 1:1   B. 2:1   C. 3:1   D. 4:1

8. The one of the following actions an operator should NOT take to stop or decrease carry-over caused by foaming in a boiler is to

    A. lower the water level in the drum
    B. blow down the boiler
    C. increase the rate of chemical feed to the boiler
    D. reduce the steam output

9. The PRIMARY reason for treating de-aerated feedwater with sodium sulphite is to

    A. remove dissolved oxygen
    B. control scale
    C. prevent carry-over
    D. increase alkalinity

10. In accordance with recommended practice, a sample of boiler water for pH analysis should be taken

    A. immediately after chemicals are added to the feedwater
    B. just before bottom blowdown
    C. when the steaming rate is high
    D. prior to putting the boiler on the line

11. Of the following oil burner types, the one in which the return oil passes through the atomizer body is the

    A. rotary cup
    B. steam atomizing
    C. mechanical pressure atomizing
    D. air atomizing

12. One advantage that the mechanical pressure atomizing oil burner has over the steam atomizing oil burner is that, with the mechanical pressure atomizing oil burner, the

    A. required oil temperature is lower
    B. required pump pressure is lower
    C. range of capacity available is wider
    D. fuel is more accurately and uniformly metered

13. Of the following, the LEAST likely cause of faulty atomization of fuel oil in a rotary cup burner is

    A. too low an oil temperature
    B. carbon formation on the rotary cup
    C. too low an oil pressure
    D. insufficient secondary air

14. The device which senses the presence of the burner flame in a rotary cup oil burner is 14.____

    A. mercury tube B. lead sulfide cell
    C. vaporstat D. selenium rectifier

15. The component present, in GREATEST amount by weight, in #6 fuel oil is 15.____

    A. carbon B. hydrogen C. nitrogen D. oxygen

16. The explosion hazard in an oil-fired boiler is usually GREATEST when 16.____

    A. lighting off
    B. securing the boiler
    C. firing at 75% of rated load
    D. firing at 100% of rated load

17. Of the following, the one which is the MOST complete and correct statement of the function of an F and T steam trap is that it removes 17.____

    A. only condensate from a steam line
    B. both condensate and non-condensable gases from a steam line
    C. only non-condensable gases from a steam line
    D. both sediment and rust particles from a steam line

18. Fire actuated fusible plugs on boilers should be renewed AT LEAST once every _____ months. 18.____

    A. 12 B. 18 C. 24 D. 30

19. A safety valve on a boiler must reach its full lift when the pressure is no GREATER than _____ above its set pressure. 19.____

    A. 3% B. 5% C. 7% D. 8%

20. A device used to calibrate a steam pressure gauge is the _____ tester. 20.____

    A. spring-scale B. dead-weight
    C. live-load D. in-line

21. The one of the following statements that is NOT correct concerning feedwater injectors is that they are 21.____

    A. inefficient pumping units
    B. practical only on large boilers
    C. highly efficient thermally
    D. unreliable when subjected to varying loads and pressures

22. A steam pressure gauge is located 10 feet below the point where the connection is made to the top of a boiler water column. If the absolute pressure in the steam drum is 125 psi, the pressure at the gauge will be MOST NEARLY _____ psig. 22.____

    A. 102 B. 116 C. 119 D. 148

23. When comparing the operation and maintenance of a Stirling boiler with that of an equivalent horizontal straight tube boiler, the one of the following statements that is MOST complete and accurate is: 23.____

A. It is much harder to get to the tubes of a Stirling boiler for maintenance work than to a straight tube boiler with box headers
B. A Stirling boiler will steam at a lower rate than a straight tube boiler
C. Leaks occur more frequently in a Stirling boiler than in a straight tube boiler
D. The water and steam circulation rates are greater in a Stirling boiler than in a straight tube boiler

24. A supplier quotes a list price of $68.00 less discounts of 25 and 20 percent for a replacement part.
The actual cost of this item is MOST NEARLY

    A. $31   B. $34   C. $37   D. $41

25. The MAIN reason for maintaining an air dome in a pressurized house tank is to

    A. increase the tank pressure above the pump pressure
    B. avoid frequent start-and-stop pump operation
    C. force the water up to the top floor
    D. aerate the water

26. In a magnetic across-the-line starter for a 10 hp motor connected to a 4-wire, 3-phase circuit with grounded neutral, the MINIMUM required number of over-current devices is

    A. one, in the neutral conductor
    B. two, in any two conductors except the neutral
    C. three, in all conductors except the neutral
    D. four, in all four conductors

27. In order to select the correct heaters for the equipment described in Question 26 from the controller manufacturer's chart, the MOST important information needed is the

    A. power factor   B. line voltage
    C. full-load motor current   D. motor horsepower

28. An electric motor, which is direct-connected to a centrifugal pump on an integral machined base, is to be replaced. In order to minimize the labor involved in replacing the motor, the specifications should include

    A. end bell size   B. serial number
    C. NEMA frame size   D. shaft size

29. A squirrel cage induction motor is rated at 5 hp when connected to a 220-volt, 3-phase, 60-cycle service.
If this motor is connected to a 208-volt, 3-phase, 60-cycle circuit, the horsepower rating would

    A. remain constant
    B. be increased by approximately 5%
    C. be decreased by approximately 10%
    D. be decreased by approximately 30%

30. A 20 hp, 230-volt DC motor operates at 75% efficiency. The full-load current, in amperes, is MOST NEARLY

    A. 45   B. 65   C. 85   D. 115

31. In a cooling tower, the water is cooled MAINLY by

    A. condensation
    B. conduction
    C. convection
    D. evaporation

32. An economizer is used with a steam boiler in order to raise the temperature of the

    A. boiler feedwater by utilizing some of the heat in the exit flue gases
    B. boiler feedwater by utilizing exhaust steam from the turbines or steam engines
    C. air used for combustion of the fuel utilizing some of the heat in the exit flue gases
    D. air used for combustion of the fuel utilizing exhaust steam from the turbines or steam engines

33. A centrifugal boiler feed pump requires 5 hp to drive it at a certain speed, total head and quantity of water delivered.
    If the speed and the quantity of water delivered are doubled and the total head quadrupled, the horsepower required will be APPROXIMATELY

    A. 10   B. 20   C. 30   D. 40

34. In a centrifugal pump installation, the available net positive suction head is NOT affected by the

    A. suction piping size and length
    B. level of the liquid supply
    C. temperature of the liquid being pumped
    D. cavitation in the pump

35. In operating a closed water circulating system, it is good practice to

    A. treat the water chemically for corrosion control
    B. drain and flush the system regularly to control corrosion
    C. leave the system undisturbed because it is sealed and needs no maintenance
    D. replace the pump shaft seals every three months

36. The function of an unloader on an electric motor-driven air compressor is to

    A. release the pressure in the cylinders in order to reduce the starting load
    B. reduce the speed of the motor when the maximum pressure is reached
    C. prevent excess pressure in the receiver
    D. drain the condensate from the cylinder head

37. The MOST highly toxic of the following refrigerants is

    A. sulphur dioxide
    B. ammonia
    C. methyl chloride
    D. freon 12

38. The MOST important objective of a safety training program should be to motivate the worker to

    A. avoid tripping hazards
    B. use hand tools properly
    C. write a clear concise accident report
    D. be constantly alert to safety hazards

39. An automatically controlled circulating water pump in a domestic hot water system is started by a device when it senses a

    A. drop in the water pressure in the circulating line
    B. drop in the water temperature in the return line
    C. rise in the water pressure in the circulating line
    D. rise in the temperature in the return line

40. In performing a hydrostatic test on an existing power boiler, the required test pressure must be controlled so that it is NOT exceeded by more than

    A. 2%   B. 4%   C. 6%   D. 8%

41. A preventive maintenance program in a boiler room should provide for routine periodic replacement of

    A. programmer electronic tubes
    B. badly leaking boiler tubes
    C. electric motors
    D. safety valve springs

42. The FIRST step to take in planning a preventive maintenance program is to

    A. replace all electric wiring
    B. make an equipment inventory
    C. replace all pump seals
    D. repair all equipment which is not in operation

43. The MOST important consideration in a fire prevention program is to

    A. train the staff to place flammables in fireproof containers
    B. know how to attack fires regardless of size
    C. see that halls, corridors, and exits are not blocked
    D. detect and eliminate every possible fire hazard

44. The type of portable fire extinguisher recommended as MOST effective for putting out oil fires is the _____ type.

    A. pump tank   B. cartridge actuated
    C. soda acid   D. foam

45. Inspecting and testing of mechanical equipment is done periodically MAINLY to

    A. help the men become more familiar with the equipment
    B. keep the men busy during slack periods
    C. encourage the men to take better care of the equipment
    D. discover minor equipment faults before they develop into major breakdowns

46. During the first stage of the high air pollution alert, plans must be made in public buildings to discontinue on-site incineration and to provide personnel and space to store the quantity of refuse that could accumulate during a period of _____ day(s).

    A. 1   B. 2   C. 5   D. 7

47. The four stages of the warning system designated by the high air pollution alert warning system are:

    A. initial, chronic, acute, penetrating
    B. forecast, alert, warning, emergency
    C. light, medium, heavy, extra heavy
    D. early, moderate, severe, toxic

48. Unless a sulphur exemption certificate is obtained, the amount of sulphur in residual fuel oil burned for heating purposes is restricted to NOT MORE than

    A. 0.2%   B. 0.3%   C. 0.55%   D. 0.7%

49. Refuse burning equipment in public buildings other than central municipal incinerators may NOT be operated except during the hours between

    A. 7 A.M. and 12 Noon
    B. 7 A.M. and 5 P.M.
    C. 9 A.M. and 3 P.M.
    D. 8 P.M. and 11 P.M.

50. The air contaminant detector required in a boiler installation must be adjusted to cause an audible and/or visible signal upon the emission of an air contaminant whose density, on the standard smoke chart, is GREATER than

    A. No. 1   B. No. 2   C. No. 3   D. No. 4

KEY (CORRECT ANSWERS)

1. B	11. C	21. B	31. D	41. A
2. C	12. D	22. B	32. A	42. B
3. A	13. D	23. D	33. D	43. D
4. C	14. B	24. D	34. D	44. D
5. A	15. A	25. B	35. A	45. D
6. D	16. A	26. B	36. A	46. C
7. B	17. B	27. C	37. A	47. B
8. C	18. A	28. C	38. D	48. B
9. A	19. A	29. C	39. B	49. B
10. B	20. B	30. C	40. A	50. A

TEST 2

DIRECTIONS: Each question or incomplete statement is followed by several suggested answers or completions. Select the one that BEST answers the question or completes the statement. *PRINT THE LETTER OF THE CORRECT ANSWER IN THE SPACE AT THE RIGHT.*

1. The one of the following grades of fuel oil that contains the GREATEST heating value in BTU per gallon is   1.____

   A. #2   B. #4   C. #5   D. #6

2. When we say that a fuel oil has a high viscosity, we mean MAINLY that the fuel oil will   2.____

   A. evaporate easily
   B. burn without smoke
   C. flow slowly through pipes
   D. have a low specific gravity

3. The type of fuel oil pump GENERALLY used with a rotary cup oil burner system is the   3.____

   A. propeller pump
   B. internal pump
   C. centrifugal pump
   D. piston

4. No. 6 fuel oil flowing to a mechanical atomizing burner should be preheated to APPROXIMATELY   4.____

   A. 185° F   B. 115° F   C. 100° F   D. 80° F

5. The flame of an industrial rotary cup oil burner should be adjusted so that the flame   5.____

   A. has a yellow color with blue spots
   B. strikes all sides of the combustion chamber
   C. has a light brown color
   D. does not strike the rear of the combustion chamber

6. The location of the oil burner *remote control switch* should GENERALLY be   6.____

   A. at the boiler room entrance
   B. on the boiler shell
   C. on the oil burner motor
   D. on a wall nearest the boiler

7. With forced draft, the approximate wind box pressure in a single-retort underfeed stoker is NORMALLY   7.____

   A. 2"   B. 5"   C. 7"   D. 9"

8. The pressure over the fire in a coal-fired steam boiler with a balanced-draft system and natural draft is MOST NEARLY   8.____

   A. +.60"   B. +.50"   C. -.02"   D. -.70"

9. Three tons of coal with an ash content of 10% will yield a weight of ash of MOST NEARLY _____ lbs.   9.____

   A. 400   B. 500   C. 600   D. 700

10. To clean and spread the coal over the grates of a coal-fired boiler, you would use a tool known as a(n)

    A. hoe   B. extractor   C. lance   D. slice bar

11. To burn the volatile matter in coal MORE efficiently, one should

    A. mix peat with the coal
    B. supply overfire draft
    C. mix it with a lower grade of coal
    D. add moisture to the coal

12. The one of the following that lists the size classifications of anthracite coal in proper order ranging from the smallest to the largest is:

    A. Chestnut, culm, pea, birdseye, egg
    B. Egg, stove, pea, broken, culm
    C. Stove, egg, birdseye, culm, broken
    D. Birdseye, pea, chestnut, stove, egg

13. The fire in a hand-fired furnace can be cleaned by a method known as

    A. ashpit to grate   B. bottom to top
    C. side to side   D. grate to crown

14. Coal is normally *tempered* when operating a chain-grate stoker for the purpose of

    A. increasing coking   B. preventing clinking
    C. collecting particles   D. promoting uniform burning

15. The one of the following coals that can legally be burned in power plants is

    A. anthracite   B. sub-bituminous
    C. non-coking   D. bituminous

16. The one of the following that is known as *rice coal* is _____ coal.

    A. pea   B. buckwheat #2   C. egg   D. culm

17. A MAJOR cause of air pollution resulting from the burning of fuel oils is _____ dioxide.

    A. sulphur   B. silicon   C. nitrous   D. hydrogen

18. The CO_2 percentage in the flue gas of a power plant is indicated by a

    A. Doppler meter   B. Ranarex indicator
    C. microtector   D. hygrometer

19. The MOST likely cause of black smoke exhausting from the chimney of an oil-fired boiler is

    A. high secondary air flow   B. low stack emission
    C. low oil temperature   D. high chimney draft

20. The diameter of the steam piston in a steam-driven duplex vacuum pump whose dimensions are given as 3 by 2 by 4 is

    A. 2   B. 3   C. 4   D. 6

21. An induced draft fan is GENERALLY connected between the

    A. condenser and the first pass
    B. stack and the breeching
    C. feedwater heater and the boiler feed pump
    D. combustion chamber and fuel oil tanks

22. The PURPOSE of an air chamber on a reciprocating water pump is to

    A. maintain a uniform flow
    B. reduce the amount of steam expansion
    C. create a pulsating flow
    D. vary the amount of steam admission

23. *Flash point* is the temperature at which oil will

    A. change completely to vapor
    B. safely fire in a furnace
    C. flash into flame if a lighted match is passed just above the top of the oil
    D. burn intermittently when ignited

24. A *sounding box* would NORMALLY be found

    A. on top of the boiler
    B. next to a compressed air tank
    C. in a fuel oil tank
    D. in a steam condenser

25. An *intercooler* is GENERALLY found on a(n)

    A. steam pump   B. air compressor
    C. steam engine   D. rotary oil pump

26. The instrument used to measure atmospheric pressure is a

    A. capillary tube   B. venturi
    C. barometer   D. calorimeter

27. The control which starts or stops the operation of the oil burner at a pre-determined steam pressure is the

    A. pressuretrol   B. air flow interlock
    C. transformer   D. magnetic oil valve

28. In a closed feedwater heater, the water and the steam

    A. come into direct contact
    B. are kept apart from each other
    C. are under negative pressure
    D. mix and exhaust to the atmosphere

29. A *knocking* noise in steam lines is GENERALLY the result of

    A. superheated steam expansion
    B. high steam pressure

C. condensation in the line
D. rapid steam expansion

30. An electrical component known as a step-up transformer operates by

    A. raising voltage and decreasing amperage
    B. decreasing amperage and raising resistance
    C. raising amperage and decreasing resistance
    D. raising voltage and amperage at the same time

31. A monometer is an instrument that is used to measure

    A. heat radiation   B. air volume
    C. eondensate water level D. air pressure

32. Three 75-gallon per hour mechanical pressure type oil burners operating together are to burn 150,000 gallons of No. 6 fuel oil.
    The number of hours they would take to burn this amount of oil is MOST NEARLY

    A. 665   B. 760   C. 870   D. 1210

33. The sum of 10 1/2, 8 3/4, 5 1/2, and 2 1/4 is

    A. 23   B. 25   C. 26   D. 27

34. A water tank measures 50 feet long, 16 feet wide, and 12 feet high. Assume that water weighs 60 pounds per cubic foot and that one gallon of water weighs 8 pounds.
    The number of gallons the tank can hold when it is half full is

    A. 21,500   B. 28,375   C. 33,410   D. 36,000

35. Assuming 70 gallons of oil cost $42.00, then 110 gallons of oil at the same rate will cost

    A. $66.00   B. $84.00   C. $96.00   D. $152.00

Questions 36-40.

DIRECTIONS: Questions 36 through 40, inclusive, are to be answered in accordance with the information contained in the following paragraph.

Fuel is conserved when a boiler is operating near its most efficient load. The efficiency of a boiler will change as the output varies. Large amounts of air must be used at low ratings and so the heat exchanger is inefficient. As the output increases, the efficiency decreases due to an increase in flue gas temperature. Every boiler has an output rate for which its efficiency is highest. For example, in a water-tube boiler, the highest efficiency might occur at 120 percent of rated capacity while in a vertical fire-tube boiler highest efficiency might be at 70% of rated capacity. The type of fuel burned and cleanliness affects the maximum efficiency of the boiler. When a power plant contains a battery of boilers, a sufficient number should be kept in operation so as to maintain the output of individual units near their points of maximum efficiency. One of the boilers in the battery can be used as a regulator to meet the change in demand for steam while the other boilers could still operate at their most efficient rating. Boiler performance is expressed as the number of pounds of steam generated per pound of fuel.

36. According to the above paragraph, the number of pounds of steam generated per pound of fuel is a measure of boiler

   A. size
   B. performance
   C. regulator input
   D. by-pass

37. According to the above paragraph, the HIGHEST efficiency of a vertical fire-tube boiler might occur at

   A. 70% of rate capacity
   B. 80% of water tube capacity
   C. 95% of water tube capacity
   D. 120% of rated capacity

38. According to the above paragraph, the MAXIMUM efficiency of a boiler is affected by

   A. atmospheric temperature
   B. atmospheric pressure
   C. cleanliness
   D. fire brick material

39. According to the above paragraph, a heat exchanger uses large amounts of air at low

   A. fuel rates
   B. ratings
   C. temperatures
   D. pressures

40. According to the above paragraph, one boiler in a battery of boilers should be used as a

   A. demand   B. stand by   C. regulator   D. safety

KEY (CORRECT ANSWERS)

1. D	11. B	21. B	31. D
2. C	12. D	22. A	32. A
3. B	13. C	23. C	33. D
4. A	14. D	24. C	34. D
5. D	15. A	25. B	35. A
6. A	16. B	26. C	36. B
7. A	17. A	27. A	37. A
8. C	18. B	28. B	38. C
9. C	19. C	29. C	39. B
10. A	20. B	30. A	40. C

TEST 3

DIRECTIONS: Each question or incomplete statement is followed by several suggested answers or completions. Select the one that BEST answers the question or completes the statement. *PRINT THE LETTER OF THE CORRECT ANSWER IN THE SPACE AT THE RIGHT.*

1. The bottom blowdown on a boiler is used to　　1.____
   A. remove mud drum water impurities
   B. increase boiler priming
   C. reduce steam pressure in the header
   D. increase the boiler water level

2. The term *spalling* refers to a boiler　　2.____
   A. flue gas content　　B. soot blower
   C. combustion chamber　　D. mud leg

3. The wrench that would NORMALLY be used on hexagonally-shaped screwed valves and fittings is the _____ wrench.　　3.____
   A. adjustable pipe　　B. tappet
   C. monkey　　D. open-end

4. The designated size of a boiler tube is GENERALLY based upon its　　4.____
   A. internal diameter　　B. external diameter
   C. wall thickness　　D. weight per foot of length

5. A fusible plug on a boiler is made PRIMARILY of　　5.____
   A. selenium　　B. tin　　C. zinc　　D. iron

6. The range of *Ph* values for boiler feed water is NORMALLY　　6.____
   A. 1 to 2　　B. 4 to 6　　C. 9 to 10　　D. 12 to 15

7. The *boiler horsepower* is defined as the evaporation of _____ lbs. of water from and at 212° F.　　7.____
   A. 900　　B. 400　　C. 345　　D. 34.5

8. A low pressure air-atomizing oil burner has an operating air pressure range of _____ lbs.　　8.____
   A. 25 to 35　　B. 16 to 20　　C. 6 to 10　　D. 1 to 2

9. A superheater is installed in a Stirling boiler MAINLY for the purpose of raising the temperature of the　　9.____
   A. secondary air
   B. steam leaving the steam drum
   C. boiler feed water
   D. primary air

83

10. The function of a counterflow economizer in a power plant is to

    A. use flue gases to heat feed water
    B. raise flue gas temperatures
    C. recirculate exhaust steam
    D. pre-heat combustion air

11. A fire due to spontaneous combustion would MOST easily occur in a pile of

    A. asbestos sheathing   B. loose lumber
    C. oil drums   D. oily waste rags

12. A *damper regulator,* used for combustion control, is operated by

    A. steam pressure   B. the water column
    C. the boiler pump   D. a pitot tube

13. The packing of an expansion joint in a firebrick wall of a combustion chamber is GENERALLY made of

    A. silica   B. brick cement
    C. silicon carbide   D. asbestos

14. An open-ended steam pipe, called a steam lance, is USUALLY used on a boiler to

    A. remove soot   B. bleed the steam header
    C. clean the mud drum   D. clean chimneys

15. A high vacuum reading on the fuel oil gauge would indicate

    A. an empty oil tank   B. high oil temperature
    C. a clogged strainer   D. worn pump gears

16. The one of the following boilers that is classified as an internally-fired boiler is the _____ boiler.

    A. cross-drum straight tube
    B. vertical tubular
    C. Stirling
    D. cross-drum horizontal box-header

17. Try-cocks are used on a boiler PRIMARILY to

    A. check the gauge glass reading
    B. release steam pressure
    C. drain the water column
    D. blow down the gauge glass

18. Scale deposits on the tubes and shell of a high-pressure boiler are UNDESIRABLE because the deposits cause

    A. protrusions or roughness   B. suction
    C. foaming   D. concentrates

19. The function of a radiation pyrometer is to measure

    A. boiler water height   B. boiler pressure
    C. furnace temperature   D. boiler drum stresses

20. An engine indicator is GENERALLY used to measure

    A. steam temperature
    B. heat losses
    C. errors in gauge readings
    D. steam cylinder pressures

21. A goose-neck is installed in the line connecting a steam gauge to a boiler to

    A. maintain constant steam flow
    B. prevent steam knocking
    C. maintain steam pressure
    D. protect the gauge element

22. A boiler steam gauge should have a range of AT LEAST

    A. one-half the working steam pressure
    B. the working steam pressure
    C. 1 1/2 times the maximum allowable working pressure
    D. twice the maximum allowable working pressure

23. A disconnected steam pressure gauge is USUALLY calibrated with a(n)

    A. Orsat instrument
    B. air pump
    C. tuyeres
    D. dead-weight tester

24. The recommended size joint for repairing firebrick wall is MOST NEARLY

    A. 1/64"   B. 1/16"   C. 1/4"   D. 1/2"

25. The acidity of boiler water is USUALLY determined by a _____ test.

    A. Rockwell
    B. soap hardness
    C. paper
    D. alkalinity

26. Electrostatic precipitators are used in power plants to

    A. remove fly ash from flue gases
    B. measure smoke conditions
    C. collect boiler impurities
    D. disperse minerals in feed water

27. Fly ash from the flue gases in a power plant is collected by a

    A. soot blower
    B. gas separator
    C. stack regulator
    D. mechanical separator

28. The installation of four new split packing rings in a stuffing box requires that the joints of the packing rings be placed _____ apart.

    A. 180°   B. 90°   C. 60°   D. 30°

29. In power plants, boiler feed water is chemically treated in order to

    A. prevent scale formation
    B. increase water foaming
    C. increase oxygen formation
    D. increase the temperature of the water

30. The soot in a fire tube boiler GENERALLY settles on the

    A. bridgewall
    B. inside tube surface
    C. combustion chamber sides
    D. outside tube surface

31. The one of the following classifications of fuel oil strainers that is generally NOT used with the heavier industrial fuel oils is a _____ strainer.

    A. wire mesh   B. metallic disc
    C. filter cloth   D. perforated metal cylinder

32. The temperature of the fuel oil leaving a pre-heater is controlled by a(n)

    A. potentiometer   B. relay
    C. low water cut-off   D. aquastat

33. A pneumatic tool is GENERALLY powered by

    A. natural gas   B. steam   C. a battery   D. air

34. The maximum steam pressure permitted in the steam coils used for heating the oil in a submerged oil storage tank is MOST NEARLY _____ psi.

    A. 40   B. 35   C. 25   D. 10

35. The water pressure used in a hydrostatic test on a boiler is GENERALLY _____ maximum working pressure.

    A. 4 times   B. 2 times the
    C. 1 1/2 times the   D. the same as

36. The one of the following valves that should be used in a steam line to throttle the flow is the _____ valve.

    A. plug   B. check   C. gate   D. globe

37. The CO (carbon monoxide) content in the flue gas from an efficiently fired boiler should be APPROXIMATELY

    A. 0% to 1%   B. 4% to 6%
    C. 8% to 10%   D. 12% to 13%

38. The CO_2 (carbon dioxide) percentage in the flue gas of an efficiently fired boiler should be APPROXIMATELY

    A. 1%   B. 12%   C. 18%   D. 25%

39. When the temperature of stack gases rises considerably above the normal operating stack temperature, it GENERALLY indicates

    A. a low boiler water level
    B. a heavy smoke condition in the stack
    C. that the boiler is operating efficiently
    D. that the boiler tubes are dirty

40. A boiler safety valve is USUALLY set above the maximum working pressure by an amount equal to _____ of the maximum working pressure.   40._____

   A. 6%   B. 10%   C. 12%   D. 14%

KEY (CORRECT ANSWERS)

1. A	11. D	21. D	31. C
2. C	12. A	22. C	32. D
3. D	13. D	23. D	33. D
4. B	14. A	24. B	34. D
5. B	15. C	25. D	35. C
6. C	16. B	26. A	36. D
7. D	17. A	27. D	37. A
8. D	18. A	28. B	38. B
9. B	19. C	29. A	39. D
10. A	20. D	30. B	40. A

EXAMINATION SECTION
TEST 1

DIRECTIONS: Each question or incomplete statement is followed by several suggested answers or completions. Select the one that BEST answers the question or completes the statement. *PRINT THE LETTER OF THE CORRECT ANSWER IN THE SPACE AT THE RIGHT.*

1. Of the following, the one that is an *inherent* boiler heat loss is the loss due to

   A. dry chimney gases
   B. excess air
   C. unburned gaseous combustibles
   D. radiation from the furnace setting

   1.____

2. The one of the following flue gases whose presence indicates that MORE excess air is being supplied to a furnace than is being used is

   A. carbon dioxide
   B. carbon monoxide
   C. nitrogen
   D. oxygen

   2.____

3. A pressure gage on a compressed air tank reads 35.3 psi at 70° F.

   If, due to a fire, the temperature of the air in the tank were to increase to 600° F, the gage reading should be MOST NEARLY _____ psi.

   A. 70   B. 75   C. 80   D. 85

   3.____

4. Of the following types of flow meters, the one that is MOST accurate is a

   A. concentric orifice
   B. venturi tube
   C. flow nozzle
   D. pitot tube

   4.____

5. A spring pop safety valve on a fired high-pressure boiler fails to pop at its set pressure. Which of the following methods should be used to free the valve before retesting it?

   A. Strike the valve body with a soft lead hammer until it pops
   B. Raise the valve lifting-lever and release it
   C. Reduce the spring compression gradually until the valve opens
   D. Unscrew the valve one-quarter turn to relieve the strain on it

   5.____

6. A device which retains the desired parts of a steam-and-water mixture while rejecting the undesired parts of the mixture is a

   A. check valve
   B. calorimeter
   C. stud tube
   D. steam trap

   6.____

7. The MAIN advantage of using water-tube boilers in preference to fire-tube boilers in an installation is that water-tube boilers can be

   A. built much larger
   B. equipped with superheaters
   C. stoker-fired
   D. made portable

   7.____

8. The PRIMARY purpose of using phosphate to treat boiler water is to

   A. precipitate the hardness constituents
   B. scavenge the dissolved oxygen
   C. dissolve the calcium
   D. dissolve the magnesium

9. Assume that the set pressure of a safety valve on a power boiler is 100 psi.
   The MINIMUM pressure at which the safety valve must close after blowing down is _____ psi.

   A. 92   B. 94   C. 96   D. 98

10. A one-pound sample of wet steam at a certain pressure has an enthalpy of 960 BTU. For this same pressure, the Steam Tables list the enthalpy of saturated liquid as 130 and of saturated vapor as 1130 BTU.
    The quality of the sample steam is MOST NEARLY

    A. 75%   B. 85%   C. 90%   D. 95%

11. The type of feedwater heater which uses hot flue gases to heat the feedwater is known as a(n)

    A. economizer   B. direct-contact heater
    C. deaerator   D. surface heater

12. The minimum recommended suction head for a centrifugal pump handling feedwater at 300° F is 155 feet.
    If the vapor pressure corresponding to the water temperature is 135 feet and the losses in the suction piping amount to 5 feet, the pump should be located AT LEAST _____ the lowest level of the water in the heater.

    A. 25 feet below   B. 15 feet below
    C. 15 feet above   D. 25 feet above

13. As compared to a power-driven triplex single-acting pump of the same size and operating at the same speed, a steam-driven duplex double-acting pump will

    A. pump more water per minute
    B. give a more uniform discharge
    C. have a higher first cost
    D. be more economical to operate

14. The MAIN advantage of operating a steam engine or steam turbine *condensing* is that it

    A. increases the mean effective pressure in the prime mover
    B. decreases the condensate temperature
    C. permits the use of exhaust steam to drive auxiliary equipment
    D. eliminates the need for separating non-condensibles from the steam

15. The automatic shut-off valves for a water gage installed on a high-pressure boiler must be _____ check valves.

    A. horizontal swing   B. vertical swing
    C. ball   D. spring-loaded

16. The efficiency of a riveted joint is defined as the ratio of the 16.____

   A. plate thickness to the rivet diameter
   B. strength of the riveted joint to the strength of a welded joint
   C. strength of the riveted joint to the strength of the solid plate
   D. number of rivets in the first row of the joint to the total number of rivets on one side of the joint

17. A pump delivers 1500 pounds of water per minute against a total head of 200 feet. The water horsepower of this pump is MOST NEARLY 17.____

   A. 10   B. 40   C. 100   D. 600

18. In the most usual type of large capacity oil burner using #6 oil, under *fully automatic* control, the atomization of the oil is produced MAINLY by the 18.____

   A. pressure from the pump
   B. pressure from the secondary air fan
   C. oil temperature from the heater
   D. rotation of the burner assembly by the motor

19. Which of the following comes the closest to indicating the number of degree-days in a normal heating season in the city? 19.____

   A. 3000   B. 4000   C. 5000   D. 6000

20. In which of the following methods of steam generation would you expect to obtain reasonably continuous values of CO_2 CLOSEST to the perfect CO_2 value? 20.____
    Automatic

   A. stoker firing with temperature recorder
   B. stoker firing with *hold fire timer*
   C. oil firing with *stack switch*
   D. oil firing with *haze regulator*

21. The loss of heat in stack gases for heavy fuel oils is HIGHEST when the CO_2 content is _____ and the stack temperature is _____. 21.____

   A. 12%; 500°   B. 8%; 600°   C. 6%; 700°   D. 14%; 600°

22. A badly sooted HRT boiler under coal firing will show a _____ than a clean boiler. 22.____

   A. *higher* CO_2 value
   B. *lower* CO_2 value
   C. *higher* stack temperature
   D. *lower* draft loss

23. A unit heater condensing 50 lbs. of low pressure steam per hour would be rated MOST NEARLY at _____ square feet E.D.R. 23.____

   A. 50   B. 100   C. 150   D. 200

24. Which of the following values MOST NEARLY equals one horsepower? 24.____

   A. 550 ft.lbs. per sec.   B. 3300 ft.lbs. per min.
   C. 5500 ft.lbs. per hour   D. 10000 ft.lbs. per min.

25. An indicator card from a steam engine is most useful to the engineer in
    A. determining the boiler pressure
    B. determining the engine speed
    C. adjusting the valve setting
    D. computing the mechanical efficiency

25.____

KEY (CORRECT ANSWERS)

1.	A	11.	A
2.	D	12.	A
3.	D	13.	A
4.	B	14.	A
5.	B	15.	C
6.	D	16.	C
7.	A	17.	A
8.	A	18.	D
9.	C	19.	C
10.	B	20.	D

21. C
22. C
23. D
24. A
25. C

TEST 2

DIRECTIONS: Each question or incomplete statement is followed by several suggested answers or completions. Select the one that BEST answers the question or completes the statement. *PRINT THE LETTER OF THE CORRECT ANSWER IN THE SPACE AT THE RIGHT.*

1. A centrifugal water pump is direct-driven by a 25 HP 900 RPM electric motor at rated load.
   In order to double the quantity of water delivered, it would be necessary to substitute a motor rated at _____ HP at _____ RPM.

   A. 40; 1200　　B. 50; 1200　　C. 100; 1800　　D. 200; 1800

   1.____

2. The angle of advance of the eccentric on a D-slide valve steam engine is equal to

   A. the lead angle minus the lap angle
   B. the lead angle plus the lap angle
   C. 90 degrees minus the lead angle
   D. 90 degrees plus the lead and the lap angle

   2.____

3. Of the following statements pertaining to a duplex steam-driven water pump, the one which is NOT true is that

   A. the slide valves have a steam and an exhaust lap
   B. there is a pause in the flow of water through the discharge valve at the end of the stroke
   C. the piston stroke can be adjusted
   D. an air chamber may be omitted on small sizes

   3.____

4. The diagram on which a steam throttling process is indicated by a straight horizontal line is the _____ diagram.

   A. PV　　　　　　　　　　B. Mollier
   C. Ringelman　　　　　　D. temperature-entropy

   4.____

5. The one of the following devices which is useful in preventing damage to a multi-stage turbine rotor due to unequal thermal expansion or contraction is the

   A. thrust bearing
   B. dummy piston and seal
   C. rupture seal
   D. motor-driven turning gear

   5.____

6. The purpose of a steam turbine's governing system is to control steam flow through the unit, usually in order to keep some other factor constant.
   When a steam turbine is driving an alternator, the factor which is usually kept constant by the governor's operation is the

   A. inlet steam pressure　　　　B. exhaust steam pressure
   C. shaft speed　　　　　　　　D. power output

   6.____

7. The speed regulation of a condensing steam turbine operating at 1800 RPM at no load and 1750 RPM at full load is MOST NEARLY

   A. 1%　　B. 3%　　C. 5%　　D. 7%

   7.____

8. The one of the following statements which is NOT true of the operation of steam turbines is that they

   A. operate most efficiently at high speed
   B. can be operated condensing or non-condensing
   C. can be used to drive centrifugal water pumps
   D. need high viscosity cylinder oil mixed with the steam supply to operate properly

9. Of the following, the one which is TRUE regarding backpressure steam turbines is that they

   A. operate on the exhaust steam from higher pressure turbines
   B. operate condensing
   C. exhaust through a very large hood
   D. convert a small part of the available heat in the steam into power

10. An aftercooler on a reciprocating air compressor is used PRIMARILY to

    A. increase compressor capacity
    B. improve compressor efficiency
    C. condense the moisture in the compressed air
    D. cool the lubricating oil

11. The one of the following tasks which is an example of preventive maintenance is

    A. replacing a leaking water pipe nipple
    B. cleaning the cup on a rotary cup burner
    C. cleaning a completely clogged oil strainer
    D. replacing a blown fuse

12. The four MAIN causes of failure of three-phase electric motors are

    A. dirt, friction, moisture, single-phasing
    B. friction, moisture, single-phasing, vibration
    C. dirt, moisture, single-phasing, vibration
    D. dirt, friction, moisture, vibration

13. Assume that an alternator running at a speed of 1800 RPM generates AC voltage at a frequency of 60 cycles per second (Hertz).
    The number of poles in this alternator is

    A. 2   B. 4   C. 6   D. 8

14. Assume that on an integrating watt-hour meter with 4 dials, the respective pointers from left to right are between 7 and 8, between 5 and 6, between 0 and 1, and between 3 and 4.
    Under these conditions, the reading is

    A. 8614   B. 7503   C. 3168   D. 3067

15. Assume that an ammeter is properly connected to a current transformer that has a ratio of 80 to 5. When the ammeter indicates 4.0 amperes, the current in the primary circuit is MOST NEARLY _____ amperes.

    A. 4.0   B. 20.0   C. 64.0   D. 80.0

16. Assume that two alternators, No. 1 and No. 2, are operating in parallel and that alternator No. 1 is taking a greater share of the load than alternator No. 2.
    Of the following, the PROPER method to reapportion the load between the two alternators is to

    A. speed up No. 2
    B. slow down No. 1
    C. increase the excitation of No. 2
    D. adjust the governors of both prime movers

    16._____

17. Which of the following CORRECTLY describes the flow of electric power in a three-phase alternator?
    The input is _____ and the output is _____.

    A. three-phase AC to the stator; single-phase AC from the rotor
    B. three-phase AC to the rotor; single-phase AC from the stator
    C. DC to the stator; three-phase AC from the rotor
    D. DC to the rotor; three-phase AC from the stator

    17._____

18. When the load on a mechanical stoker fired boiler plant furnishing steam for slide valve engine generators drops by 30%, the

    A. stoker should be shut down
    B. fan should be speeded up and the stoker slowed
    C. stoker should be speeded up and the air supply reduced
    D. stoker speed and air supply should be adjusted by reducing both

    18._____

19. Which of the following statements is MOST NEARLY correct?

    A. All types of mechanical stokers may be used with equal efficiency under all types of boilers.
    B. Most stokers are designed with a weak member.
    C. The best type of stoker to use is not dependent upon the type of fuel available.
    D. The advisability of installing stokers is not dependent upon the load.

    19._____

20. The number and size of safety valves required on a high pressure boiler is dependent upon the

    A. size of the boiler drums
    B. amount of heating surface
    C. number of pounds of fuel burned per square foot of grate per hour
    D. size of the steam main

    20._____

21. In changing over a boiler from high pressure (150 lbs. per square inch) to 10 lbs. per square inch, it is USUALLY necessary to

    A. *increase* the size of the safety valves
    B. *decrease* the grate area
    C. *increase* the size of the feedwater piping
    D. *increase* the size of the blow down piping

    21._____

22. A boiler feed injector becomes temporarily steam bound. To correct this condition, the MOST proper action to take is to

   A. increase boiler pressure
   B. reduce suction lift
   C. wrap it with cold rags
   D. bank fire

23. If in your plant the volume of air in cu.ft. per min. for combustion is represented by X, which of the following lowing values of X would MOST NEARLY represent the Cfm of stack gas, under usual conditions, that an induced draft fan would have to handle?

   A. X B. $2X$ C. $3X$ D. $4X$

24. If the stack switch of an oil burner becomes excessively sooted, a condition that is MOST likely to result is

   A. continuous shutting down of the burner shortly after it starts up
   B. excessive flow of oil to the burner resulting in a smoky fire
   C. excessive fire due to failure to cut off current to the burner motor
   D. failure of the warp switch of the relay to operate

25. In the usual high pressure electric generating plant in large buildings, heating the feedwater from 70° F to 180° F with exhaust steam usually will *decrease* the fuel consumption by

   A. 5%   B. 10%   C. 15%   D. 20%

KEY (CORRECT ANSWERS)

1. D		11. B	
2. B		12. D	
3. A		13. B	
4. B		14. B	
5. D		15. C	
6. C		16. D	
7. B		17. D	
8. D		18. D	
9. D		19. B	
10. C		20. B	

21. A
22. C
23. B
24. A
25. B

BASIC FUNDAMENTALS OF REFRIGERATION

TABLE OF CONTENTS

	Page
I. Fundamentals of Refrigeration	1
A. Heat	1
B. Heat and Temperature	1
C. Sensible Heat and Latent Heat	1
D. Specific Heat	2
E. Heat Flow	2
F. Refrigeration Ton	2
II. Pressure, Temperature, and Volume	2
III. Mechanical Refrigeration Systems	3
IV. Main Parts of the R-12 System	5
A. Thermostatic Expansion Valve	5
B. Evaporator	6
C. Compressor	8
D. Condenser	8
E. Receiver	9
F. Accessories	9
V. Operating Procedures for an R-12 System	15
A. Starting the Compressor	16
B. Operating an R-12 Plant in Automatic	16
C. Securing the Compressor	17
VI. Maintenance of R-12 Systems	17
A. Defrosting the Coding Coils	17
B. Pumping Down a Refrigerant System	18
C. Testing for Refrigerant Leaks	20
D. Testing for Air and Noncondensable Gases	22
E. Checking Compressor Oil	23
F. Care of V-Belts	25
G. Setting Control and Safety Devices	25
VII. Characteristics of Refrigerants	30
VIII. Safety Precautions	31

BASIC FUNDAMENTALS OF REFRIGERATION

From practical experience, you will probably learn how to start, operate, stand watch on, and secure these systems. To do your job properly, you must have a thorough understanding of the operating principles of refrigeration systems. This understanding can be attained through study.

The refrigeration systems most commonly used utilize R-12 as a refrigerant.

Chemically, R-12 is dichlorodifluoromethane (CCl_2F_2). The boiling point of R-12 is so low that the substance cannot exist as a liquid unless it is confined and put under pressure. It also has the advantage of being practically nontoxic, nonflammable, nonexplosive, and non-corrosive; and it does not poison or contaminate foods. The information given in this chapter is, therefore, primarily concerned with R-12 systems. It should be noted that the cycle of operation and the main components of R-12 systems are basically the same for refrigeration and air conditioning plants.

I. FUNDAMENTALS OF REFRIGERATION

Refrigeration is a general term used to describe the process of removing heat from spaces, objects, or materials and to maintain them at temperatures below the temperature of the surrounding atmosphere. In order to produce a refrigeration effect, it is merely necessary to expose the material to be cooled to a colder object or environment and allow heat to flow in its NATURAL direction that is, from the warmer material to the colder material. The term is usually applied to an artificial means of lowering the temperature. Mechanical refrigeration may be defined as a mechanical system or apparatus so designed and constructed that, through its function, heat is transferred from one substance to another.

Refrigeration is more readily understood if you know the relationships among temperature, pressure, and volume, and how pressure affects liquids and gases.

A. HEAT

The purpose of refrigeration is to maintain spaces at low temperatures. Remember, however, that you can't cool anything by adding coolness to it; you have to REMOVE HEAT from it. Refrigeration, therefore, is a process of cooling by removing heat.

B. HEAT AND TEMPERATURE

It is important to distinguish between heat and temperature. HEAT is a form of energy. TEMPERATURE is the intensity of heat. The quantity or amount of heat is measured in terms of a standard unit called a BRITISH THERMAL UNIT (Btu). Temperature, as you know, is measured in degrees, which indicate the intensity of the heat in a given substance; it does not indicate the number of Btus in the substance. For example, let's consider a spoonful of very hot water and a bucketful of warm water. Which has the higher temperature? Which has more heat? The heat in the spoonful of hot water is more intense; therefore, its temperature is higher. The bucketful of warm water has more Btu (more heat energy), but its heat is less intense.

C. SENSIBLE HEAT AND LATENT HEAT

In the study of refrigeration, it is necessary to distinguish between sensible heat and latent heat. SENSIBLE HEAT is the term applied to the heat that is absorbed or given off by a substance that is NOT in the process of changing its physical state. When a substance is not in the process of changing its state, the addition or removal of heat always causes a change in the temperature of the substance. Sensible heat can be sensed, or measured with a thermometer.

LATENT HEAT is the term used to describe the heat that is absorbed or given off by a substance while it is changing its physical state. When a substance is in process of changing its physical state, the heat absorbed or given off does NOT cause a temperature change in the substance the heat is latent or hidden. In other words, sensible heat is the term used to describe heat that affects the temperature of things; latent heat is the term used to describe heat, that affects the physical state of things.

D. SPECIFIC HEAT

Substances vary with respect to their ability to absorb heat or to lose heat. The ability of a substance to absorb heat or to lose it is known as the SPECIFIC HEAT of the substance. The specific heat of water is taken to be 1.0, and the specific heat of each other substance is measured by comparison with this standard. Thus, if it takes only 1/2 Btu to raise the temperature of 1 pound of a substance 1F, the specific heat of that substance is 0.5, or one-half the specific heat of water. If you look up the specific heat of ice in a table, you will find it to be about 0.5.

E. HEAT FLOW

Heat flows only from objects of higher temperature to objects of lower temperature. When two objects at different temperatures are placed near each other, heat will flow from the warmer object to the cooler one until both objects are at the same temperature. Heat flow takes place at a greater rate when there is a large temperature difference than when there is only a slight temperature difference. As the temperature difference approaches zero, the rate of heat flow also approaches zero. Heat flow may take place by radiation, by conduction, by convection, or by some combination of these methods.

F. REFRIGERATION TON

The unit which measures the amount of heat removal and thereby indicates the capacity of a refrigeration system is known as the REFRIGERATION TON. The refrigeration ton is based on the cooling effect of 1 ton (2000 pounds) of ice at 32 F melting in 24 hours. The latent heat of fusion of ice (or water) is 144 Btu. Therefore, the number of Btu required to melt 1 ton of ice is 144 x 2000, or 288,000. The standard refrigeration ton is defined as the transfer of 288,000 Btu in 24 hours. On an hourly basis, the refrigeration ton is 12,000 Btu per hour (288,000 divided by 24).

It should be emphasized that the refrigeration ton is the standard unit of measure used to designate the heat-removal capacity of a refrigeration unit. It is not necessarily a measure of the ice-making capacity of a machine, since the amount of ice that can be made depends upon the initial temperature of the water and other factors.

II. PRESSURE, TEMPERATURE, AND VOLUME

In studying refrigeration, it is important to understand some of the ways in which pressure affects liquids and gases, and some of the relationships between pressure, temperature, and volume in gases.

The boiling point of any liquid varies according to the pressure on the liquid the higher the pressure, the higher the boiling point. It is well to remember that condensing a gas to a liquid is just the reverse process of boiling a liquid until it vaporizes, and that the same pressure and temperature relationship is required to produce either change of state.

Water boils at 80°F under a vacuum of 29 inches of mercury; at 212°F at atmospheric pressure; and at 489°F at a pressure of 600 psig. Refrigerants used in vapor compressor cycle equipment usually have much lower boiling points than water, under any given pressure, but these boiling points also vary according to pressure. R-12, for example, boils at -21°F at atmospheric pressure; at 0°F at 9.17 psig; at 50°F at 46.69 psig; and at 100°F at 116.9 psig. From these figures, you can see that R-12 cannot exist as a liquid at ordinary temperatures unless it is confined and put under pressure.

If the temperature of a liquid is raised to the boiling point corresponding to its pressure, and if the application of heat is continued, the liquid begins to boil and vaporize. The vapor which is formed remains at the same temperature as the boiling liquid, as long as it is in contact with the liquid. A vapor CANNOT be superheated as long as it is in contact with the liquid from which it is being generated.

The pressure-temperature-volume relationships of gases are expressed by Boyle's law, Charles' law, and the general gas law or equation.

BOYLE'S LAW states that the volume of any dry gas varies inversely with its absolute pressure, provided the temperature remains constant. This law may also be expressed as an equation:

$$V_1 P_1 = V_2 P_2$$

where V_1 is the original volume of the gas, P_1 its original absolute pressure, V_2 its new volume, and P_2 its new absolute pressure.

CHARLES' LAW states that the volume of a gas is directly proportional to its absolute temperature, provided the pressure is kept constant. The equation for this law is:

$$V_1 T_2 = V_2 T_1$$

THE GENERAL GAS EQUATION combines Boyle's law and Charles' law, and expresses the relationship between the volume, the absolute pressure, and the absolute temperature of gases. The general gas law is expressed by the equation:

$$\frac{P_1 V_1}{T_1} = \frac{P_2 V_2}{T_2}$$

These equations indicate the nature of the relationship between the pressure, the volume, and the temperature of any gas. You will probably not find it necessary to use the equations themselves, but you should have a thorough understanding of the principles which they express. Let's summarize them:

1. When temperature is held constant, increasing the pressure on a gas causes a proportional decrease in volume; decreasing the pressure causes a proportional increase in volume.

2. When pressure is held constant, increasing the temperature of a gas causes a proportional

increase in volume; decreasing the temperature causes a proportional decrease in volume.

3. When the volume is held constant, increasing the temperature of a gas causes a proportional increase in pressure; decreasing the temperature causes a proportional decrease in pressure.

In this discussion of the effects of pressure on a gas, we have noted that the volume and the temperature of the gas are different AFTER the pressure has been changed. It is important to note, however, that a temperature change normally occurs in a gas WHILE the pressure is being changed. Compressing a gas raises its temperature; allowing a gas to expand lowers its temperature. As we will see, this fact is of importance in the refrigeration cycle.

III. MECHANICAL REFRIGERATION SYSTEMS

Various types of refrigerating systems are used for refrigeration and air

conditioning. The most generally employed is the vapor compression cycle with reciprocating compressors. Vapor compression cycle refrigerating systems with centrifugal compressors as described are sometimes used for air conditioning. Centrifugal units are generally used to cool a secondary refrigerant; brine for cargo refrigeration and fresh water for air conditioning application.

The STEAM-JET REFRIGERATION SYSTEM is used for air conditioning purposes. As shown in figure 1, the steam-jet plant consists of a flash tank, a booster ejector, a condenser, air ejectors, and the necessary pumps and piping. The flash tank (sometimes called the evaporator) is maintained under exceptionally high vacuum by the air ejector on some other vacuum producing device. As water is sprayed into the flash tank, part of each drop flashes into vapor and thereby cools the unvaporized portion of each drop to about 50°F or lower, depending upon the capacity of the unit. The vapor formed by this evaporation is removed or "pumped" to the condenser by the steam jet booster ejector. The cooled water falls to the bottom of the shell; it is then pumped to the cooling coils, and returned to the flash tank at a temperature of about 55°F.

The vapor compression cycle with reciprocating compressors using R-12 is used for most refrigerating plants. Figure 2 gives a general idea of this type of refrigeration cycle. As you study this system, try to understand what happens to the refrigerant as it passes through each part of the cycle. In particular, be sure that you understand why the refrigerant changes from liquid to vapor and from vapor to liquid, and what happens in terms of heat because of these changes of state. It will be helpful to trace the refrigerant through its entire cycle, beginning with the thermostatic expansion valve.

Liquid refrigerant enters the expansion valve from the high pressure side of the system and passes through an orifice, which reduces the pressure of the refrigerant. Due to the reduction in pressure, the liquid refrigerant begins to boil and to flash into vapor.

From the thermostatic expansion valve, the refrigerant passes into the cooling coil (or evaporator). The boiling point of the refrigerant under the low pressure in the evaporator is about 20°F lower than the temperature of the space in which the cooling coil is installed. As the liquid boils and vaporizes, it picks up its latent heat of vaporization from the surroundings, thereby removing heat from the space. The refrigerant continues to absorb latent heat of vaporization until all the liquid has been vaporized. By the time the refrigerant is ready to leave the cooling coil, it has not only absorbed this latent heat of vaporization, but has also picked up some additional heat that is, the vapor has become superheated. As a rule, the amount of superheat is 4°F to 12°F.

REFRIGERATION

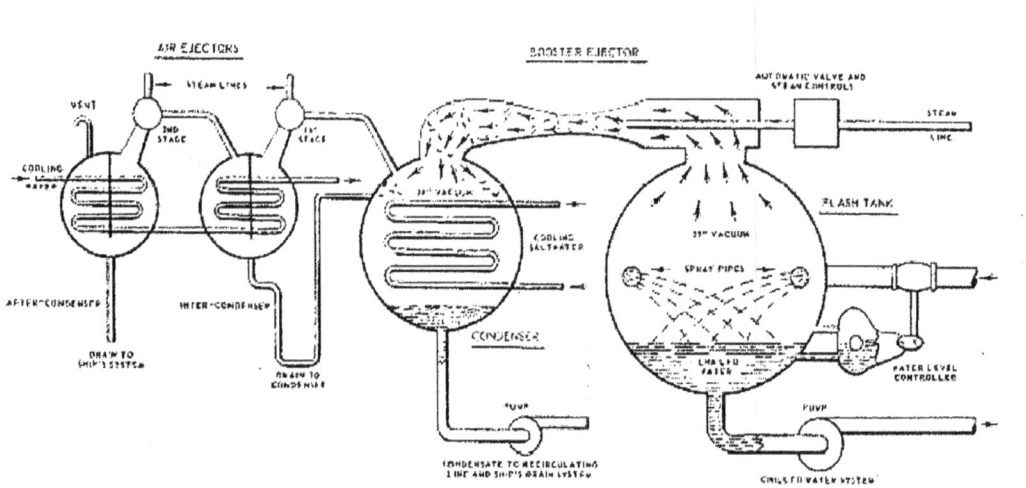

Figure 1.—Steam-jet refrigeration system.

The refrigerant leaves the evaporator as a low pressure superheated vapor, having absorbed heat and thus cooled the space to the desired temperature. The remainder of the cycle is concerned with disposing of this heat and converting the refrigerant back into a liquid state so that it can again vaporize in the evaporator and thus again absorb the heat.

The low pressure superheated vapor is drawn out of the evaporator by the compressor, which also keeps the refrigerant circulating through the system. In the compressor cylinders, the refrigerant is compressed from a low pressure, low temperature vapor to a high pressure vapor, and its temperature rises accordingly.

The high pressure R-12 vapor is discharged from the compressor into the condenser. Here the refrigerant condenses, giving up its superheat (sensible heat) and its latent heat of vaporization to the ambient air in an air-cooled condenser or the cooling water in a water-cooled condenser. The refrigerant, still at high pressure, is now a liquid again.

From the condenser, the refrigerant flows into a receiver, which serves as a storage place for the liquid refrigerant in the system. From the receiver, the refrigerant goes to the thermostatic expansion valve, and the cycle begins again.

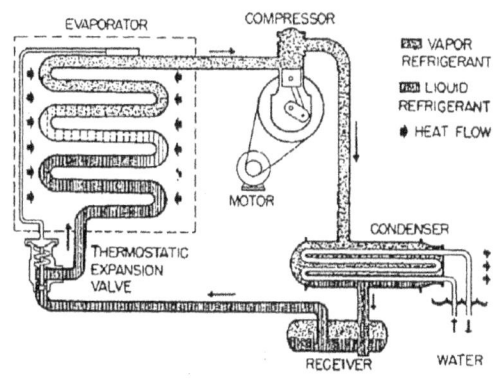

Figure 2.—R-12 refrigeration cycle.

As you can see from this description of the compression cycle, this type of refrigeration system has two pressure sides. The LOW PRESSURE SIDE extends from the orifice of the thermostatic expansion valve up to and including the intake side of the compressor cylinders. The HIGH PRESSURE SIDE extends from the discharge valve of the compressor to the thermostatic expansion valve.

IV. MAIN PARTS OF THE R-12 SYSTEM

The main parts of an R-12 refrigeration system are shown diagrammatically in figure 3. The primary components of the system are the thermostatic expansion valve, the evaporator, the compressor, the condenser, and the receiver. Additional equipment required to complete the plant includes piping, pressure gages, thermometers, various types of control switches and control valves, strainers, relief valves, sight-flow indicators, dehydrators, and charging connections. Figure * 4 shows most of the components on the high pressure side of an R-12 system, as actually installed on board ship.

In the following discussion, we will deal with the R-12 system as though it had only one evaporator, one compressor, and one condenser. As you will see from figure 3 however, a refrigeration system may (and usually does) include more than one evaporator; and it may include additional compressor and condenser units.

A. Thermostatic Expansion Valve

The thermostatic expansion valve is essentially a reducing valve between the high pressure side and the low pressure side of the system. The valve is designed to regulate the rate at which the refrigerant enters the cooling coil in proportion to the rate of evaporation of the liquid refrigerant in the coil; the amount depends of course, on the amount of heat being removed from the refrigerated space.

A thermal control bulb for the thermostatic expansion valve is clamped to the cooling coil, near the outlet. The bulb contains R-12. Control tubing connects the bulb with the area above the diaphragm in the thermostatic expansion valve. When the temperature at the control bulb rises, the R-12 expands and transmits a pressure to the diaphragm; this causes the diaphragm to be moved downward, thus opening the valve and allowing more refrigerant to enter the cooling coil. When the temperature at the control bulb falls, the pressure above the diaphragm is decreased and the valve tends to close. Thus, the temperature near the evaporator outlet controls the operation of the thermostatic expansion valve.

B. Evaporator

The evaporator consists of a coil of copper tubing installed in the space to be refrigerated. Figure 11-5 illustrates some of this tubing. As mentioned before, the liquid R-12 enters the tubing at a very much reduced pressure and with, therefore, a very much lowered boiling point. In passing through the expansion valve, part of the

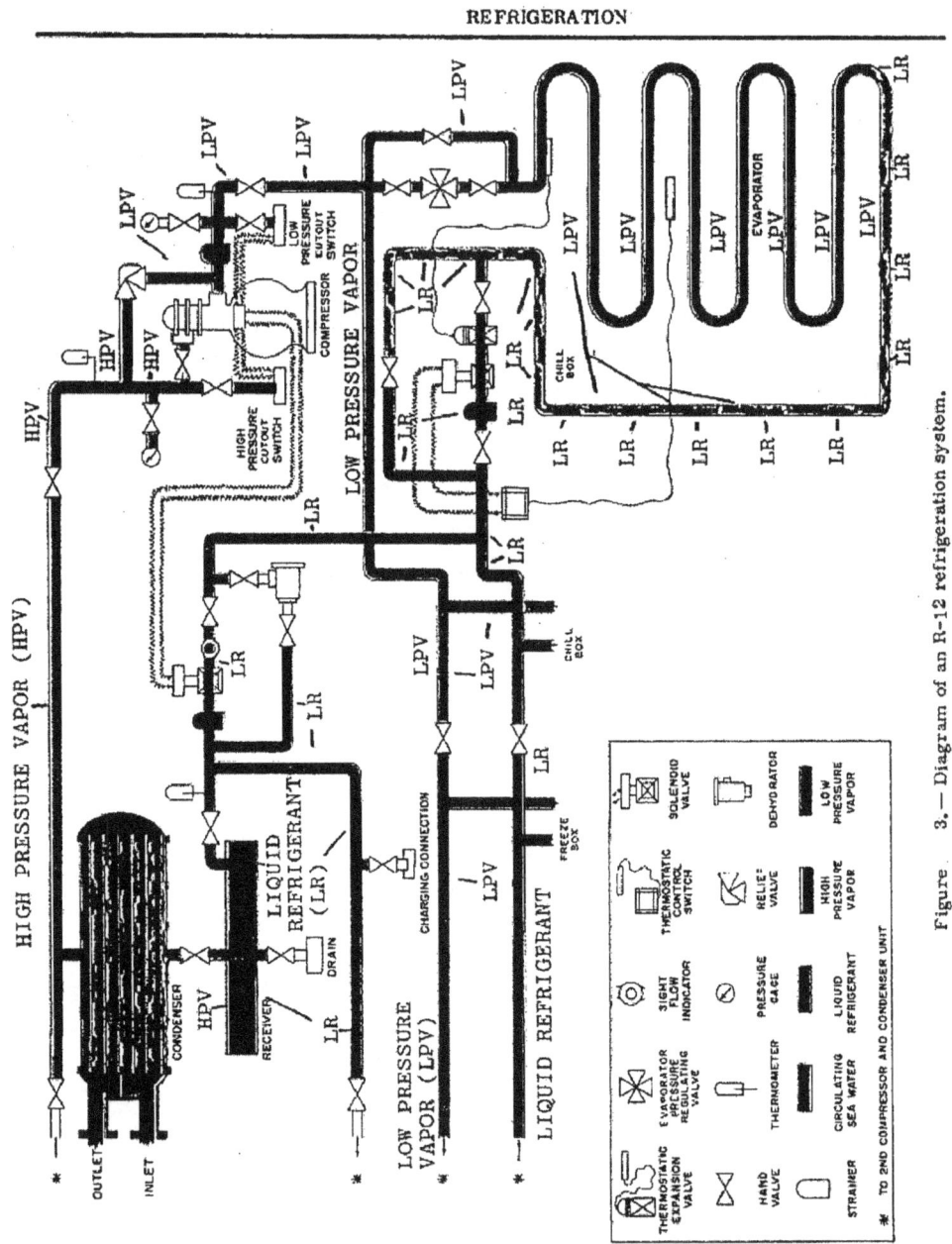

Figure 3. — Diagram of an R-12 refrigeration system.

refrigerant boils and vaporizes, due to the reduced pressure, and the remaining liquid refrigerant is cooled to its boiling point. Then, as the refrigerant passes through the evaporator, the heat flowing to the coil from the surrounding air causes the rest of the liquid refrigerant to boil and vaporize. After the refrigerant has absorbed its latent heat of vaporization (that is, after it is entirely vaporized), the refrigerant continues to absorb heat until it becomes superheated by about 10°F. The amount of superheat is determined by the amount of liquid refrigerant admitted to the

Figure 4.—R-12 installation.

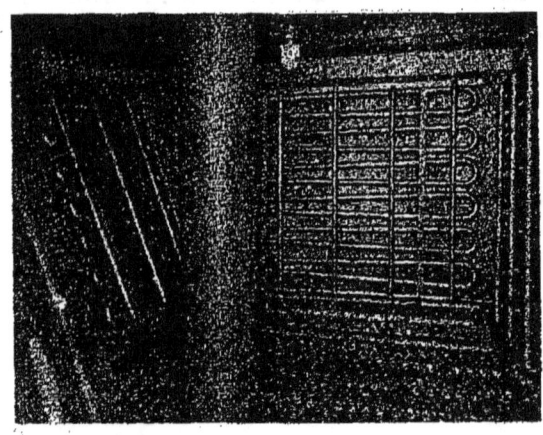

Figure 5. — Evaporator tubing.

evaporator; and this, in turn, is controlled by the spring adjustment of the thermostatic expansion valve. A temperature range of 4 to 12° F of superheat is considered desirable because it increases the efficiency of the plant and because it evaporates all of the liquid, thus preventing liquid carryover into the compressor.

C. Compressor

The compressor in a refrigeration system is essentially a pump. It is used to pump heat "uphill" from the cold side to the hot side of the system.

The heat absorbed by the refrigerant in the evaporator must be removed before the refrigerant can again absorb latent heat. The only way in which the vaporized refrigerant can be made to give up the latent heat of vaporization that it absorbed in the evaporator is by cooling and condensing it. In view of the relatively high temperature of the available cooling medium, the only way to make the vapor condense is by first compressing it.

The vapor drawn into the compressor is at very low pressure and very low temperature. In the compressor, both the pressure and the temperature are raised. Since an increase in pressure causes a proportional rise in temperature, and since the condensation point of any vapor is dependent upon the pressure, raising the pressure of the vaporized refrigerant provides a condensation temperature high enough to permit the use of sea water as the condensing and cooling medium. The compressor raises the pressure of the vaporized refrigerant sufficiently high to permit condensation to take place in the condenser.

In addition to this primary function, the compressor also serves to keep the refrigerant circulating and to maintain the required pressure difference between the high pressure side and the low pressure side of the system.

Many different types of compressors are used in refrigeration systems. The designs of compressors vary depending upon the application of the refrigerants used in the system. Figure 6 shows a motor-driven, single acting, two-cylinder, reciprocating compressor such as is commonly used in naval refrigeration plants.

Compressors used in R-12 systems may be lubricated either by pressure lubrication or by splash lubrication. Splash lubrication, which depends upon maintaining a fairly high oil level in the compressor crankcase, is usually satisfactory for smaller compressors. High speed, or large capacity, compressors use pressure lubrication systems.

D. Condenser

The compressor discharges the high pressure, high temperature refrigerant vapor to the condenser, where it flows around the tubes through which sea water is being pumped. As the vapor gives up its superheat (sensible heat) to the sea water, the temperature of the vapor drops to the condensation point. As soon as the temperature of the vapor drops to its boiling or condensing temperature at the existing pressure, the vapor condenses, giving off its latent heat of vaporization in the process. The refrigerant, now in liquid form, is subcooled slightly below its boiling point (condensation point) at this pressure to ensure that it will not flash into vapor.

A water-cooled condenser for an R-12 refrigeration system is shown in figure 7. Circulating water is obtained through a branch connection from the firemain, or by means of an individual pump taking suction from the sea. The purge connection shown in figure 7 is on the refrigerant side; it is used to remove air and other noncondensable gases that are lighter than the R-12 vapor.

Most condensers used for refrigeration plants are of the water-cooled type. However,

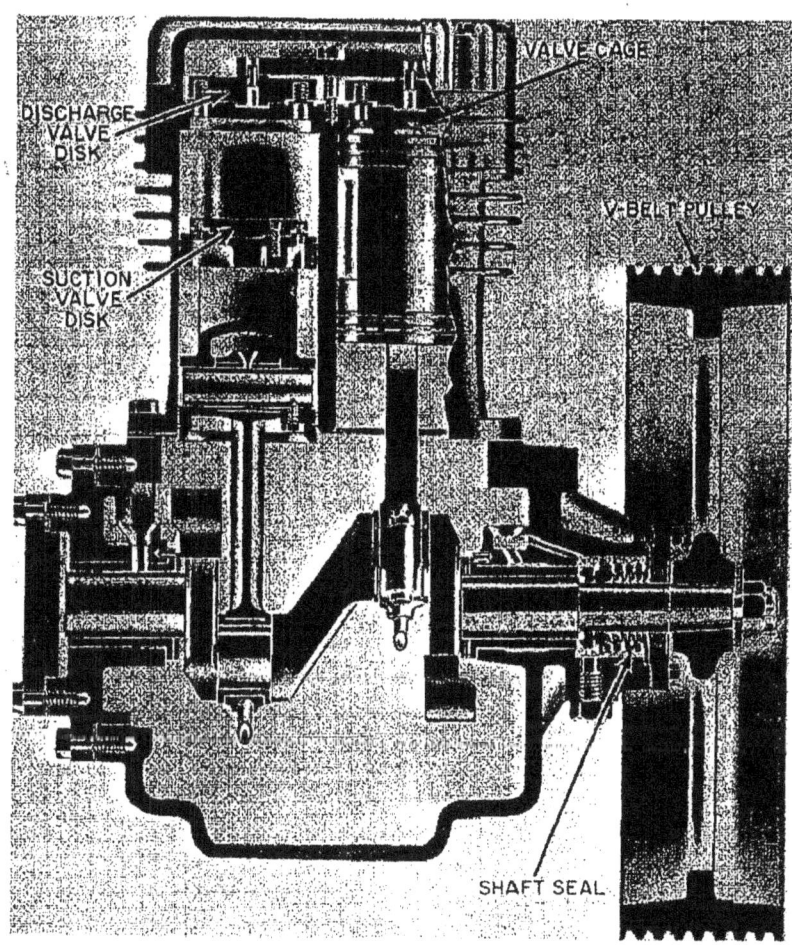

Figure 6. — Reciprocating compressor.

it should be mentioned that some small units have air-cooled condensers. These consist of tubing with external fins to increase the heat transfer surface. Most air-cooled condensers have fans to ensure positive circulation of air around the condenser tubes.

E. Receiver

The receiver, shown in figure 8, acts as a temporary storage space and surge tank for the liquid refrigerant which flows from the condenser. The receiver also serves as a vapor seal, to prevent the entrance of vapor into the liquid line to the expansion valve. Receivers may be constructed for either horizontal or vertical installation.

F. Accessories

In addition to the five main components just described, a refrigeration system requires a number of controls and accessories. The most important of these will be described briefly.

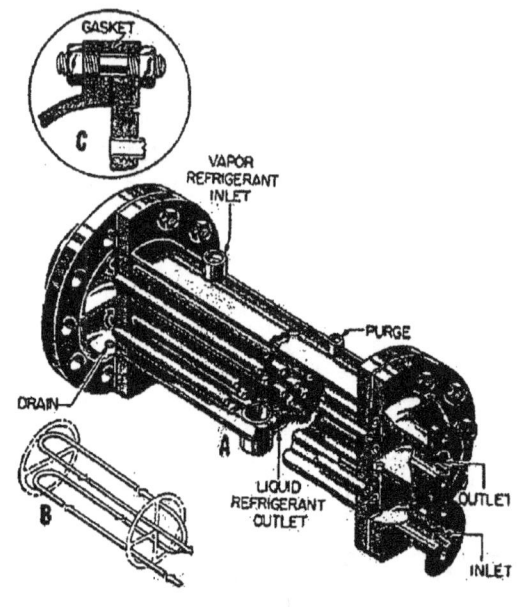

Figure 7.—Water-cooled condenser for R-12 refrigeration system. A. Cutaway view. B. Water-flow diagram. C. Arrangement of heat joint.

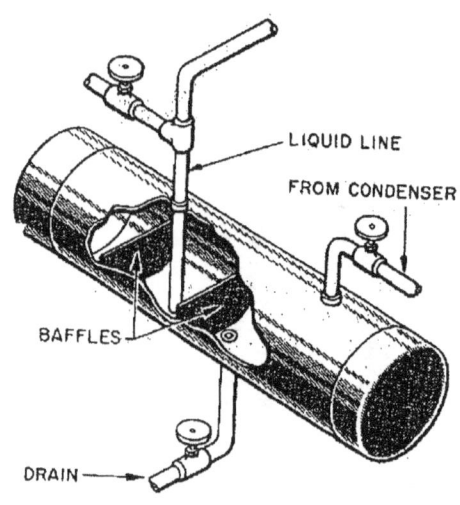

Figure 8.—Receiver.

A DEHYDRATOR, or dryer, is placed in the liquid refrigerant line between the receiver and the thermostatic expansion valve. In older installations, bypass valves allow the dehydrator to be cut in or out of the system. In newer installations, the dehydrator is installed in the liquid refrigerant line without any bypass arrangement. A MOISTURE INDICATOR is either located in the liquid refrigerant line or built into the dehydrator. A dehydrator is shown in figure 9. The moisture indicator indicates the presence of moisture by means of a chemically treated element which changes color on an increase of moisture in the refrigerant. The color change is reversible and will change back to a DRY reading when the moisture is removed from the refrigerant. Excessive moisture or water will damage the moisture indicator element and turn it gray.

A SOLENOID VALVE is installed in the liquid line leading to each evaporator. Figure 10 shows a solenoid valve and the thermostatic control switch that operates it. The thermostatic control switch is connected by long flexible tubing to a thermal control bulb which is located in the refrigerated space. When the tempsrature in the refrigerated space drops to the desired point, the thermal control bulb causes the thermostatic control switch to open, thereby closing the solenoid valve and

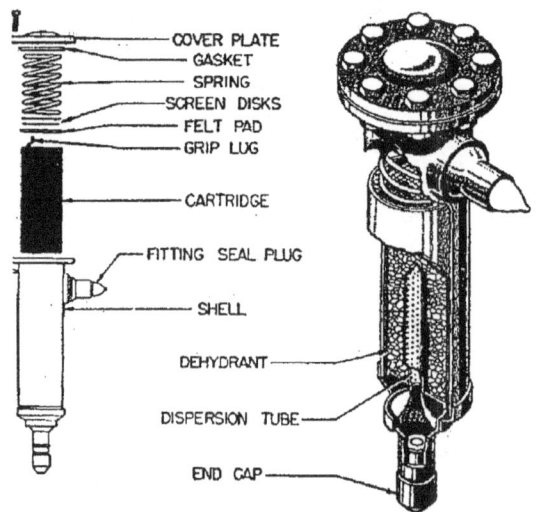

Figure 9.—Refrigerant dehydrator.

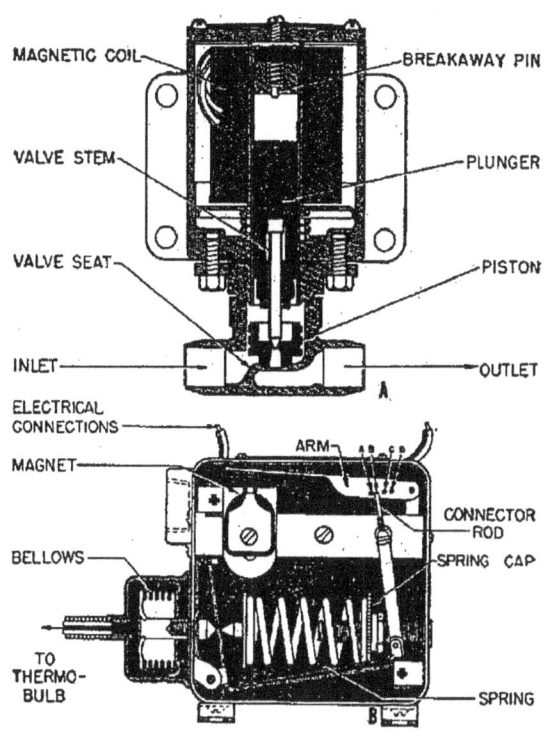

Figure 10.—Solenoid valve and thermostatic control switch.

shutting off all flow of liquid refrigerant to the thermostatic expansion valve. When the temperature in the refrigerated space rises above the desired point, the thermostatic control switch closes, the solenoid valve opens, and liquid refrigerant once again flows to the thermostatic expansion valve.

The solenoid valve and its related thermostatic control switch serve to maintain the proper temperature in the refrigerated space. If the thermostatic expansion valve controls the amount of refrigerant admitted to the evaporator, why is the solenoid valve necessary? Actually, the solenoid valve is not necessary on units having only one evaporator. In systems having more than one evaporator, where there is wide variation in load, the solenoid valve provides the additional control required to prevent the spaces from becoming too cold at light loads.

In addition to the solenoid valve installed in the line to each evaporator, a large refrigeration plant usually has a main liquid line solenoid valve installed just after the receiver. If the compressor stops for any reason except normal suction pressure control, the main liquid solenoid valve closes and prevents liquid refrigerant from flooding the evaporator and flowing to the compressor suction. Extensive damage to the compressor can result if liquid is allowed to enter the compressor suction.

Whenever several refrigerated spaces of varying temperatures are to be maintained by one compressor, an EVAPORATOR PRESSURE REGULATING VALVE is installed at the outlet of each evaporator EXCEPT the evaporator in the space in which the lowest temperature is to be maintained. The evaporator pressure regulating valve is set to keep the pressure in the coil from falling below the pressure corresponding to the lowest evaporator temperature desired in that space.

Suction pressure regulating valves may be installed in the suction line at the outlet of the evaporator where minimum temperature must be maintained as in certain types of water cooler applications or where high humidities are desired, as in fruit and vegetable rooms, or where two or more spaces are maintained at different temperature levels from a single compressor unit. (Pressure regulating valves are designed to maintain a substantially constant pressure within the cooling coil higher than the suction pressure downstream and independent of suction pressure fluctuations.) Valve adjustment is obtained by compression of the adjusting spring to a point where a predetermined coil pressure is established. The automatic operation is maintained by diaphragm balance resulting from small fluctuation in coil pressures permitting positioning of the valve seat to adjust the refrigerant flow.

Suction pressure regulating valves function to decrease the temperature difference which would otherwise exist between the compartment temperature and the surface of the cooling coils. Since the amount of heat which can be transferred into the evaporating refrigerant is directly proportional to the temperature difference, the employment of suction pressure regulating valves requires the provision of more coil surface in a given compartment than would be otherwise necessary.

Suction pressure regulating valves are ADJUSTED by changing the pressure exerted by an auxiliary spring against the valve disk.

For a given setting the valve maintains a substantially constant pressure in the cooling coil regardless of changes in the compressor suction pressure, provided that the suction pressure is about 4 psi or more lower than that which the regulator is set to maintain in the coil. Adjustment to increase the spring pressure tending to close the valve increases the evaporating pressure and vice versa. A test gage is temporarily connected to the cooling coil side of the valve when adjustment is to be made.

The pressure setting for any individual application is dependent on coil design and the amount of coil surface available. In general, settings are not critical where the same refrigerant circuit is also controlled by a solenoid valve except that the pressure setting must be maintained sufficiently low to provide a temperature differential between the refrigerant evaporating temperature and the compartment temperature. Where temperature and humidity control depend on the pressure regulating valve, the setting must be sufficiently high to permit the control desired, keeping in mind the temperature differential required for satisfactory coil operation. Where the medium being cooled is water, as in process and drinking-water coolers, the setting of the suction pressure regulating valve is VERY CRITICAL and, if improperly or hastily adjusted, may cause derangement. A change in pressure setting of 1 pound will appreciably change the temperature of the delivered water. Too low a pressure setting will result in an almost immediate freezing of the water in the cooler with possible rupture. Consequently, adjustment of this valve in a water-cooler application should be very carefully made. Turn the adjusting screw only one-eighth turn at a time and take frequent samples of delivered water to check the temperature.

Figure 11 shows an exploded view of a typical valve which demonstrates the ease of disassembly for repair or replacement of the parts without disturbing soldered piping joints. Dirt or foreign matter under the seat or in moving parts can cause erratic operation.

The LOW PRESSURE CUTOUT SWITCH, or suction pressure control switch, is the control that causes the compressor to go on or off, as required for normal operation of the refrigeration plant. This switch is located on the suction side of the compressor, and is actuated by pressure changes in the suction line. When the solenoid valves in the lines to the various evaporators are closed, so that the flow of refrigerant to the evaporators is stopped,

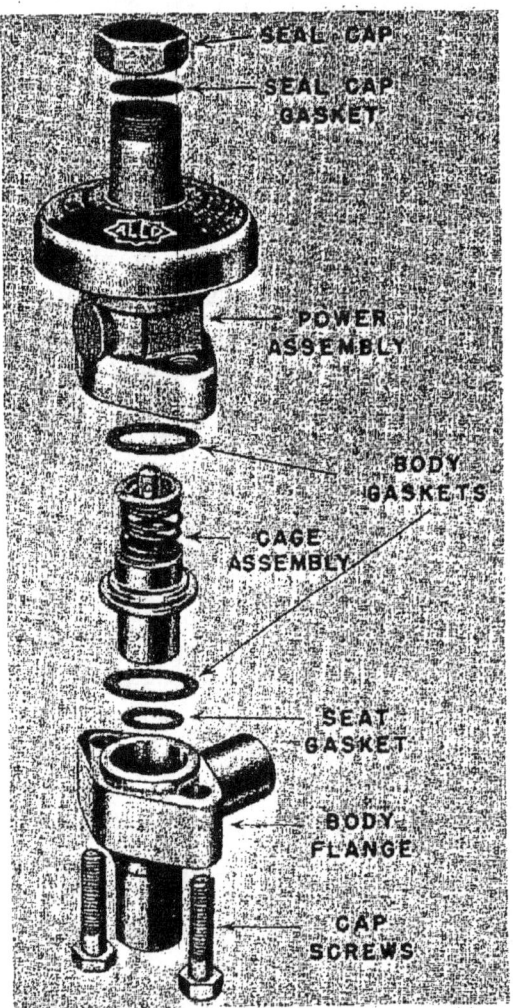

Figure 11.—Exploded view of typical suction pressure regulating valve.

the pressure of the vapor in the compressor suction line drops quickly. When the suction pressure has dropped to the desired pressure, the low pressure cutout switch causes the compressor motor to stop. When the temperature in the refrigerated spaces has risen enough to operate one or more of the solenoid valves, refrigerant is again admitted to the cooling coils, and the compressor suction pressure builds up again. At the desired pressure, the low pressure cutout switch closes, starting the compressor again and repeating the cycle.

A HIGH PRESSURE CUTOUT SWITCH is connected to the compressor discharge line to protect the high pressure side of the system against excessive pressures. The design of this switch is essentially the same as that of the low pressure cutout switch, however, the low pressure cutout switch is made to CLOSE when the suction pressure reaches its upper normal limit, whereas the high pressure cutout switch is made to OPEN when the discharge pressure is too high. The high pressure switch is normally set to stop the compressor when the pressure reaches 160 psi and to start it again when the pressure drops to 140 psi. As mentioned before, the low pressure cutout switch is the compressor control for normal operation of the plant; the high pressure cutout switch, on the other hand, is a safety device only and does not have control of compressor operation under normal conditions.

An OIL FAILURE SWITCH is provided where high speed compressors are used. This switch is designed to prevent operation of the compressor in the event of low oil pressure. The switch is installed with one bellow connected to the oil pressure on the discharge of the compressor oil pump and the other to the compressor suction refrigerant pressure. The switch is set to open the electrical circuit and stop the compressor when the oil pressure drops to 5 psi above compressor crankcase pressure and to close the electrical circuit and start the compressor when the oil pressure reaches 10 psi above the crank-case pressure.

In order that the compressor can be started after it has been stopped and the contacts of the oil failure switch have opened, a time delay mechanism is used with the compressor motor starter. The time delay switch will open 10 to 30 seconds after the compressor motor has been started. The oil pressure normally will be built-up in this time interval so that the oil pressure switch will have made contact to keep the compressor motor electrical circuit energized after the time delay switch opens. If the oil pressure has not built-up within about 30 seconds after the compressor is started, the contacts of the oil pressure differential switch will not have closed, and the compressor will stop because the time delay relay switch is open.

A SPRING LOADED RELIEF VALVE is installed in the compressor discharge line as an additional precaution against excessive pressures. The relief valve is set to open at about 225 psi; therefore, it functions only in case of failure or improper setting of the high pressure cutout switch. If the relief valve opens, it discharges high pressure vapor to the suction side of the compressor.

A WATER REGULATING VALVE is installed to control the quantity of circulating water flowing through the refrigerant condenser. The water regulating valve is actuated by the refrigerant pressure in the compressor discharge line; this pressure acts upon a diaphragm (or, in some valves, a bellows arrangement) which transmits motion to the valve stem. The primary function of the water regulating valve is to maintain a constant refrigerant condensing pressure. Basically two variable conditions exist, the amount of refrigerant to be condensed and changing water temperatures. The valve maintains a constant refrigerant condensing pressure by controlling the water flow through the condenser. By sensing the refrigerant pressure it permits only that quantity of water through the condenser that is necessary to condense the amount of refrigerant vapor coming from the compressor. The quantity of water required to condense a given amount of refrigerant varies with the water temperature. Thus, the flow of cooling water through the condenser is automatically maintained at the rate actually required to condense the refrigerant under varying conditions of load and temperature.

A WATER FAILURE SWITCH is provided to stop the compressor in the event of failure of the circulating water Supply. This is a pressure-actuated switch, generally similar to the low pressure cutout switch and the high pressure cutout switch previously described. If the water failure cutout switch should fail to function, the refrigerant pressure in the condenser would quickly build up to the point where the high pressure switch would function.

Because of the solvent action of R-12, any particles of grit, scale, dirt, and metal that the system may contain are very readily circulated through the refrigerant lines. To avoid damage to the compressor from such foreign matter, a STRAINER is installed in the compressor suction connection.

In addition, a LIQUID STRAINER of the type shown in figure 11 12 is installed in the liquid line leading to each evaporator; these strainers serve to protect the solenoid valves and the thermostatic expansion valves.

A number of PRESSURE GAGES and THERMOMETERS are used in refrigeration systems. Figure 13 shows a compound refrigerant gage. The temperature markings on this gage show the boiling point (or condensing point) of the refrigerant at each pressure; the gage cannot measure temperature directly. The short pointer (red in color) is a stationary pointer that can be set manually to indicate the maximum working pressure.

A water pressure gage is installed in the circulating water line to the condenser, to give visual indication of failure of the circulating water supply.

Standard thermometers of appropriate range are provided for the refrigerant system.

REFRIGERANT PIPING in modern naval installations is made of copper. Copper is good for this purpose because (1) it does not become corroded by refrigerants; (2) the internal surface of the tubing is smooth enough to minimize

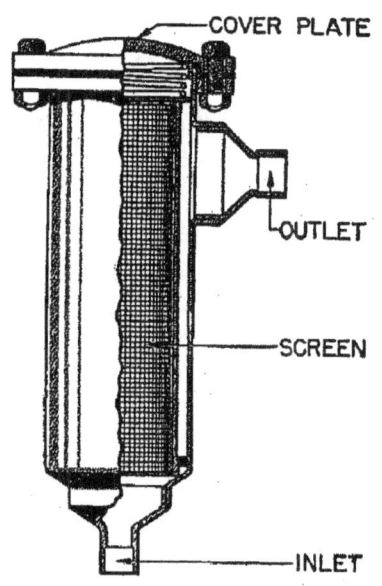

Figure . 12.—Strainer for liquid refrigerant.

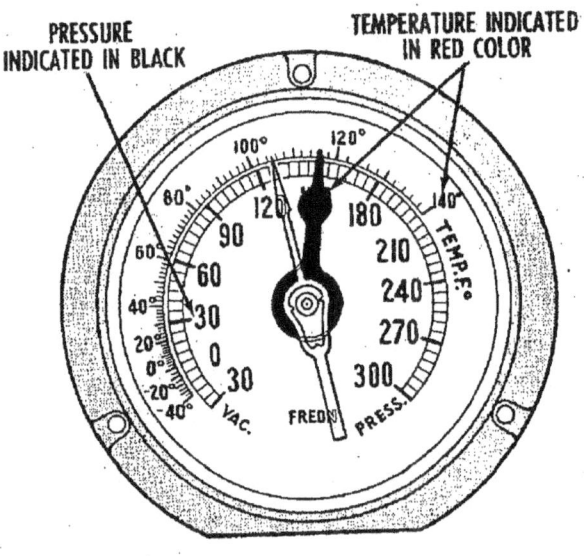

Figure 13.—Compound R-12 pressure gage.

friction; and (3) copper tubing is easily shaped to meet installation requirements.

Nearly all hand-operated valves in large refrigeration systems are PACKLESS VALVES of the type shown in figure 14. In this type of valve, the upper part of the valve is sealed off from the lower part by a diaphragm. An upward-seating ball check in the lower valve stem makes it possible for the spring to lift the lower stem regardless of pressure differences developed while the valve was closed. Thus, the valve will operate properly regardless of direction of flow. By backseating the valve, the diaphragm can be changed without placing the system or unit out of operation.

V. OPERATING PROCEDURES FOR AM R-12 SYSTEM

Learning how to do all of the tasks related to refrigeration system operation will require a good deal of practical experience and attentive observation of the procedures followed by those qualified in refrigeration system operation and maintenance.

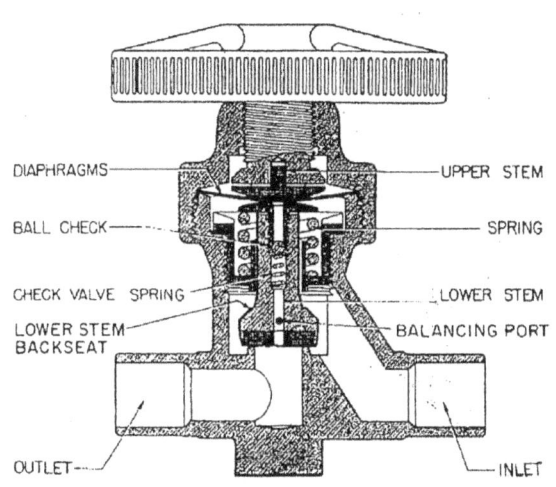

Figure 14. — Packless valve for refrigeration system.

The intervals of time between plant inspections will vary depending upon the purpose for which the plant is used. The temperatures and pressures throughout the system and the oil level in the compressor crankcase are checked and the results recorded every two hours unless watch-standing instructions specify otherwise. The results of these checks can be used to determine whether the plant is operating properly. One of the best methods for checking plant operation is to compare the existing temperatures and pressures with those recorded during a period when the plant was known to be operating properly, under conditions similar to the-present conditions.

The following information on operating procedures applies to refrigeration systems in general.

1. Open the compressor discharge valve; open all stop valves in the circulating water supply and in the discharge lines for the condenser.

2. Open the condenser refrigerant outlet valve and open the thermal expansion stop valves on the chill and freeze boxes.

3. Start all air circulating fans. On water cooling applications (soda fountains, drinking water coolers, and air conditioning water chillers), admit the water to be cooled, and purge the water circuit of air.

4. If water is taken from the firemain, make certain that the pressure-reducing valve ahead of the water regulating valve is adjusted to provide a water pressure of 35 psi or less ahead of the water regulating valve.

5. When no pressure-reducing valve is installed, regulate the firemain connection stop valve manually so that the required water pressure ahead of the water regulating valve is maintained.

6. When an individual circulating pump is used to supply condenser circulating water, be sure that any valves which permit transmission of pump discharge pressure to the water failure switch are open.

7. If the compressor unit is equipped with an air-cooled condenser, make certain that the air flow passages to the condenser are unobstructed, and that the air circulating fans are clear.

8. Open the compressor discharge-line valve, the stop valve in the line connecting the condenser and the liquid receiver, and the main liquid-line valve.

A. Starting the Compressor

Too much stress cannot be placed on the need for thoroughness and care at the time the compressor is started. Bent crankshafts, distorted valves, and blown gaskets are a few of the casualties which may occur if proper procedures and applicable precautions are not followed. After accomplishing or checking the items listed under the posted prestarting instructions, proceed as follows:

1. Set the AUTOMATIC-MANUAL selector switch in the MANUAL position.

2. Close the maintaining-contact START button in the pump control circuit to prepare the pump motor for starting.

3. Close the momentary-contact START switch in the compressor control circuit to start the pump motor which also energizes the main line solenoid valve circuit.

As the pump circulates the water, the water failure switch closes automatically and completes the circuit of the compressor-motor contactor coil. When this circuit is closed, the compressor motor starts. In installations where a pump motor and a pump control circuit are not installed, closing the momentary-contact START switch energizes the compressor control circuit and starts the compressor motor.

4. Start and stop the motor and compressor several times by manual control, to check their operating condition; then, stop the compressor and check the oil level.

5. After it has been determined that the motor and the compressor are in operating condition, crack the suction stop valve and set the controls on AUTOMATIC. This arrangement will eliminate the possibility of the pressure in the system from decreasing below that of the atmosphere and drawing air into the compressor.

Open the compressor suction valve slowly, with the compressor running, so as to limit the quantity of suction gas handled by the compressor.

The suction gage should be watched as the compressor suction valve is opened to ensure that the suction pressure is within the limits of the automatic control low pressure suction setting. The valve should be opened gradually, at a rate so that there will be neither a rapid fluctuation in suction pressure nor a rapid drop of pressure in the compressor crank-case. This will prevent the rapid boiling off of refrigerant from the oil and the carrying of oil into the system. Unusual noise or knocking in the compressor and frosting of crankcase or suction valve are indications of liquid refrigerant being drawn into the compressor.

6. If lubrication of the compressor is by forced feed, check the pressure on the oil pressure gage.

Unless specific instructions indicate otherwise, the oil pressure should be between 15 and 30 psi above the compressor suction pressure within a few seconds after the compressor is started. If the compressor is designed for automatic capacity control, oil pressure of 50 to 60 psi above suction pressure is required.

7. Make certain that the proper quantity of circulating water is flowing through the condenser before the compressor discharge pressure reaches 125 psi.

8. Open the receiver outlet valve and the main solenoid outlet valve.

In systems not equipped with water regulating valves, normal operating conditions generally produce condensing pressures of less than 125 psi, since the condensing water temperature is usually less than 85°F. In systems equipped with water regulating valves, the valves should be adjusted to maintain the condensing pressure at 125 psi. Wh3n the valves are so adjusted, the quantity of cooling water required decreases rapidly with decreasing circulating water temperatures. In systems equipped with air-cooled condensers, condensing pressures may exceed 125 psi when the temperature of the surrounding air is higher than normal.

B. Operating an R-12 Plant in Automatic

After the prescribed operating pressures and temperatures have been established with the selector switch set in the

AUTOMATIC position, the suction-pressure control is so connected by electrical means, that it starts and stops the compressor automatically, on the basis of load conditions. If the automatic control valves and switches are in proper adjustment, the operation of the plant, after proper starting, will be entirely automatic.

When the selector switch is set for automatic operation, the closing of the water failure switch, the high pressure switch, or the low pressure switch through automatic operation will energize their respective circuits. Other control devices require the intervention of an operator before the compressor can be restarted. Some high pressure switches are provided with manual reset devices which must be reset by the operator after the switches have been opened by excessive pressure.

Some installations are designed so that the supply of condenser cooling water is available either from a centrifugal pump or from the fire and flushing main directly. If cooling water is obtained from the fire and flushing main instead of from the pump, the pump controller switch is opened manually. The water failure switch remains closed regardless of the source of condenser cooling water.

C. Securing the Compressor

If a compressor is to be secured for only a short period, it is not necessary to pump down the system. The compressor however, must be pumped down. To do this, first close the compressor suction valve slowly, to prevent too rapid a reduction in crankcase pressure. Then allow the compressor to run until it is stopped by the low pressure control switch; push the fTOP button on the motor-control panel. Next, close the compressor discharge shutoff valve; shut off the water supply to the condensers. Finally, close the main liquid valve after the receiver.

If a refrigeration system is to be secured for an extended period, the system must be pumped down. The pumping-down procedure involves pumping most of the R-12 out of the coils of the evaporator, and storing the refrigerant in the receiver. If the quantity of liquid refrigerant contained in the system is in excess of the capacity of the receiver, the surplus liquid must be drawn off into refrigerant drums.

D. Notes on Compressor Operation

An R-12 compressor should not remain idle for an extended period of time. When two or more compressors are installed for a particular plant, the compressors should be operated alternately so that the total operating time on each of the compressors is approximately the same. An idle compressor should be operated at least once a week.

Only one compressor should serve a cooling coil circuit. When compressors are operated in parallel on a common cooling coil circuit, lubricating oil may be transferred from one compressor to another. Such transfer of oil may result in serious damage to all compressors on the circuit.

VI. MAINTENANCE OF R-12 SYSTEMS

In order for you to perform your share of the required maintenance of a refrigerating system, you must be familiar with the proper procedures for the following jobs: defrosting the cooling coils, pumping down a system and checking for non-condensable gases, purging a system of non-condensable gases, using a halide torch to test for refrigerant leaks, checking compressor oil, taking care of V-belts, and setting and adjusting refrigeration system controls and safety devices. Most of these maintenance items are covered by the Planned Maintenance System and will be scheduled accordingly.

A. Defrosting of Cooling Coils

The cooling coils should be defrosted as often as necessary to maintain the effectiveness of the cooling surface. Excessive accumulations of frost on the coils will result in reduced cooling capacity, low compressor-suction pressure, and a tendency for the compressor to short cycle. The maximum permissible time interval between defrosting operations depends on many factors, such as refrigerant evaporating temperature, free-moisture content of supplies placed in the refrigerated space, temperature of refrigerated spaces, frequency of opening of cold-storage compartment doors, and atmospheric humidity. In the average cold-storage refrigeration installation it is good practice to defrost cooling coils before the average frost thickness reaches 3/16 inch. This is not a hard and fast rule, however; sometimes the frost layer may become appreciably thicker without seriously interfering with plant operation. At other times it may be necessary to defrost more often to maintain satisfactory operation of the plant and proper compartment temperature.

The most COMMON METHOD OF DEFROSTING a cooling coil in the average refrigeration installation is (1) to shut off the supply of R-12 to the coil to be defrosted, by closing the liquid-line stop valve ahead of the expansion valve; and (2) to permit the temperature in the compartment to rise above 32 F, by leaving the entrance door open. The frost will melt off the coils or may be easily brushed off. Since the cooling coils are made of tinned copper or galvanized steel tubing, care should be taken not to damage the evaporator coil if a scraper is used to remove frost.

Most installations now in use are provided with HOT-GAS DEFROSTING lines to facilitate defrosting where compartment temperatures are maintained at 32°F or less. The principal advantage of hot-gas defrosting is that this process permits defrosting of the freeze room coils while the rest of the plant operates normally.

In the following paragraphs, defrosting procedures will refer only to freeze room coils.

A hot-gas defrosting line leads from the compressor discharge piping to the tail-coil of the freeze room cooling coil. The hot-gas line joins the suction line, between the freeze room and the suction valve; therefore, hot gas admitted to the freeze room cooling coil flows "backwards" through the coil that is, the hot gas flows in a direction opposite to the flow of refrigerant under normal operating conditions.

When it is desired to defrost the coils of the freeze room, the normal refrigerant-liquid supply and suction return-line valves of the freeze room cooling coil are closed. The valve in the hot-gas supply line is then opened; compressed refrigerant-gas is admitted to the coil. As the frost melts on the exterior coil surfaces, the gas is condensed in the coils and becomes a liquid. The liquid is led, from the inlet end of the freeze room cooling coil, to the main liquid supply line and is utilized in the other compartments.

Upon completion of the defrosting process, the system is returned to its normal operating condition by closing the defrosting valves and opening the valves in the refrigerant-liquid supply line to the freeze room coil, and the suction return valve from the freeze room coil. Care must be taken that all liquid refrigerant has been discharged from the freeze room coil before the suction line valve from the compartment is opened. Proceed as previously outlined in step 5 for starting the compressor using the tail coil suction valve, vice the compressor suction valve, as the control valve. If all the liquid has not been discharged, liquid slugs may be returned to the compressor.

B. Pumping Down a Refrigerant System

The pumping-down procedure to be followed will depend on the maintenance to be done. In some cases, the necessary maintenance can be performed on the charged system after a part to be repaired or replaced has been isolated. Generally, it is possible to pump down any part of a charged system except the condenser, the liquid receiver, and the compressor discharge line. When repairs are to be made to a major portion of the system, the refrigerant system must be pumped down to return all refrigerant to the receiver. If repairs are to be made to the receiver, the condenser, or the compressor discharge line, the entire system must be drained into spare refrigerant drums. However, in systems having valves to isolate the compressor discharge line and condenser, and where it is not objectionable to release refrigerant

(which may still be trapped in the condenser after the system has been pumped down to the receiver) to the atmosphere, repairs to the compressor discharge line and condenser may be made with this section isolated.

Whenever it is necessary to open a charged system in order to make repairs or replacements or to clean strainers, the refrigerant pressure within the part of the system to be opened should be pumped down to a pressure slightly above atmospheric (1/2 to 2 psig) before any connections are broken. It is generally possible to pump down any part of the system (except the condenser, the liquid receiver, and the compressor discharge line) by proper manipulation of cutout valves. As a part of the system which contains liquid R-12 is pumped down, its temperature will decrease as a result of the evaporation of the liquid refrigerant. When the temperature of such a part of the system begins to rise to normal again, while the low pressure in the part is maintained, it is reasonably certain that all R-12 liquid within the part has been evaporated; If, in the final evacuation of a part of the system, a pressure of less than 0 psig is reached, sufficient refrigerant should be immediately bled into the evacuated part of the system to raise the pressure to between 1/2 and 2 psig. Connections may then be opened; and repairs, replacements of parts, or other necessary service operations may be accomplished.

When a refrigerant system is opened, the free ends of the refrigerant lines should be temporarily plugged in order to prevent the entrance of air and dirt. When the connections are remade, one connection is made tight while the other connection is left loose, temporarily, so that the air or other foreign gases in the section of the system which is serviced can be swept out through the free end as this section of the system is slowly purged with refrigerant-gas bled from the charge in the system. The other connection (or connections) is then quickly tightened. Refrigerant, oil-charging, gage, and control lines, although generally of small size and short length, should be purged with refrigerant-gas immediately before they are connected to the system. Where connecting lines which have been removed are to be used again, the ends of the lines should be capped to protect the connecting fitting and to ensure that the tube will be clean when it is used again.

When MAJOR REPAIRS are to be made to a major portion of the system or when the system is to be secured for an extended period, the refrigerant system must be pumped down to return all refrigerant to the receiver. Sufficient refrigerant-gas should be retained within the system to create a positive pressure of approximately 2 psig throughout the circuit, except within the compressor-discharge line and the condenser, and between the receiver and the main liquid-line shutoff valve. To pump down the system, close the main liquid-line shutoff valve and the dehydrator-bypass valve (if installed), and open the cooling-coil solenoid valves. Allow the compressor to operate on manual control until the suction pressure reaches approximately 1/2 to 2 psig; then stop the compressor. Repeat the operation until the liquid refrigerant in the circuit has evaporated and the suction pressure remains relatively constant at 1/2 to 2 psig. During the pump-down period, the evaporation of liquid refrigerant can be traced to the liquid line back to the main liquid-line shutoff valve by the formation of frost and its subsequent melting as the liquid refrigerant is evaporated and superheated. Open the power-supply switch to the compressor; close the compressor suction and discharge shutoff valves. Shut off the water supply to the condenser and drain the condenser water. Where the amount of liquid refrigerant contained in the system is in excess of the capacity of the receiver, the surplus liquid refrigerant must be drawn off into separate refrigerant drums.

To drain the refrigerant charge from the system when it is necessary to make repairs to the condenser, the liquid receiver, or the compressor discharge line, or for any other reason, proceed as follows:

1. Start the compressor and pump down the cooling coil and suction-line pressure, with the liquid-line valve at the receiver outlet closed, to the point at which the low pressure control switch stops the unit.

2. When the compressor is stopped by the low pressure cutout switch, restart the unit manually and continue the pumping-down procedure until the suction pressure reaches approximately 2 psig and stop the compressor. Repeat the operation in periodic cycles until the liquid refrigerant in the circuit has evaporated and the suction pressure remains relatively constant between 1/2 and 5 psig.

3. Close the compressor discharge line valve; close all liquid valves at the cooling coils.

4. Connect an empty R-12 service drum to the refrigerant drain valve. (Before connecting

the drum to the R-12 system, cool the drum thoroughly and thus permit rapid draining of the refrigerant into the drum.) Always use a clean R-12 service drum containing no air or water so that the drained R-12 may be kept in suitable condition for future use.

5. Purge the air out of the line connecting the drain valve and the drum by leaving the connection at the drum valve open as you slowly flush refrigerant through the line and out at the connection; then close the connection. The R-12 may now be drained into the cooled drum by opening the drain valve and the service drum valve.

6. When the service drum is full, doge the drain valve and permit the R-12 liquid in thfe drain line to evaporate; then close the service drum valve and disconnect the drum from the system.

7. Weigh the drum while filling, to be certain that it is not overcharged. The net and gross weights are stamped on the drum. (These weights include that of the cast iron protector cap which fits over the cylinder valve.)

> CAUTION: Never fill a service drum beyond its rated capacity; drum rupture may result from hydraulic pressure upon rise in temperature.

8. Discharge the R-12 vapor, which remains in the condenser and receiver to the atmosphere through the purge valve.

C. Testing for Refrigerant Leaks

Refrigerant leaks mean the loss of the refrigerating effect and loss of refrigerant. Various tests are used to determine the existence of leaks in refrigerant systems. Pressure tests are used after the installation of a system and after extensive repairs or replacement of parts have been made. Pressure tests are made before the system is charged with refrigerant. Charged systems are tested for leakage either with a halide leak detector, electronic refrigerant gas detector, or with soapsuds; which of the three methods to be used will depend largely Mapon the size of the leak, and upon the type of space in which the test is to be performed. "Moreover, you will be required to know how to use the detectors and how to use soapsuds to check for the refrigerant leakage.

In addition to those tests for leaks which are made at periodic intervals, tests should be made before the compressors are started and at any other time that a shortage of refrigerant in the system is suspected. Unusual operating conditions which indicate a shortage of refrigerant in the system are:

1. High suction-line temperatures.
2. Relatively high crankcase and cylinder temperatures.
3. Excessively high refrigerant temperature in the liquid line.

4. Bubbles in the refrigerant sight-flow indicator.

5. Liquid refrigerant carrying partially through the coil, with considerable superheat at the thermal element.

6. Short cycle or compressor running continuously.

7. Excessive oil seepage at shaft seal connection.

8. Oil seepage at refrigerant-system piping and compressor connections.

A shortage of refrigerant in the system nearly always indicates the presence of leaks. When a shortage of refrigerant is found the entire system should be tested for leaks by one of the following methods.

The use of a HALIDE LEAK DETECTOR is the most positive method of detecting leaks in a refrigerant system. Such a detector consists essentially of a torch burner, a copper reactor plate, and an exploring hose. (See fig. 17.)

Most detectors use either acetylene gas or alcohol as a fuel. Pressure for detectors which use alcohol is supplied by a pump. If a pump-pressure type of alcohol-burning detector is used, be sure that the air pumped into the fuel tank is pure.

Atmosphere suspected of containing R-12 vapor is drawn, by injector action, through the exploring hose into the torch burner of the detector. Here the air passes over the copper reactor plate, which is heated to incandescence. If there is a minute trace of R-12 present, the color of the torch flame will change from a blue (neutral) to green as the R-12 comes in contact with the reactor plate. The shade of green will depend upon the relative amount of R-12 present; a pale green indicates small concentrations and a darker green shows heavier concentrations. Excessive quantities of R-12 will cause the flame to burn with a vivid purple color. Extreme concentrations of R-12 may extinguish

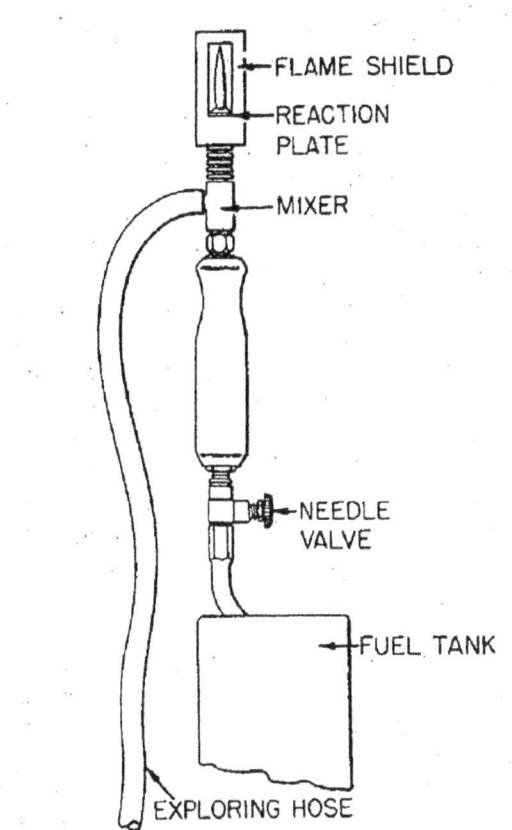

Figure 17.—Halide leak detector.

the flame by crowding out the oxygen available from the air.

When a leak detector is used, best results are obtained if the following precautions are observed:

1. Be sure that the reactor plate is properly in place.

2. Adjust the flame so that it does not extend beyond the end of the burner. (A small flame is much more sensitive than a large flame. If difficulty is experienced in lighting the torch when it is adjusted to produce the necessary small flame, block the end of the exploring hose until the fuel ignites; this will reduce the amount of oxygen drawn in. Then gradually open the hose.)

3. Clean out the exploring tube if the flame continues to have a white or yellow color. (A white or yellow flame indicates that the exploring tube is partially blocked with dirt.)

4. Check to see that air is being drawn into the exploring tube; this check can be made, from time to time, by holding the end of the tube to your ear.

5. Hold the end of the exploring tube close to the joint being tested; this prevents dilution of the sample by stray air currents.

6. Move the end of the exploring hose tube slowly and completely around each joint being tested. (Leak testing cannot be safely hurried. There is a definite time lag between the moment when air enters the exploring tube and the moment it reaches the reactor plate; permit sufficient time for the sample to reach the reactor plate.)

7. If a greenish flame is noted at any time, repeat the test in the same vicinity until the source of the refrigerant is determined.

A halide torch or an electronic refrigerant gas detector is so sensitive that it is useless if the atmosphere is contaminated by excessive leakage of R-12. This is most likely to happen in a small or poorly ventilated compartment. If a compartment is contaminated by R-12 and cannot be ventilated, the SOAPSUDS TEST must be used.

In using the soapsuds test, prepare the soap-and-water solution so that it has the consistency of liquid hand soap, and will work up a lather on a brush. (The lather will remain wet for a longer period if a few drops of glycerin are added to the solution.)

Apply the lather all the way around the joint; then look carefully for bubbles. If a joint is so located that a part of it is not visible, use a small mirror when inspecting that part.

Remember that it sometimes takes a minute or more for bubbles to appear, if the leak is "mall. Doubtful spots should be lathered and examined a second time.

Always follow a definite procedure in testing for refrigerant leaks, so that no joints will be missed. The extra time spent in testing all joints will be justified. Even the smallest leak is not to be considered negligible. However insignificant the leak may seem, it eventually empties the system of its charge to the point of faulty plant operation.

Because R-12 is practically odorless, the first indication that leakage exists is the loss of refrigerating effect. A refrigerant system should never be recharged until all leaks are discovered and definitely repaired.

Never use oil to test for R-12 leaks. Oil is not reliable because of the capacity of the oil for absorbing R-12. If a small leak should exist where oil has been applied, the R-12, will

be absorbed by the oil and will show no indication (bubbles) of the leak until the oil is saturated with R-12. Furthermore, if a halide torch is used to test a joint that has been tested previously with oil, the torch will give a false indication because of the R-12 released from the oil.

D. Testing for Air and Noncondensable Gases

It is essential that every resonable precaution be taken to keep air and noncondensable gases out of a refrigerant system. When ^ir enters the system the condenser must ,be purged, with a resultant loss of refrigerant. Atmospheric air always contains some moisture, which will enter the system when air does. A refrigerant system must be kept as moisture-free as possible to eliminate such troubles as the freezing of water at the expansion valves, internal oxidation or corrosion of parts, and emulsification or sludging of lubricating oils.

Air and noncondensable gases in a refrigerant system are pumped through the system and are discharged by the compressor into the condenser. These gases are trapped in the condenser by the liquid seal maintained over the receiver outlet. These gases are, in general, lighter than the relatively dense R-12 vapor; they tend to collect, therefore, in the upper part of the condenser when the compressor is stopped. The purge valve for discharging these gases to the atmosphere is located either in the upper part of the condenser shell or in the compressor discharge line above the condenser. While the compressor is in operation, any noncondensable gases in the system are thoroughly mixed with the R-12 vapor. This mixing is caused by the turbulence produced by the rapidly pulsating discharge of refrigerant into the condenser. Therefore, it is not advisable to attempt to purge noncondensable gases from the system while the compressor is in operation. Noncondensable gases in a condenser cause excessive condensing pressures with a resultant loss in plant efficiency.

The best time to check an R-12 system for noncondensable gases is immediately before the compressor starts after a shutdown period. When a condenser is to be checked for non-condensable gases, it is essential that the gages and thermometers used be accurate and that the system have sufficient refrigerant charge so that the liquid refrigerant present in the receiver will seal the liquid-line connection.

The following procedure should be followed when checking a refrigerant system for non-condensable gases:

1. Close the liquid-line valve.
2. Shut off the compressor and close the suction-line valves.
3. Determine the actual condensing temperature of the refrigerant.

A service gage should be installed in the compressor discharge connection if a discharge-pressure gage is not already provided. An approximation of the actual condensing temperature of the refrigerant will be reached when no further decrease is noted in the discharge pressure. (On water-cooled condensers, the reduction in pressure can be accelerated by permitting circulation of condenser water until discharge pressure is reduced.) The thermometer provided on most ships in the liquid line at the receiver will indicate the actual condensing temperature. If a thermometer is not installed in an air-cooled condenser application, one should be placed near the condenser to record the ambient temperature at that location. When the temperature of an air-cooled condenser has dropped to the ambient temperature, the reading of the thermometer will approximate the actual condensing temperature.

4. On the compound pressure gage, read the condensing temperature which corresponds to the condensing pressure registered by the high pressure gage; the temperature indicated on the temperature scale is the condensing temperature of pure R-12 at the pressure indicated by the gage.

5. Subtract the existing condensing temperature from the condensing temperature of pure R-12 at the existing condenser pressure. If the difference between these two temperatures is more than 5F, it will be necessary to purge the condenser of noneondensable gases.

If the above test indicates the need for PURGING, slowly release the noncondensable gases. When a purge valve is not provided, purge the gases by opening the discharge pressure gage connection.

The proportion of R-12 gas that will mix with the condensable gases and escape while the condenser is being purged will depend upon the rate of purging and upon the concentration of the noncondensable gases in the condenser. No practical test is available aboard ship to determine definitely when an excessively high proportion of R-12 gas is being purged with the noncondensable gases. To keep the R-12 loss to a minimum whcn the condenser is being purged, purge slowly; and frequently check the condenser for noncondensable gases. R-12 is odorless in concentrations of less than 20 percent by volume in air; in heavier concentrations, however, it resembles carbon tetrachloride in odor. If you can get close to the purge-valve discharge, you may be able to determine by the odor of the purged gases when purging should be discontinued and when the check for non-condensable gases should be repeated. Protect your eyes with goggles when you are checking the odor of purged gases.

E. Checking Compressor Oil

If the apparent oil level observed immediately after a prolonged shutdown period is lower than normal, it is almost certain that the actual working oil level is far too low. After a sufficient quantity of oil has been added to raise the apparent oil level to the center of the bull's-eye sight-glass, the actual oil level should be checked as follows:

1. Operate the compressor on MANUAL control for at least one hour. If the compressor is operating on a water cooler or other coil which is apt to freeze, observe the temperature and interrupt compressor operation as necessary to prevent freezing. Repeat cycling until the total running time (one hour) is obtained. Then slowly close the suction line stop valve.

2. Stop the compressor. If the compressor is fdVce lubricated, immediately observe the oil level in the sight-glass. If the compressor is splash lubricated, turn the flywheel until the crankshaft and connecting rod ends are immersed in the lubricating oil, then check the oil level.

To check the oil level when the compressor has been running on its normal cycle, with no abnormal shutdown period, proceed as follows:

1. Wait until the end of a period of operation; if the operation is continuous, wait until the compressor has been in operation at least 1/2 hour, then stop the compressor.

2. As soon as the compressor stops, observe the oil level in the sight-glass on force-lubricated compressors. If the compressor is splash lubricated, turn the flywheel until the crankshaft and connecting rod ends are satisfactorily immersed in the lubricating oil; then check the oil level.

Do not remove oil from the crankcase because of an apparent high level unless too much oil has been previously added, or unless it is apparent that oil from the crankcase of one compressor of the plant has been inadvertently deposited in the crankcase of another.

However, if the oil level is lower than its recommended height on the glass, a sufficient quantity of oil should be added to obtain the desired level. Do not add more oil than is necessary; too much oil can result in excessive oil transfer to the cooling coils.

ADDING OIL. There are two common methods of adding oil to a compressor. In one type of installation, a small oil-charging pump is furnished for adding oil to the compressor crankcase. In another type, oil is placed in the compressor by means of a clean, well-dried funnel. In either installation, care must be taken to prevent the entrance of air or foreign matter into the compressor.

When performing hourly checks of the compressors, you may observe no oil in the crankcase, or a very low oil level on the sight-glass. This indicates that the oil has left the compressor and is circulating in the system; and it will be necessary to add oil and operate the system. After the compressor has reclaimed the excessive oil in the system, the excess oil should be drained.

REMOVING OIL. To remove oil from the compressor crankcase, reduce the pressure in the crankcase to approximately 1 psi by gradually closing the suction line stop valve. Then stop the compressor, and close the suction and discharge line valves, loosen the lubricating oil drain plug near the bottom of the compressor crankcase, and allow the required amount of oil to drain out. Since the compressor crank-case is under a slight pressure, do not fully remove the drain plug from the compressor, but allow the oil to seep out around the threads of the loosened plug. When the desired amount of oil has been removed, tighten the drain plug, open the suction and discharge line valves, and start the compressor. If an oil drain valve is provided in lieu of a plug, the required amount of oil may be drained without pumping down the compressor.

RENEWING THE LUBRICATING OIL. When clean copper tubing is used for R-12 systems, and reasonable care has been taken to prevent the entrance of foreign matter and moisture during installation, the oil in the compressor crankcase will probably not become so contaminated that it requires renewal more than once a year. When iron or steel pipe and fittings are used in the R-12 system, a sample of oil from the compressor crankcase should be withdrawn into a clean glass container every 3 months. If the sample shows contamination, all the lubricating oil should be renewed. It is good practice to check the cleanliness of the lubricating oil after each cleaning of the compressor suction scale trap.

F. Care of V-Belts

Excessive looseness will cause slippage, rapid wear, and deterioration of V-belts. On the other hand, a belt that is too tight will cause excessive wear of both the belt and the main bearing of the compressor. In extreme cases it may cause a bad seal leak. When properly tightened, a belt can be depressed 1/2 to 3/4 inch, by the pressure of one finger, at a point midway between the flywheel and the motor pulleys.

When replacement of one belt of a multiple V-belt drive is necessary, a complete new set of matched belts should be installed. Belts stretch considerably during the first few hours of operation. Replacement of a single belt will upset the load balance between the new and old belts and will be a potential source of trouble. It is better practice to run the unit temporarily with a defective belt removed than to attempt to operate a new belt in conjunction with two or more seasoned belts.

V-belts, motor pulleys, and compressor flywheels should be kept dry and free of oil. Belt dressing should never be used.

G. Setting Control and Safety Devices

A refrigeration plant cannot operate EFFICIENTLY and SAFELY unless the control and safety devices are in good working order and set properly. When a new control or safety device is installed in a refrigeration system, it must be adjusted or set to function at pressures or temperatures in accordance with the plant design. Periodic tests and inspections may indicate faulty plant operation that is due to improperly adjusted control or safety devices.

This section contains information on some of the more common types of control and safety devices used.

The methods of setting the low pressure switch, the water failure switch, and the ther-rhbstatic switch are similar; however, these switches differ as to operating range, purpose, and setting. Also, the high pressure switch and the water failure switch are safety devices while the low pressure switch and the thermo-static switches are control devices.

The HIGH PRESSURE SWITCH has an operating range of 60 to 350 psig and an adjustable differential (difference between the cut-in point and cutout point). As mentioned earlier in the chapter, the switch should be set to cut out at 160 psig and to cut in at 140 psig. To set the switch, first remove the cover plate. Then the two adjusting screws; one labeled differential, the other labeled range, are easily accessible. Turning the range adjusting screw to the right raises both the cut-in point and cutout point. Turning it to the left lowers these points. The differential adjustment affects only the cutout point. Turning it to the right raises the cutout point and turning it to the left lowers the cutout point. Start the compressor and control the discharge pressure by throttling the circulating water through the condenser. Turn the differential screw all the way to the left and turn the range screw all the way to the right. Raise the compressor discharge to 150 psig. Turn the range screw to the left until the contactor in the switch opens, thereby stopping the compressor. When the discharge pressure drops to 140 psig, turn the range screw to the right until the contacts close, starting the compressor. The cut-in point is now set. With the compressor running, turn the differential screw all the way to the right, then raise the discharge pressure to 160 psig. Turn the differential screw to the left until the contacts open, stopping the compressor. The cutout point is now set.

The LOW PRESSURE SWITCH has an operating range of 20 inches of vacuum to 80 psig and an operating differential of 9 psig to 30 psig.

To set the low pressure switch, start the compressor and control the suction pressure by throttling the compressor suction valve. Turn the range and differential adjustment screws to the left. Lower the suction pressure to about 10 psig below the desired cut-in pressure and turn the range screw to the right until the switch contacts open, stopping the compressor. Allow the suction pressure to rise to the desired cut-in pressure and turn the range screw to the left until the switch contacts close, starting the compressor. The cut-in point is now set. Turn the differential screw all the way to the right, throttle the suction valve to lower the suction pressure to the desired cutout pressure. Turn the differential screw to the left until the switch contacts open, stopping the compressor. The cutout point is now set.

The WATER FAILURE SWITCH should be set to cut in at 15 psig and to cut out at 5 psig. To set the water failure switch, turn the differential screw to the left limit for minimum differential since the required differential (difference between cut-in and cut-out points) is 10 psig. Throttle water overboard valve until a pressure of 15 psig is maintained at the condenser inlet. Turn the range screw clockwise until the switch contacts open, then turn counterclockwise slowly until contacts close. Slowly shut off water supply, decreasing the pressure. The contacts should open at 5 psig.

The THERMAL EXPANSION VALVE is generally factory set and seldom needs adjustment. The design and construction of expansion valves vary greatly. Figure ' 18 shows a cross sectional assembly view of a type which is generally used aboard ship. Other designs may have different arrangements for adjustment, sealing, and control.

Figure 19 shows a sketch of a thermal expansion valve and a cooling coil operating under assumed conditions of 40 evaporating temperatures with a valve adjusted to operate with a 10 superheat and with negligible pressure loss in the cooling coil. The 40 has a corresponding pressure of approximately 37 psig. As long as any liquid exists in the coil at this pressure the refrigerant temperature will remain at 40. As the liquid approaches point B on the cooling coil, it becomes evaporated due to the rate of liquid feed by the valve and due to the absorption of heat equal to the latent heat of vaporization of the refrigerant from the surrounding atmosphere. The refrigerant as a gas continues along the coil at a pressure of 37 pounds until at point C its temperature has increased to 50 due to the continued absorption

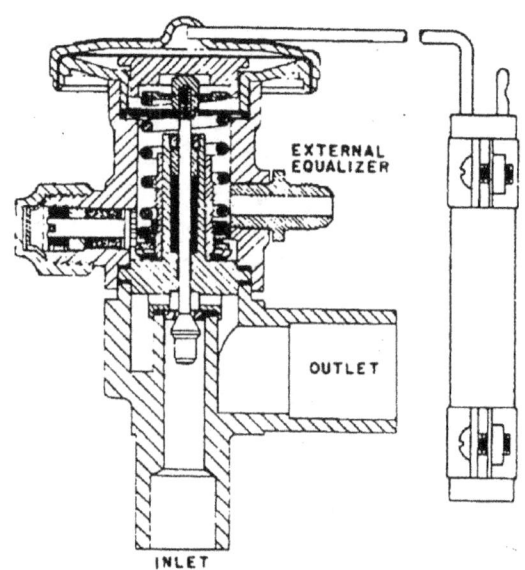

Figure 18.—Single outlet thermal expansion valve.

of heat from outside the coil. This then represents the 10 superheat (50°-40°). The amount of the superheat is dependent upon the amount of refrigerant fed by the expansion valve and the load to which the cooling coil is exposed.

Since the cooling coil temperature at C is 50°, the thermal bulb strapped to the coil at this point also will be 50°. The temperature of the thermal bulb affects the pressure of the refrigerant within the bulb so that it has an internal pressure equal to 46.7 psig. This pressure, shown as P_1, is the pressure exerted on top of the diaphragm. The pressure, P_2, exerted on the underside of the diaphragm is a result of the pressure of 37 psig at point A (expansion valve has an internal equalizer). The pressure, P_3, is that exerted by the spring under compression.

The movement of the diaphragm in response to pressure operates the valve stem to modulate the valve opening and to control flow. When the cooling load decreases, the rate of refrigerant feed would extend beyond point B resulting in a temperature lower than 50° at point C with a smaller superheat condition. The thermal bulb,

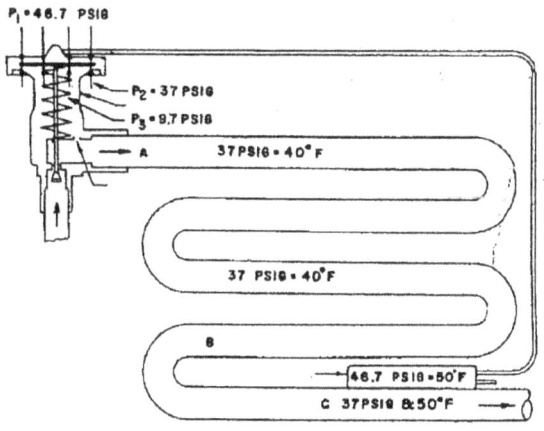

Figure 19.—Thermal expansion valve with internal equalizer on evaporator with no pressure drop.

in turn, would have lower temperature with a correspondingly lower pressure so that the reduced pressure exerted on top of the diaphragm would cause the valve to start to close until a balancing point was reached reducing the flow of refrigerant. On the other hand if the cooling load is increased, liquid refrigerant would be vaporized before it reached point B, resulting in more superheat by the time the gas passed point C. This in turn would raise the temperature of the thermal element increasing the pressure on top of the diaphragm causing the valve to open to admit more refrigerant. It will be noted in the example that the valve attempted to maintain a predetermined superheat represented by the spring pressure, P_3. The pressure is adjustable to increase or decrease the superheat setting and is usually maintained from 5° to 10° depending on the application.

An external equalizing connection, shown in figure 11-18 is required where the refrigerant pressure loss through the cooling coil is of any consequence: such as, above 2 1/2 pounds for air conditioning, 1 1/2 pounds for middle range refrigeration and 1/2 pound for frozen food applications. The need for an external equalizing port can be described by using figure 11-20. Assume the pressure loss through the coil is 10 pounds. This would result in a pressure at point B of 37 psig minus 10 psig or 27 psig

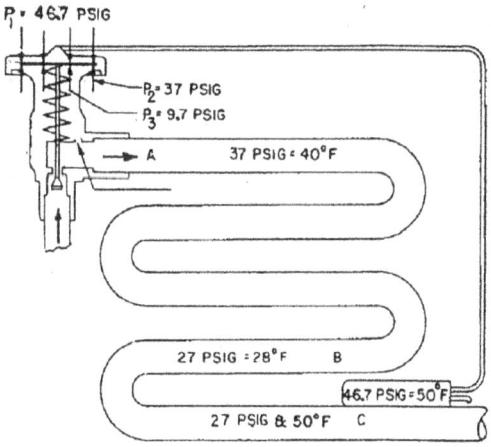

Figure 20.—Thermal expansion valve with internal equalizer on evaporator with 10 psi drop.

which is equivalent to an evaporating temperature of approximately 28°. Pressure at point A would still be 37 psig and the pressure at the underside of the diaphragm would still be 37 psig plus 9.7 psig or 46.7 psig. The required pressure above the diaphragm for equalization purposes would be 46.7 psig equivalent to a thermal bulb temperature of 50°. However, the difference between the superheated temperature at 50° at point C and 28° evaporating temperature at point B results in a 22° superheat.

This increase in superheat from 10° to 22° makes it necessary to use more of the cooling coil surface for superheating the vapor rather than for absorption of latent heat by the liquid and so the cooling coil is not fully utilized. The thermal expansion valve provided with an external equalizer must be used where such a condition exists. Figure 21 shows the connection with external equalizer, resulting in using the pressure of 27 psig at C and applying it directly to the underside of the diaphragm P_2 for a true response to superheat temperature. Thermal expansion valves are rated by the manufacturer in tons of refrigeration for various refrigerant evaporating temperatures and pressure differentials across the valve. These ratings are based generally on an assumed 1° sub-cooling of the liquid refrigerant at the entrance to the valve. This requires that each

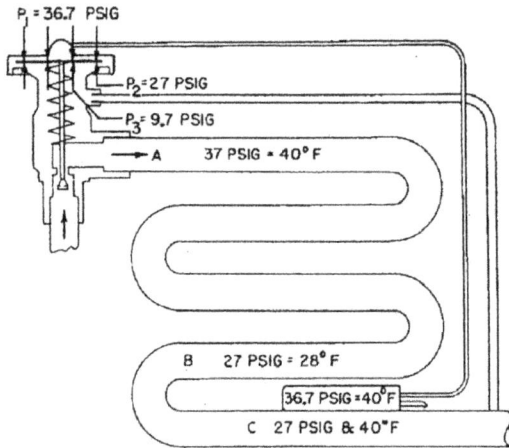

Figure 21.—Thermal expansion valve with external equalizer on evaporator with 10 psi pressure drop.

valve be selected not only for the tonnage needed for the cooling coil it serves but also for the conditions of pressure and temperature of the refrigerant at the inlet and downstream of the valve for its specific location in the refrigerating piping system. Thus, it becomes necessary to determine pressure losses including vertical rise of liquid and anticipate realistic operating conditions in order to properly select a valve of adequate size.

When the thermostatic expansion valve is operating properly, the temperature at the outlet side of the valve is much lower than that at the inlet side. If this temperature difference does not exist when the system is in operation, the valve seat is probably dirty and clogged with foreign matter.

Once a valve is properly adjusted, further adjustment should not be necessary. The major trouble encountered can usually be traced to moisture or dirt collecting at the valve seat and orifice. The symptoms of improper valve operation should be carefully analyzed before concluding that the valve is out of adjustment. Once a valve is properly adjusted, additional adjustment should not be necessary unless changes are made to the cooling coil arrangement or thermal element location.

By means of a gear and screw arrangement, the thermostatic expansion valve is adjusted to maintain a superheat ranging approximately from 4°F to 12°F at the cooling coil outlet. The proper superheat adjustment varies with the design and service operating conditions of the valve, and the design of the particular plant. Increased spring pressure increases the degree of superheat at the coil outlet and decreased pressure has the opposite effect. Many thermo-static expansion valves are initially adjusted by the manufacturer to maintain a predetermined degree of superheat, and no provision is made for further adjustments in service.

If expansion valves are adjusted to give a high degree of superheat at the coil outlet, or if the valve is stuck shut, the amount of refrigerant admitted to the cooling coil will be reduced. With an insufficient amount of refrigerant, the coil will be "starved" and will operate at a reduced capacity. Compressor lubricating oil carried with the refrigerant may tend to collect at the bottom of the cooling coils, thus robbing the compressor crankcase, and providing a condition whereby slugs of lubricating oil may be drawn back to the compressor. If the expansion valve is adjusted for too low a degree of superheat, or if the valve is stuck open, liquid refrigerant may flood from the cooling coils back to the compressor. Should the liquid collect at a low point in the suction line or coil, and be drawn back to the compressor intermittently in slugs, there is danger of injury to the moving parts of the compressor.

In general, the expansion valves for air conditioning and water cooling plants (high temperature installations) must be adjusted for higher superheat than are the expansion valves for cold storage refrigeration and ship's service store equipment (low temperature installations).

If it is impossible to adjust expansion valves to the desired settings, or if it is suspected that the expansion valve assembly is defective and requires replacement, appropriate tests must be made. (First be sure that the liquid strainers are clean, that the solenoid valves are operative, and that the system is sufficiently charged with refrigerant.)

The major equipment required for expansion valve tests is as follows:

1. A service drum of R-12, or a supply of clean dry air at 70 to 100 psig. The service drum is used to supply gas under pressure. The gas used does not have to be the same as that employed in the thermal element of the valve being tested.

2. A high pressure and a low pressure gage. The low pressure gage should be accurate and in good condition so that the pointer does not have any appreciable lost motion. The high pressure gage, while not absolutely necessary, will be useful in showing the pressure on the inlet side of the valve. Refrigeration plants are provided with suitable spare and test pressure gages.

The procedure for testing is as follows:

1. Connect the valve inlet to the gas supply with the high pressure gage attached so as to indicate the gas pressure to the valve, and with the low pressure gage loosely connected to the expansion valve outlet. The low pressure gage is connected up loosely so as to provide a small amount of leakage through the connection.

2. Insert the expansion valve thermal element in a bath of crushed ice. Do not attempt to perform this test with a container full of water in which a small amount of crushed ice is floating.

3. Open the valve on the service drum or in the air supply line. Make certain that the gas supply is sufficient to build up the pressure to at least 70 psi on the high pressure gage connected in the line to the valve inlet.

4. The expansion valve can now be adjusted. If it is desired to adjust for 10°F superheat, the pressure on the outlet gage should be 22.5 psig. This is equivalent to an R-12 evaporating temperature of 22°F, and since the ice maintains the bulb at 32°F, the valve adjustment is for 10° superheat (difference between 32 and 22). For a 5° superheat adjustment, the valve should be adjusted to give a pressure of approximately 26.1 psig. There must be a small amount of leakage through the low pressure gage connection while this adjustment is being made.

5. To determine if the valve operates smoothly, tap the valve body lightly with a small weight. The low pressure gage needle should not jump more than 1 psi.

6. Now tighten the low pressure gage connection so as to stop the leakage at the joint, and determine if the expansion valve seats tightly. With the valve in good condition, the pressure will increase a few pounds and then either stop or build up very slowly. With a leaking valve, the pressure will build up rapidly until it equals the inlet pressure.

7. Again loosen the gage so as to permit leakage at the gage connection; remove the thermal element, or control bulb, from the crushed ice, and warm it with the hand or place it in water that is at room temperature. When this is done, the pressure should increase rapidly, showing that the power element has not lost its charge. If there is no increase in pressure, the power element is dead.

8. With high pressure showing on both gages as outlined above, the valve can be

tested to determine if the body joints or the bellows leak. This can be done by using a halide leak detector. When performing this test, it is important that the body of the valve have a fairly high pressure applied to it. In addition, the gages and other fittings should be made up tightly at the joints so as to eliminate leakage at these points.

If it is evident that the expansion valve is defective, it must be replaced. Often it is possible to replace a faulty power element or other part of the valve without having to replace the entire assembly. When replacement of an expansion valve is necessary, it is important to replace the unit with a valve of the same capacity and type, designed for R-12 systems.

The WATER REGULATING VALVE should be adjusted to maintain a compressor discharge pressure of approximately 125 psig. To raise the valve opening point, turn the adjusting nuts clockwise, increasing tension on the main springs. Increasing main spring tension increases the amount of pressure required to open the valve. Turning the adjusting nuts counterclockwise decreases the main spring tension, therefore decreasing the amount of pressure required to open the valve. If the ambient temperature is high, pressure (gas) in the compressor discharge line and condenser may remain high and cause the water regulating valve to partly open when the compressor is idle. In such instances, the point of valve opening should be raised just enough to cause the valve to close during compressor shutdown.

The valve may be flushed by opening it with an outside force, a screwdriver or similar tool may be used to force the spring yoke.

The THERMOSTATIC SWITCH which operates the solenoid valve is similar to the low pressure switch. Tubing connects a bellows in the thermostatic switch to a thermal bulb in the compartment being cooled. The thermal bulb and tubing are charged with R-12 or some other volatile liquid. Temperature changes in the refrigerated compartment cause corresponding pressure changes of the actuating medium in

the thermal bulb. These pressure changes are transmitted to the thermostatic switch, through the connecting tubing. To set or adjust the cut-in and cutout points of the thermostatic switch, the same procedure is used as in setting and adjusting the low pressure switch.

When condenser circulating water is obtained from the firemain, the pressure must be reduced. For this pressure reduction, an AUTOMATIC REDUCING VALVE is installed in the branch line leading from the firemain to the condenser. The reducing valve is installed just ahead of the regulating valve.

Mate may have to adjust the reducing valve to raise or lower the outlet pressure. The outlet pressure can be varied by turning the adjusting screw, which is located under the cap. Turning the adjusting screw clockwise increases the pressure applied by the spring to the top of the diaphragm, thus opening the valve wider and increasing the outlet pressure. Turning the adjusting screw counterclockwise decreases the spring pressure on the top of the diaphragm, thus tending to decrease the discharge pressure.

VII. CHARACTERISTICS OF REFRIGERANTS

Pure R-12 (CCl_2F_2) is colorless. In concentrations of less than 20 percent by volume in air, R-12 is odorless; in higher concentrations, its odor resembles that of carbon tetrachloride. It has a boiling point of -21 F at atmospheric pressure. At ordinary temperatures R-12 is a liquid when under a pressure of about 70 to 75 psig.

Mixtures of R-12 vapor and air, in all proportions, are nonirritating to the eyes, nose, throat, and lungs. The refrigerant will not contaminate or poison foods or other supplies with which it may come in contact. The vapor is nonpoisonous; it will not support respiration, however, and it produces mild anesthesia when it is inhaled in sufficient quantities. In view of its low boiling point at atmospheric pressure, care must be taken to prevent liquid R-12 from coming in contact with the eyes; the liquid will freeze the tissues of the eyes. Always wear goggles if you are to be exposed to R-12.

R-12 in either a liquid or vapor state is nonflammable and nonexplosive. R-12 will not corrode the metals commonly used in refrigerating systems.

One hazard which may be introduced through the use of R-12 as a refrigerant is the very remote health hazard which may be presented should leakage of a large amount of the vapor come in direct contact with an open flame of high temperature (about 1,000°F) and be decomposed. In order to be a health hazard, the leakage of R-12 must be within a confined and poorly ventilated space and the vapor must come in direct contact with a high temperature flame. When these conditions exist, however, the products of decomposition are pungent and irritating, rendering them noticeable even when they are present only in minute quantities; ample warning is available before concentrations dangerous to health are reached.

R-12 is a stable compound capable of undergoing without decomposition, the physical changes required of it in refrigeration service. It is an excellent solvent and has the ability to loosen and remove all particles of dirt, scale, and oil with which it comes in contact within a refrigerating system.

R-22 ($CHC1F_2$) and R-11 ($CC13F$) are colorless, nonexplosive, nonpoisonous refrigerants with many properties similar to those of R-12.

VIII. SAFETY PRECAUTIONS

Refrigerants are furnished in cylinders for use in refrigeration systems. The following precautions must be observed in the handling, use, and storage of these cylinders:

1. Never drop cylinders nor permit them to strike each other violently.

2. Never use a lifting magnet or a sling (rope or chain) when handling cylinders. A crane may be used if a safe cradle or platform is provided to hold the cylinders.

3. Caps provided for valve protection must be kept on cylinders except when the cylinders are being used.

4. Whenever refrigerant is discharged from a cylinder, the cylinder should be weighed immediately and the weight of the refrigerant remaining in the cylinder should be recorded.

5. Never attempt to mix gases in a cylinder.

6. NEVER put the wrong refrigerant into a refrigeration system! <u>No refrigerant accept the one for which the system was designed should ever be introduced into the system.</u> Check the equipment nameplate or the manufacturer's technical manual to determine the proper refrigerant type and charge. Putting the wrong refrigerant into a system may cause a violent explosion.

7. When a cylinder has been emptied, close the cylinder valve immediately to prevent the entrance of air, moisture, or dirt. Also, be sure to replace the valve protection cap.

8. Never use cylinders for any purpose other than their intended purpose. DO NOT use them as rollers, supports, etc.

9. DO NOT tamper with the safety devices in the valves or cylinders.

10. Open cylinder valves slowly. Never use wrenches or other tools except those provided by the manufacturer.

11. Make sure that the threads on regulators or other connections are the same as those on the cylinder valve outlets. Never force connections that do not fit.

12. Regulators and pressure gages provided for use with a particular gas must NOT be used on cylinders containing other gases.

13. Never attempt to repair or alter cylinders or valves.

14. Never fill R-12 cylinders beyond 80 percent of capacity.

15. Store cylinders in a cool, dry place, in an upright position. If the cylinders are exposed to excessive heat, a dangerous increase in pressure will occur. If cylinders

must be stored in the open, take care that they are protected against extremes of weather. NEVER allow a cylinder to be subjected to a temperature above 125 °F.

16. NEVER allow R-12 to come in contact with a flame or red-hot metal! When exposed to excessively high temperatures, R-12 breaks down into PHOSGENE gas, an extremely poisonous substance.

Because R-12 is such a powerful freezing agent that even a very small amount can freeze the delicate tissues of the eye, causing permanent damage; it is essential that goggles be worn by all personnel who may be exposed to a refrigerant, particularly in its liquid form. If refrigerant does get in the eyes, the person suffering the injury should receive medical treatment immediately in order to avoid permanent damage to the eyes. In the meantime, put drops of clean olive oil, mineral oil, or other nonirritating oil in the eyes, and MAKE SURE that the person does not rub his eyes. CAUTION: DO NOT use anything except clean, nonirritating oil for this type of eye injury.

If R-12 comes in contact with the skin, it may cause frostbite. This injury should be treated as any other case of frostbite. Immerse the affected part in a warm bath for about 10 minutes, then dry carefully. DO NOT rub or massage the affected area.

Although R-12 is generally classed as non-toxic, it IS poisonous in high concentrations such as might occur from excessive R-12 leakage in a confined or poorly ventilated space. If a person should be overcome by R-12 remove him IMMEDIATELY to a well-ventilated place and get medical attention at the earliest opportunity. Watch his breathing. If the person is not breathing, begin artificial respiration.

BASIC FUNDAMENTALS OF AIR CONDITIONING AND REFRIGERATION

TABLE OF CONTENTS

	Page
I. Operation	1
A. Using the Dehydrator	1
B. V-Belt Drive	1
C. Checking Compressor Oil	2
II. Maintenance	3
A. Compressor Maintenance	3
B. Removing Shaft Seal	5
C. Installing Shaft Seal	5
D. Lapping Shaft Seal	6
III. System Maintenance	6
A. Charging the System	6
B. Purging Air from the System	7
C. Cleaning Suction Strainers	7
D. Cleaning Liquid Line Strainer	7
E. Cleaning Oil Filters and Strainers	7
IV. Condensers	8
A. Checking Condenser Performance	8
B. Cleaning Condenser Tubes	8
C. Cleaning Air-Cooled Condensers	9
D. Testing for Leaks	9
E. Retubing Condensers	9
V. Expansion Valves	10
A. Thermostatic Expansion Valve	10
B. Automatic Expansion Valve	12
C. Hand Expansion Valve	13
D. Switches	13
E. Evacuating and Dehydrating the System	13
F. Reactivating the Drying System	14
G. Cleaning the System	16
VI. Detecting and Correcting Troubles	16
A. Trouble-Diagnosis Chart	17

BASIC FUNDAMENTALS OF AIR CONDITIONING AND REFRIGERATION

I. OPERATION

Proper operation of any unit of machinery is an important part of maintaining it. To ensure proper operation of the refrigeration plant, it is necessary to understand the principles of operation of the unit. It is also necessary to make periodic inspections and tests. It is good practice to make an hourly check of all temperatures and pressures throughout the system and to check the oil level in the compressor crankcase.

One of the best methods, and probably the easiest, for checking plant operation is to compare the temperatures and pressures of the plant with corresponding temperatures and pressures which were recorded during a period when the plant was known to be operating properly. The value of the comparison will depend on the similarity of the conditions existing when each set of readings was taken.

A daily operating log for refrigeration equipment should be maintained and used for a continuous analysis of the operating conditions found in a refrigeration plant.

Refrigeration plants are equipped with automatic controls and once the plant is in normal operation, very little attention is required. However, these plants are, like all units of machinery, liable to casualties, so periodic checks must be made to ensure that the plant is operating normally. The main purpose of the operating log is to ensure that abnormal operating conditions do not go undetected.

Usually the personnel assigned to operate and maintain refrigeration plants are graduates of an air conditioning and refrigeration school. However, in small shops, the men assigned to make the periodic checks on the refrigeration plants may or may not have attended this school. These men must be properly indoctrinated as to how to take and record the temperatures and pressures in a refrigeration plant and also as to why these readings are important for the operation of the plant.

A. USING THE DEHYDRATOR

A dehydrator is installed in the liquid line between the receiver and the expansion valve to absorb moisture that has entered the system. The dehydrator is installed with a bypass so that it may be cut in or out of the system. The dehydrator should be put into use when the system is being charged, at any time the system is opened for repairs, or at any time the presence of moisture is suspected.

Dehydrators can absorb only small quantities of moisture and are installed to minimize the effects of moisture. If large quantities of moisture are present in the refrigeration system, more than one dehydrator must be used, or other means must be taken to rid the system of moisture. Another drying-out process is described in this chapter under "Evacuating and Dehydrating the System."

B. V-BELT DRIVE

Belts must be properly tightened. Excessive looseness will cause slippage, rapid wear, and deterioration of V-belts. On the other hand, a belt that is too tight will result in excessive wear of both the belt and main bearing of the compressor. In extreme cases, it may cause a bad seal leak. If a belt is properly tightened, it should be possible to depress it, by the pressure of one finger, as much as 1/2 to 3/4 inch, at a point midway between the flywheel and motor pulleys.

When replacement of one belt of a multiple V-belt drive is necessary, a complete new set of matched belts should be installed. Belts stretch considerably during the first few hours of operation. Replacement of a single belt will upset the load balance between the new and old belts and be a potential source of trouble. It is better practice to run the unit temporarily with a defective belt removed than to attempt to operate a new belt in conjunction with two or more seasoned belts.

V-belts, motor pulleys, and compressor flywheels should be kept dry and free of oil. Belt dressing should never be used.

C. CHECKING COMPRESSOR OIL

If the apparent oil level observed immediately after a prolonged shutdown period is lower than normal, it is almost certain that the actual working oil level is far too low. After a sufficient quantity of oil has been added to raise the apparent oil level to the center of the bull's-eye sight glass, on the side of the compressor, the actual oil level should be checked as follows:

1. Operate the compressor or manual control for at least one hour. Then slowly close the suction line stop valve. If the compressor is operating on a water cooler or other coil which is apt to freeze, observe the temperature and interrupt compressor operation as necessary to prevent freezing. Repeat cycling until the total running time (one hour) is obtained.

2. Stop the compressor, turn the flywheel until the crankshaft and connecting rod ends are immersed in the lubricating oil, and immediately observe the oil level in the sight glass.

To check the oil level when the compressor has been running on its normal cycle, with no abnormal shutdown, proceed as follows:

1. Wait until the end of a period of operation; if the operation is continuous, wait until the compressor has been in operation at least 1/2 hour.

2. As soon as the compressor stops, turn the flywheel until the crankshaft and connecting rod ends are immersed in the lubricating oil, and observe the oil level in the sight glass.

Do not remove oil from the crankcase because of an apparent high level unless it is known that too much oil has been previously added, or unless it is apparent that oil from the crankcase of one compressor of the plant has been inadvertently deposited in the crankcase of another.

However, if the oil level is lower than its recommended height on the glass, additional oil should be added. Do not add more oil than is necessary to obtain the desired level. Too much oil can result in excessive oil transfer to the cooling coils.

Adding Oil

There are two common methods of adding oil to a compressor. In one type of installation a small oil-charging pump is furnished for adding oil to the compressor crankcase. In another type, oil is placed in the compressor by means of a clean, well-dried funnel. In either case, care must be taken to prevent the entrance of air or foreign matter into the compressor.

When performing hourly checks of the compressors, you may observe no oil in the crank-case, or a very low oil level on the sight glass. This indicates that the oil has left the compressor and is circulating in the system; and that it will be necessary to add oil to the normal level and operate the system. After the compressor has reclaimed the excessive oil in the system, the added oil should be drained.

Removing Oil

To remove oil from the compressor crank-case, reduce the pressure in the crankcase to approximately 1 psi by gradually closing the suction line stop valve. Then stop the compressor, close the suction and discharge line valves, loosen the lubricating oil drain plug near the bottom of the compressor crankcase, and allow the required amount of oil to drain out. Since the compressor crankcase is under a slight pressure, do not fully remove the drain plug from the compressor, but allow the oil to seep out around the threads of the loosened plug.

When the desired amount of oil has been removed, tighten the drain plug, open the suction and discharge line valves, and start the compressor. If an oil drain valve is provided in lieu of a plug, the required amount of oil may be drained without the necessity of pumping down the compressor.

Changing Oil

When clean copper tubing is employed for the mains and evaporators, and reasonable care has been taken to prevent the entrance of foreign matter during installation, the oil in the compressor crankcase will probably not become sufficiently contaminated to require renewal. When iron or steel pipe and fittings are used in the system, a sample of oil from the compressor crankcase should be withdrawn into a clean glass vessel every three months. If the sample shows contamination, the entire lubricating oil charge should be renewed. It is good practice to check the cleanliness of the lubricating oil after each cleaning of the compressor suction scale trap.

II. MAINTENANCE

In order for you to perform the required maintenance you must understand the proper operating and maintenance procedures. In most instances, personnel who are assigned to maintain refrigeration plants are graduates of an Air Conditioning and

Refrigeration School. While this school teaches most operating and maintenance procedures, the manufacturer's technical manuals should be referred to for the details of the plants on your ship.

A. COMPRESSOR MAINTENANCE

Refrigeration compressors vary to such an extent that this training course could not cover each type. The manufacturer's technical manuals must be referred to for details of any specific unit. Compressors range from small reciprocating types (for drinking water coolers) to very large centrifugal units used for air conditioning on large ships. Compressors may be splash lubricated or forced-feed lubricated. Centrifugal compressors are seldom used on plants smaller than 110 tons. They operate on the same principle as a centrifugal pump, except that they are designed to pump a gas instead of a liquid. Reciprocating compressors are used for air conditioning on most ships.

If a compressor cannot be pumped down and is damaged to the extent that it has to be opened fox repairs, it is necessary to first close the suction and discharge valves and then allow all refrigerant in the compressor to vent to the atmosphere, through a gage line.

To service a compressor correctly, it is necessary to be familiar with the manufacturer's technical manual. These manuals usually give a step-by-step procedure for disassembling the compressor and for renewing any part of the unit.

Before disassembling a compressor, make certain that the faulty operation of the unit is not caused by trouble in some other part of the system. Disassemble only the part of the compressor that is necessary to correct the fault. As internal machined parts are removed, every precaution should be taken to protect them from being damaged in handling and from corrosion.

Before starting to reassemble a compressor, all partsincluding replacement parts should be carefully washed in an approved solvent and permitted to dry in air. The final rinse should be made with clean solvent. The parts should be wiped with a lintfree cloth before the unit is assembled. Every precaution should betaken to prevent dirt, lint, water, or other foreign matter from entering the compressor during reassembly.

When it becomes necessary to remove, replace, or repair internal parts of the compressor, the following precautions should be observed:

1. Carefully disassemble and remove parts, noting the correct relative position so that errors will not be made when reassembling.

2. Inspect all those parts that become accessible due to the removal of other parts requiring repair or replacement.

3. Make certain that all parts and surfaces are free of dirt and moisture.

4. Apply compressor oil freely to all bearing and rubbing surfaces of parts being replaced or reinstalled.

5. If the compressor is not equipped with an oil pump, make certain the oil dipper on the lower connecting rod is in correct position for dipping oil when the unit is in operation.

6. Position the ends of the piston rings so that alternate joints come on the opposite side of the piston.

7. Care should be taken not to score gasket surfaces.

8. Renew all gaskets.

9. Clean the crankcase and renew the oil.

Whenever repairs to a compressor are of such a nature that any appreciable amount of air enters the unit, the compressor should be evacuated, after assembly is completed. The proper procedure is as follows:

1. Disconnect a connection in the compressor discharge gage line, between the discharge line stop valve and the compressor.

2. Start the compressor and let it run until the greatest possible vacuum is obtained.

3. Stop the compressor and immediately open the suction stop valve slightly in order to blow refrigerant through the compressor valves and purge the air above the discharge valves through the open gage line.

4. Close the discharge gage line and open the discharge line stop valve.

5. Remove all oil from the exterior of the compressor, and test the compressor joints for leakage, using the halide leak detector.

Testing Suction and Discharge Valves

A compressor should not be opened for inspection or repair until it has definitely been determined that the faulty operation of the system is or is not due to leaky suction or discharge valves.

Faulty compressor valves may be indicated either by a gradual or a sudden decrease in the normal compressor capacity. Either the compressor will fail to pump at all, or else the suction pressure cannot be pumped down to the designed value, and the compressor will run for abnormally long intervals or even continuously. If the compressor shuts down for short periods, the compressor valves may be leaking.

If the refrigeration plant is not operating satisfactorily, it will be best to first shift the compressors and then check the operation of the plant. If the operation of the plant is still not satisfactory when the compressors have been shifted, the trouble is in the system, and not in the compressor.

The compressor discharge valves may be tested by pumping down the compressor to 2 psig, and then stopping the compressor and quickly closing the suction and discharge line valves. If the discharge pressure drops at a rate in excess of 3 pounds in a minute and the crankcase suction pressure rises, there is evidence of compressor discharge valve leakage. If it is necessary to remove the discharge valves with the compressor pumped down, open the connection to the discharge pressure gage in order to release discharge pressure on the head. Then remove the compressor top head and discharge valve plate, being careful not to damage the gaskets.

If the discharge valves are defective, the entire discharge valve assembly should be replaced. Any attempt to repair them would probably involve relapping, and would require highly specialized equipment. Except in an emergency, such repair should never be undertaken aboard ship.

The compressor internal suction valves may be checked for leakage as follows:

1. Start the compressor by using the manual control switch on the motor controller.

2. Close the suction line stop valve gradually, to prevent violent foaming of the compressor crankcase lubricating oil charge.

3. With this stop valve closed, pump a vacuum of approximately 20 inches Hg. If this vacuum can be readily obtained, the compressor suction valves are satisfactory.

Do not expect the vacuum to be maintained after the compressor stops, because the Refrigerant-12 is being released from the crankcase oil. Do not attempt to check compressor suction valve efficiency of new units until after the compressor has been in operation for a minimum of 3 days. It may be necessary for the valves to wear in.

However, if any of the compressor suction valves are defective, the compressor should be pumped down, opened, and the valves inspected. Defective valve(s) or pistons should be replaced with spare assemblies.

Crankshaft Seal Repairs

On reciprocating compressors, the crankshaft extends through the compressor housing to provide a mount for the pulley wheel. At this point the shaft must be sealed to prevent leakage of lubricating oil and refrigerant. There are several types of crankshaft seals, depending on the manufacturer. The crankshaft seal is bathed in lubricating oil at a pressure equal to the suction pressure of the refrigerant. The first indication of crankshaft failure is excessive oil leaking at the shaft.

When the seal requires replacement, or signs of abnormal wear or damage to the running surfaces are present, a definite reason for the abnormal conditions exists and an inspection should be made. It is very important to locate and correct the trouble or the failure will reoccur.

Seal failure is very often the result of faulty lubrication, usually due to the condition of the crankcase oil. Dirty or broken oil is generally caused by one or both of the following conditions:

1. Dirt or foreign material in the system or system piping. Dirt frequently enters the system at the time of installation. After a period of operation, foreign material will always accumulate in the compressor crankcase, tending to concentrate in the oil chamber surrounding the shaft seal. When the oil contains grit, it is only a matter of time until the highly finished running faces become damaged, causing failure of the shaft seal.

2. Moisture is frequently the cause of an acid condition of the lubricating oil. Oil in this condition will not provide satisfactory lubrication and will promote failure of the compressor parts. If the presence of moisture is suspected, a dryer should be used when the compressor is put into operation. At any time foreign mate rial is found in the lubricating oil, the entire system (piping, valves, and strainers) should be cleaned thoroughly.

B. REMOVING SHAFT SEAL.— In the event a shaft seal must be repaired or renewed, proceed as follows:

If the seal is broken to the extent that it permits excessive oil leakage, do not attempt to pump the refrigerant out of the compressor, air (containing moisture) will be drawn into the system through the damaged seal. Moisture in the air may cause expansion valves to freeze. If oil is leaking excessively, close the compressor suction and discharge valves and relieve the pressure to the atmosphere by loosening a connection on the compressor discharge gage line. If the condition of the seal does permit, pump down the compressor as previously explained in this chapter.

Next drain the oil from the compressor crankcase. Since the oil contains refrigerant, it will foam while being drained. The oil drain valve or plug should be left open while you are working on the seal, so that refrigerant escaping from the oil remaining in the crankcase will not build up a pressure and unexpectedly blow out the seal while it is being removed.

Remove the compressor flywheel (or coupling) and carefully remove the shaft seal assembly. If the assembly cannot be readily removed, build up a slight pressure in the compressor crankcase by slightly opening the compressor suction valve, taking the necessary precautions to support the seal to prevent it from being blown from the compressor and damaged.

C. INSTALLING SHAFT SEAL.— When the replacement is made, the entire seal assembly should be replaced. The parts should be clean and should be replaced in accordance with the manufacturer's instructions.

Wipe the shaft clean with a linen or silk cloth, do not use a dirty or lint-bearing cloth. Unwrap the seal, being careful not to touch the bearing surfaces with the hands. Rinse the seal in an approved solvent and allow to air-dry. (Do not wipe the seal dry.) Dip the seal in clean refrigerant oil. Insert the assembly in accordance with the instructions found in the manufacturer's technical manual and bolt the seal cover in place, tightening the bolts evenly. Replace the flywheel and belts and test the unit for leaks by opening the suction and discharge valves and using a halide leak detector.

D. LAPPING SHAFT SEAL.— Due to the difficulty of properly lapping the rubbing surfaces of a shaft seal, a seal leak should be corrected by renewing the assembly. If, however, a new shaft seal is not available, and it is possible to use the existing seal by refinishingthe rubbing surfaces, the seal can be lapped as follows:

1. Thoroughly clean the surfaces of the shaft shoulder and seal collar.

2. Lap the back of the shaft seal collar to the crankshaft shoulder. This joint must form an absolute seal so the importance of this lapping cannot be overemphasized. Only jeweler's rouge or the equivalent should be used for the lapping. The abrasive must be used sparingly to avoid getting it into the shaft bearings or crankcase. As the lapping proceeds, use less and less abrasive and finish the lapping with compressor lubricating Oil.

3. After the lapping has been completed, thoroughly clean the shaft shoulder and permit it to dry without wiping. With the shaft seal shoulder and collar dry and clean, lap the two surfaces together as a final lapping operation.

4. The surfaces are properly lapped when the surface of both the shaft shoulder and the shaft seal collar form a perfect contact and are free of all mars, scratches, or other imperfections. It is good practice to make the final examination with the aid of a good magnifying glass.

5. In some instances, a molded synthetic rubber gasket is provided instead of the metal-to-metal joint between the shaft seal collar and the crankshaft shoulder. In any case, it is extremely important that these parts be properly fitted and that the gasket be kept in good condition in order that a tight seal be maintained at this point.

When a shaft seal is lapped in, it should be regarded as a temporary repair and a new assembly should be installed as soon as possible.

III. SYSTEM MAINTENANCE

A refrigeration system that has been properly installed and properly operated will need little maintenance. However, certain tests, inspections, and maintenance procedures must be carried out to ensure that the system will operate at its rated capacity.

Learning to start and secure a refrigeration system is not enough to do your job properly. As a mechanic you must know the operating principles of the entire system, how each unit of the system operates, and why it is necessary; how each control and safety device works, and the reason for its being installed on the system. This understanding can be attained only through study, either by attending an Air Conditioning and Refrigeration School or by studying the manufacturer's technical manuals.

For men who have not attended an Air Conditioning and Refrigeration School, a training program should be set up to ensure an adequate number of qualified personnel to operate and maintain the air conditioning and refrigeration equipment.

A. Charging the System

Information concerning the charging of refrigeration systems may be found in a technical manual. The amount of refrigerant charge must be sufficient to maintain a liquid seal between the condensing and evaporating sides of the system. When the compressor stops, under normal operating conditions, the receiver of a properly charged system is about 85 percent full of refrigerant. The proper charge for a specific system or unit can be found in the manufacturer's technical manual or on the blueprints.

A refrigeration system should not be charged if there are leaks or if there is reason to believe that there is a leak in the system. The leaks must be found and corrected. Immediately following or during the process of charging, the system should be carefully checked for leaks.

A refrigeration system must have an adequate charge of refrigerant at all times; otherwise its efficiency and capacity will be impaired.

B. Purging Air From The System

Operate the system for 30 minutes. Observe the pressure and temperature as indicated on the high pressure gage. Read the thermometer in the liquid line, and compare it with the temperature conversion figures shown on the discharge pressure gage. If the temperature of the liquid leaving the receiver is more than 15° F lower than the temperature corresponding to the discharge pressure, the system should be purged. While the system is still operating, slightly open the purge valve on the condenser. Purge very slowly, at intervals, until the air is expelled from the system and the temperature difference drops below 15° F.

C. Cleaning Suction Strainers

When putting a new unit into operation, the suction strainers should be cleaned after a few hours of operation. Refrigerants have a solvent action and will loosen any foreign matter in the system. This foreign matter will eventually reach the suction strainers. After a few days of operation, the strainers will need another cleaning. They should be inspected frequently during the first few weeks of plant operation, and then cleaned as found necessary.

The suction strainers are located in the compressor housing or in the suction piping. The procedure for cleaning the strainers is as follows:

    1. Pump down the compressor.
    2. Remove the strainer and inspect it for foreign matter.
    3. Clean the strainer screen by dipping it in an approved solvent and then allow it to dry.
    4. Replace the strainer and evacuate the air from the compressor.
    5. Test the housing for leaks by wiping up all oil and then using a halide leak detector.

D. Cleaning A Liquid Line Strainer

Where a liquid line strainer is installed, it should be cleaned at the same intervals as the suction strainer. If a liquid line strainer becomes clogged to the extent that it needs cleaning, a loss of refrigeration effect will take place. The tubing after the strainer will be much colder than the tubing ahead of the strainer.

To clean the liquid line strainer, secure the receiver outlet valve and wait a few minutes to allow any liquid in the strainer to flow to the cooling coils. Then close the strainer outlet valve and very carefully loosen the cap which is bolted to the strainer body. (Use goggles to protect the eyes.) When all of the pressure is bled out of the strainer, remove the cap and lift out the strainer screen. Clean the strainer screen, using an approved solvent and a small brush. Reassemble the spring and screen in the strainer body, then replace the strainer cap loosely. Purge the air out of the strainer, by blowing refrigerant through it, then tighten the cap. After the assembly is complete, test the unit for leaks.

E. Cleaning Oil Filters and Strainers

Compressors arranged for forced feed lubri-' cation are provided with lubricating oil strainers in the suction line of the lube oil pump and an oil filter may be installed in the pump discharge line. A gradual decrease in lubricating oil pressure indicates that these units need cleaning. This cleaning may be accomplished in much the same manner as described for cleaning suction strainers.

When cleaning is necessary, the lubricating oil in the crankcase should be drained from the compressor and a new charge of oil should be added before restarting the unit.

When the compressor is put back into operation, the lube oil pressure should be adjusted to the proper setting by adjustment of the oil pressure regulator.

IV. CONDENSERS

The compressor discharge line terminates at the refrigerant condenser. In shipboard R-12 installations, these condensers are usually of the multipass shell-and-tube type, with water circulating through the tubes. The tubes are expanded into grooved holes in the tube sheet so as to make an absolutely tight joint between the shell and the circulating water. Refrigerant vapor is admitted to the shell, and condenses on the outer surfaces of the tubes.

Any air which may accidentally enter the refrigeration system will be drawn through the piping and eventually discharged into the condenser with the R-12 gas. The air accumulated in the condenser is lighter than the refrigerant gas and will rise to the top of the condenser when the plant is shut down. A purge valve, for purging accumulated air from the refrigeration system (when necessary), is installed at the top of the condenser, or at a high point in the compressor discharge line.

A. Checking Condenser Performance

An overall check for water-cooled condenser performance may be used after, AND ONLY AFTER, the condenser has been properly purged. After the condition of the condensing surface has been determined, make preliminary preparations to the system as outlined in the procedure, discussed earlier in the chapter, used to check for noncondensable gases. Then proceed as follows:

1. Record the condensing temperature which corresponds to the pressure in the condenser, while the compressor is in operation.
2. Record the temperature of the water leaving the condenser.
3. Subtract the temperature of the water leaving the condenser from the condensing temperature obtained in (1). The temperature of the water leaving the condenser will be several degrees below the condensing temperature of pure R-12.
4. Clean the water side of the condenser, if the difference between the temperature of the outlet circulating water and the temperature corresponding to the condensing pressure increases 5° F to 10° F above the temperature difference obtained when the condenser was in good condition and operating under similar heat loads, and if this difference is not caused by an overcharge of refrigerant or noncondensable gases.

B. Cleaning Condenser Tubes

In order to clean the condenser tubes properly, it is necessary first to drain the cooling water from the condenser and then to remove the water connections and water chests. When the water chests are removed, be careful not to damage the gaskets between the tube sheet and the water side of the water chest. Tubes should be inspected as often as practicable and be cleaned as necessary by the use of an approved method for cleaning steam condenser tubes.

Rubber plugs and an air or water lance should be employed when necessary to remove foreign deposits. It is essential that the tube surfaces be kept clear of particles of foreign matter; however, care must be taken not to destroy the thin protective coating of corrosion products on the inner surfaces of the tubes. If the tubes become badly corroded, they should be replaced in order to avoid the possibility of losing the R-12 charge and admitting salt water to the R-12 system.

C. Cleaning Air-Cooled Condensers

Although the large plants are equipped with water-cooled condensers, auxiliary units are commonly provided with air-cooled condensers, and this eliminates the necessity for circulating water pumps and piping.

The exterior surface of the tubes and fins on an air-cooled condenser should be kept free of dirt or any matter that might obstruct heat flow and air circulation. The finned surface should be brushed clean with a stiff bristle brush as often as necessary. When installations are exposed to salt spray and rain through open doors or hatches, care should be taken to minimize corrosion of the exterior surfaces. The finned surface is usually coated with solder and should never be painted; it may be retinned if necessary.

D. Testing for Leaks

To prevent serious loss of refrigerant through leaky condenser tubes, the condenser should be tested for leakage once every two weeks. The test should always be conducted on a condenser that has not been in use for the preceding 12 hours. Slowly open the vent valves on the water side, one at a time, and insert the exploring tube of a leak detector. If this test indicates that R-12 gas is present, the exact location of the leak may be detected by the following method:

1. Remove the water heads and listen at each section for the hissing sound that indicates gas leakage. If the leak cannot be definitely located, all the, tubes must be checked. However, if the probable location of the leaky tubes is found, treat that section as follows:

2. Wash the tube heads, and with a cloth or ball of cotton clean all tubes (while wet) until the inner walls are dry and shining. Then hold the exploring tube in one end of each condenser tube for about 10 seconds. As soon as fresh air is drawn into the tube, drive a cork into each end of the tube. If necessary, repeat this procedure with all the tubes in the condenser. Before proceeding further, allow the condenser to remain in this condition for 48 hours.

3. After the tubes have been corked up for 48 hours, put three men on the job, one to remove corks at one end, another to remove corks at the other end and handle the exploring tube, and the third man to watch the color of the flame in the lamp. Start with the top row of tubes in the section being inspected, remove the corks simultaneously at each end of the tube, and insert the exploring tube for 5 seconds.

4. Mark any leaky tubes for later identification.

5. Leakage of any of the tube joints is indicated by the presence of oil at the joint, after the 48-hour period.

To date, this procedure has been found to be the only method which gives conclusive evidence; in most cases, this method has given satisfactory results.

E. Retubing Condensers

The general procedure for retubing condensers has been outlined in chapter 6 of this training course. One specific illustration of retubing a refrigerant condenser is as follows:

1. Drill into both ends of the faulty tube or tubes, with a 19/32-inch drill, to a depth of 1/16 inch less than the actual thickness of the tube sheet.

2. Insert the condenser knockout bar. Then insert, in the other end of the tube, a bar 1/2 inch x 6 inches.

3. Proceed to the other end of the condenser and drive out the faulty tube by using the knockout bar.

4. Follow the above procedure for any further tube removal.

5. Cut the new tube 1/8 inch longer than the overall length of the condenser (heads removed).

6. Both ends of the tubes must be square and all inside and outside burrs removed.

7. Insert the new tube in the condenser, leaving 1/16 of an inch protruding from each end.

8. Secure the spacing bar over one end of the tube.

9. Oil the rolling tool, insert it in the tube, and roll the tube into serrations.

10. Remove the spacing bar and roll that end of the tube by the above method.

11. Insert the belling tool and keep rotating while belling. Do not strike too hard on the belling tool.

12. After belling both ends of the tube, grind off the ends flush with the tube sheet.

13. Open the discharge line valve into the condenser, and open any other valves necessary to get gas from the compressor into the condenser.

14. Using the pressure thus obtained, test the condenser for leaks, with the halide torch.

15. If any small leaks exist, reroll the leaking tube. (Spacers are used on the rolling tool to prevent the use of maximum rolling effect on a preliminary rolling operation. Additional rolling effect may be obtained by removing one of these spacers.)

16. Reassemble the condenser.

V. EXPANSION VALVES

In order to diagnose troubles in a refrigeration plant, it is essential that the mechanic ' have a thorough understanding of the principles and ope ration of expansion valves.

A. Thermostatic Expansion Valve

FUNCTION.– The thermostatic expansion valve controls the quantity of refrigerant admitted to the cooling coil and reduces the pressure of this refrigerant to that pressure maintained in the coil. The valve also operates to feed into the coil the amount of refrigerant necessary to keep the coil working at maximum effectiveness and in accordance with heat load variation, and to prevent the flooding back of liquid refrigerant to the compressor.

OPERATION. – It is apparent that, if the suction gas leaving the cooling coil is at the saturated vapor temperature of the refrigerant and the R-12 in the control bulb is also at this temperature, the control bulb pressure transmitted to the top of the valve diaphragm will be equal to the suction pressure transmitted to the lower side of the diaphragm through the equalizing line. The valve needle will be in the closed position, because of upward pressure exerted by the valve spring. The continued operation of the compressor maintains or lowers the cooling coil suction pressure, but since the valve is closed and no liquid refrigerant is supplied to the coil, the temperature of the coil rises because of the heat absorbed from the space being cooled. The R-12 in the control bulb is in turn heated; and its pressure increases to maintain a saturated pressure corresponding to the cooling coil suction gas temperature. The pressure on top of the power element diaphragm increases, overcomes the spring pressure, and causes the valve needle to open, thus permitting the flow of refrigerant liquid into the coil.

The liquid refrigerant is evaporated during its passage through the coil. Upon leaving the outlet end, the cold vapor cools the R-12 in the control bulb and decreases the upper diaphragm pressure, tending to close the valve. This reduction in valve opening reduces the quantity of refrigerant fed to the cooling coil and permits evaporation of all the liquid before the refrigerant reaches the outlet end where the control bulb is located. The refrigerant vapor becomes superheated during its passage through that part of the coil beyond the point where all liquid is evaporated.

The amount of superheat depends on the valve spring pressure exerted on the diaphragm. For a given spring setting, the valve maintains a relatively constant degree of superheat at the coil outlet, ensuring that all R-12 liquid is evaporated before it leaves the coil to return to the compressor.

EXTERNAL EQUALIZER. – The external equalizing connection is provided for relatively large cooling coil installations where a considerable pressure loss may be expected to occur because of the length of coil travel or the distribution method. This equalizing line is connected to the cooling coil at a convenient point where the desired operating pressures will be reflected. practically equal to that at the coil outlet where the control bulb is located; in such an installation the external equalizing line is unnecessary. Instead, the expansion valve is provided with an internal equalizing port, to adjust the pressure on the lower side of the diaphragm so that it will equal the pressure at the valve outlet.

For small installations the pressure drop through the coil is correspondingly small, and the refrigerant pressure at the valve outlet.

TESTING AND ADJUSTMENT. When the thermostatic expansion valve is operating properly, the temperature at the outlet side of the valve is much lower than that at the inlet side. If this temperature difference does not exist when the system is in operation, the valve seat is probably dirty and clogged with foreign matter.

Once a valve is properly adjusted, further adjustment should not be necessary. The major trouble encountered can usually be traced to moisture or dirt collecting at the valve seat and orifice.

By means of a gear and screw arrangement, the thermostatic expansion valve is adjusted to maintain a superheat ranging approximately from $4°$ F to $12°$ F at the cooling coil outlet. The proper superheat adjustment varies with the design and service operating conditions of the valve, and the design of the particular plant. Increased spring pressure increases the degree of superheat at the coil outlet and decreased pressure has the opposite effect. Many thermostatic expansion valves are initially adjusted by the manufacturer to maintain a predetermined degree of superheat, and no provision is made for further adjustments in service.

If expansion valves are adjusted to give a high degree of superheat at the coil outlet, or if the valve is stuck shut, the amount of refrigerant admitted to the cooling coil will be reduced. With an insufficient amount of refrigerant, the coil will be "starved" and will operate at a reduced capacity. Compressor lubricating oil carried with the refrigerant may tend to collect at the bottom of the cooling coils, thus robbing the compressor crankcase, and providing a condition whereby slugs of lubricating oil may be drawn back to the compressor. If the expansion valve is adjusted for too low a degree of superheat, or

if the valve is stuck open, liquid refrigerant may flood from the cooling coils back to the compressor. Should the liquid collect at a low point in the suction line or coil, and be drawn back to the compressor intermittently in slugs, there

is danger of injury to the moving parts of the compressor.

In general, the expansion valves for air conditioning and water cooling plants (high temperature installations) must be adjusted for higher superheat than are the expansion valves for cold storage refrigeration and ship's service store equipment (low temperature installations).

If it is impossible to adjust expansion valves to the desired settings, or if it is suspected that the expansion valve assembly is defective and requires replacement, appropriate tests must be made. (First be sure that the liquid strainers are clean, that the solenoid valves are operative, and that the system is sufficiently charged with refrigerant.)

The major equipment required for expansion valve tests is as follows:

1. A service drum of R-12, or a supply of clean dry air at 70 to 100 psig. The service drum is used to supply gas under pressure. The gas used does not have to be the same as that employed in the thermal element of the valve being tested.

2. A high pressure and a low pressure gage. The low pressure gage should be accurate and in good condition so that the pointer does not have any appreciable lost motion. The high pressure gage, while not absolutely necessary, will be useful in showing the pressure on the inlet side of the valve. Refrigeration plants are provided with suitable spare and test pressure gages.

The procedure for testing is as follows:

1. Connect the valve inlet to the gas supply with the high pressure gage attached so as to indicate the gas pressure to the valve, and with the low pressure gage loosely connected to the expansion valve outlet. The low pressure gage is connected up loosely so as to provide a small amount of leakage through the connection.

2. Insert the expansion valve thermal element in a bath of crushed ice. Do not attempt to perform this test with a container full of water in which a small amount of crushed ice is floating.

3. Open the valve on the service drum or in the air supply line. Make certain that the gas supply is sufficient to build up the pressure to at least 70 psi on the high pressure gage connected in the line to the valve inlet.

4. The expansion valve can now be adjusted. If it is desired to adjust for 10° F superheat, the pressure on the outlet gage should be 22.5 psig. This is equivalent to an R-12 evaporating temperature of 22° F, and since the ice maintains the bulb at 32° F, the valve adjustment is for 10 superheat (difference between 32 and 22). For a 5 superheat adjustment, the valve should be adjusted to give a pressure of approximately 26.1 psig. There must be a small .amount of leakage through the low pressure gage connection while this adjustment is being made.

5. To determine if the valve operates smoothly, tap the valve body lightly with a small weight. The low pressure gage needle should not jump more than 1 psi.

6. Now tighten the low pressure gage connection so as to stop the leakage at the joint, and determine if the expansion valve seats tightly. With the valve in good condition, the pressure will increase a few pounds and then either stop or build up very slowly. With a leaking valve, the pressure will build up rapidly until it equals the inlet pressure.

7. Again loosen the gage so as to permit leakage at the gage connection; remove the thermal element, or control bulb, from the crushed ice, and warm it with the hand or place it in water that is at room temperature. When this is done, the pressure should increase rapidly, showing that the power element has not lost its charge. If there is no increase in pressure, the power element is dead.

8. With high pressure showing on both gages as outlined above, the valve can be tested to determine if the body joints or the bellows leak. This can be done by using a halide leak detector. When performing this test, it is important that the body of the valve have a fairly high pressure applied to it. In addition, the gages and other fittings should be made up tightly at the joints so as to eliminate leakage at these points.

REPLACEMENT OF VALVE. — If it is evident that the expansion valve is defective, it must be replaced. Often it is possible to replace a faulty power element or other part of the valve without having to replace the entire assembly. When replacement of an expansion valve is necessary, it is important to replace the unit with a valve of the same capacity and type, designed for R-12 systems.

B. Automatic Expansion Valve

Automatic expansion valves are generally similar in construction to thermostatic valves except that the thermostatic element is omitted. The refrigerant pressure in the cooling coil operates on the lower side of the diaphragm and atmospheric pressure operates on the upper side. The amount of valve opening depends upon the pressure existing in the coil. As the operation of the compressor lowers the coil pressure, there is a corresponding decrease in pressure on the lower side of the diaphragm; when this pressure becomes less than the atmospheric pressure on the upper side, the diaphragm is depressed and the valve opens. The pressure at which the valve will open can be predetermined by an adjustment of the valve. As the compressor continues to operate, the needle valve remains open enough to maintain the refrigerant evaporating pressure. When the compressor stops, the coil pressure increases and the valve automatically closes. Thermostatic expansion valves have proved to be more satisfactory than automatic expansion valves for refrigeration plant applications.

C. Hand Expansion Valve

A bypass line equipped with a manually operated expansion valve is installed around the strainer and the cooling coil liquid control valve assembly to permit repair or cleaning. The hand expansion valve is generally similar in design to the other refrigerant stop valves installed in refrigeration systems, except that the valve disk is sometimes specially shaped to permit accurate adjustment of flow. Hand expansion valves should be used only for emergency purposes, since there is the possibility of flooding liquid refrigerant back to the compressor.

D. Switches

In order to trouble-shoot or diagnose switch troubles, it is essential that you have a good understanding of pressurestats and thermostats. A pressurestat is an electric switch actuated by pressure from an outside source. The thermostat is actuated by temperature or heat on a specially prepared thermo-bulb, filled with a substance that expands and contracts with any change in temperature.

A switch that cuts out when there is an increase in pressure or temperature is known as a direct acting switch. When the pressure or temperature is decreased, the switch cuts in. The high pressure switch is a direct acting switch. A reverse acting switch is one that cuts in on an increase of pressure or temperature and cuts out on a decrease of pressure or temperature. The low pressure cutout, thermostat, and water-failure switches are reverse acting switches.

E. Evacuating and Dehydrating the System

Where moisture accumulation must be corrected, the system should first be cleared of refrigerant and air. The time required for these processes will depend upon the size of the system and the amount of moisture present. It is good engineering practice to circulate heated air through a large dehydrator and system for several hours, or as long as the dehydrator drying agent remains effective, before proceeding with the evacuation process. If possible, the dehydrated air should be heated to about $240°$ F.

Large dehydrators, suitable for preliminary dehydration of R-12 systems, are usually available at naval shipyards, and aboard tenders and repair ships.

After the preliminary dehydration, remaining moisture is evacuated by means of a two-stage high-efficiency vacuum pump having a vacuum indicator. (These vacuum pumps are available aboard tenders and repair ships.)

The vacuum indicator shown in figure 10-1 consists of an insulated test tube containing a wet bulb thermometer with its wick immersed in distilled water. The indicator is connected in the vacuum pump suction line. The suction line from the vacuum pump is connected to the charging connection in the refrigeration system. The refrigerant circuit should be closed to the atmosphere and the charging connection opened to the vacuum pump.

A two-stage pump is started for operation in parallel so that maximum displacement may be secured during the initial pumpdownstages. When the indicator shows a temperature of about $55°$ F (0.43 inch Hg, absolute), the pumps are placed in series operation (wherein the discharge from the first step enters the suction of the second step pump). The dehydration process will be reflected in the temperature drop of the vacuum indicator, as shown in figure 10-2. Readings will initially reflect ambient temperatures, then show rapidly falling temperatures until the water in the system starts to boil.

When most of the evaporated moisture has been evacuated from the system, the indicator will show a decrease in temperature. When the temperature reaches $35°$ F (0.2 inch Hg, absolute), open the system at a point farthest from the pump; at this point, air should be drawn into the system through a chemical dehydrator, and meanwhile the pump should be operated to permit dilution of moisture present in the system. Close off the opening and re-evacuate until the indicator again shows a temperature of $35°$ F. At this point the dehydration process is complete; close the charging valve and then stop the pump.

Sometimes it will be impossible to obtain a temperature as low as 35° F in the vacuum indicator; the probable reasons for such a failure, and the corrective procedures to take, are as follows:

1. Presence of excess moisture in the system. The dehydration procedure should be conducted for longer periods.

2. Presence of absorbed refrigerant in the lubricating oil contained in the compressor crankcase. Remove the lubricating oil from the crankcase before proceeding with the dehydration process.

3. Leakage of air into the system. The leak must be found and stopped. It will be necessary to repeat the procedure required for detecting leaks in the system.

4. Inefficient vacuum pump or defective vacuum indicator. The defective unit(s) should be repaired or replaced.

F. Reactivating the Drying System

Immediately after each period of use, or after the system has been opened for repairs, the drying agent in the dehydrator should be replaced. If a replacement cartridge is not available, the drying agent can be reactivated and used until a replacement is available.

Reactivation is accomplished by removing the drying agent and heating it, for 12 hours, to a temperature of 300° F to bake out the moisture. The drying agent may be placed in an oven, or a stream of hot air may be circulated through the cartridge. These methods are satisfactory for reactivating commonly used dehydrating agents such as activated alumina and silica gel. Where special drying agents are employed, they should be reactivated in accordance with specific instructions furnished by the manufacturer.

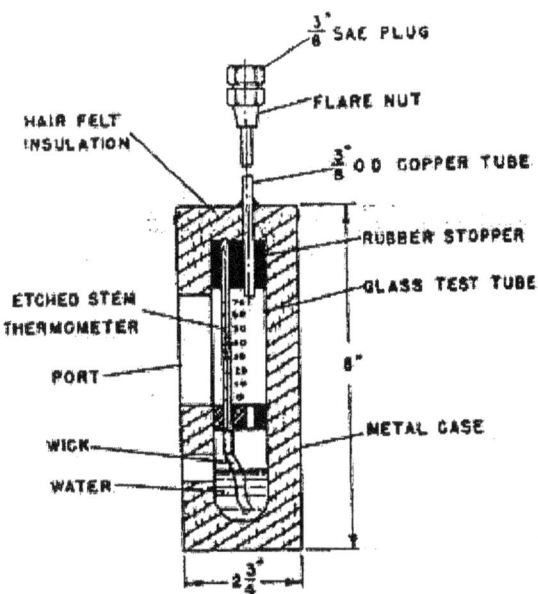

Figure 1.—Dehydrator vacuum indicator.

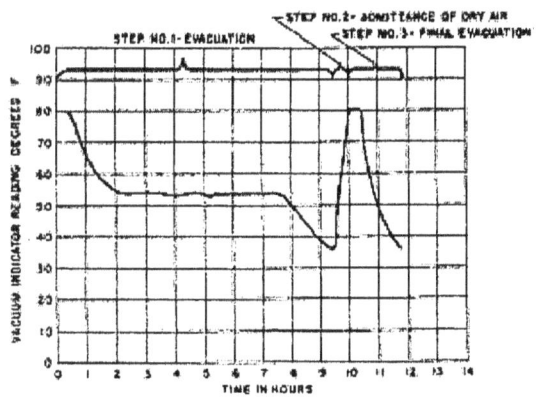

Figure 2.—Vacuum indicator readings plotted during dehydration.

After reactivation, the drying agent should be replaced in the dehydrator shell and sealed as quickly as possible, in order to prevent absorption of atmospheric moisture. When the drying agent becomes fouled or saturated with lubricating oil, it must be replaced by a fresh spare charge, or dehydrator cartridge, taken from a sealed container.

Remember that the dehydrators permanently installed in R-12 systems for naval ships are designed to remove only the minute quantities of moisture unavoidably introduced into the system. Extreme care must be taken to prevent moisture, or moisture-laden air, from entering the system.

G. Cleaning The System

Systems may accumulate dirt and scale as a result of improper techniques used during repair or installation. If such dirt is excessive and a tank-type cleaner is available, connect the cleaner to the compressor suction strainer. Where such a cleaner is not available, a hard wool felt filter, about 5/16 inch thick, should be inserted in the suction strainer screen. The plant should be operated with an operator in attendance, for at least 36 hours or until cleaned, depending upon the size and condition of the plant.

IV. DETECTING AND CORRECTING TROUBLES

Faulty operation of the refrigerating plant is indicated by various definite symptoms. These symptoms may indicate the presence of one or more conditions in the plant. Each condition must be eliminated by specific corrective measures. Space does not permit a detailed discussion here of abnormal plant conditions, but you can find complete information in the manufacturer's technical manual furnished with each refrigeration plant.

The following chart, listing symptoms, their causes, and the corrective measures to be taken, will assist you in correcting faulty operation quickly and efficiently.

| A. Trouble-Diagnosis Chart |||
Symptom or difficulty	Condition may be due to	Correction
High suction pressure	Overfeeding of expansion valve	Regulate expansion valve, check thermal element attachment.
	Leaky suction valves	Examine valve disks, or piston rings; replace if defective.
	Improper functioning of low-pressure control switch Discharge valves leak slightly	Readjust or replace switch. Examine valves. If leaking, replace if necessary.
Low suction pressure	Restricted liquid line, expansion valve, or suction strainers	Remove, examine, and clean strainers.
	Insufficient refrigerant in system	Check for refrigerant shortage.
	Too much oil circulating in system	Check for too much oil in circulation. Remove oil. (See "Oil leaves crank-case.") Adjust valve to give more flow.
	Improper adjustment of expansion valves	
	Coils in refrigerators clogged with frost	Defrost coils.
	Thermal bulb of expansion valve has lost charge	Detach thermal bulb from suction line and hold in the palm of one hand, with the other hand gripping the suction line; if flooding through is observed, bulb has not lost its charge. If no flooding through is noticed, test and replace expansion valve if necessary.
	Forced air cooler airflow restricted or fan inoperative One or more solenoid valves closed Compressor capacity in excess of existing compartment heat load	Check for air obstruction, dirty filters, or faulty electrical operation. Check electrical solenoid circuit for failure, and repair. Reduce speed of compressor or adjust compressor capacity reduction where provided.
Low suction line temperature	Excessive liquid refrigerant circulating in system	Check expansion valve adjustment and regulate.
High suction line temperature	Shortage of refrigerant in system	Check, test for leaks and add refrigerant as required.

Trouble-Diagnosis Chart — Continued

Symptom or difficulty	Condition may be due to	Correction
High discharge pressure	Air or noncondensable gas in system Inlet water warm No water or insufficient quantity of water flowing through condenser Condenser tubes clogged Too much refrigerant in system (condenser tubes submerged in liquid refrigerant) Condenser improperly vented Air-cooled condenser dirty or receiving insufficient air	Purge air from condenser. Increase quantity by adjusting water-regulating valve. Adjust water-regulating valve, open manual valves, or start pump. Clean condenser tubes and water boxes. Draw off excess refrigerant into service drum. Vent condenser water boxes. Clean or remove obstructions. Check space ventilation for adequate supply of cool air and correct.
Low discharge pressure	Too much water flowing through condenser Water too cold or unthrottled Liquid refrigerant flooding back from cooling coils Leaky discharge valve	Regulate water valve. Reduce quantity of water. Change expansion valve adjustment, examine fastening thermal element. Examine. If leaking, replace.
High discharge temperature	Air or noncondensable gas in system	Purge air from condenser.

Trouble-Diagnosis Chart — Continued		
Symptom or difficulty	Condition may be due to	Correction
Low discharge temperature	Excessive liquid refrigerant in system	Check expansion valve setting and adjust.
Low oil pressure	Dirt in oil pump or strainer	Stop compressor. Check oil gage for accuracy. Clean, repair, or replace oil strainer and pump.
Excessive oil pressure	Clogged oil distribution lines	Stop compressor. Check oil gage for accuracy. Pump down, clean oil lines.
Oil leaves crankcase	Refrigerant flooding back to compressor Leaking piston rings or worn cylinder Expansion valves leaking Overcharge of oil	Adjust expansion valve and check for proper mounting of thermal elements. Replace rings, cylinder sleeves, or compressor. Rebore and refit. Valve seats and stem may be corroded from passage of refrigerant vapor. Check and replace if required. Check oil sight glass and remove excess. Check for continuing return and repeat process until oil level is constant.
Oil does not return to crankcase	Expansion valve not supplying cooling coil with sufficient refrigerant Valve in oil return line closed or stuck shut Oil trap or pocket in cooling coil or suction line piping	Check operation of expansion valve and adjust, if required. Open. Locate, open, and drain.
Oil sight glass shows presence of oil foaming	Excessive liquid refrigerant returning to compressor	Check expansion valve adjustment or leaking hand expansion valves. Adjust, repair, or replace.
Crankcase and cylinder temperature relatively warm with low suction pressure	Shortage of refrigerant	Test for shortage, add refrigerant if required, test for leaks.
Crankcase temperature relatively cooler than suction line with low pressure suction	Excessive oil is circulating in system	See "Oil leaves crankcase."
Crankcase and cylinder temperature relatively cold, sweating, or frosting	Liquid refrigerant being returned to compressor	Check expansion valve setting, adjust. Check for proper mounting of thermal element.
Compressor noisy	Vibration because the compressor is not rigidly	Bolt down rigidly.

Trouble-Diagnosis Chart — Continued		
Symptom or difficulty	Condition may be due to	Correction
Compressor noisy— (Continued)	bolted to foundation Too much oil in circulation causing hydraulic knock Slugging due to flooding back of refrigerant Wear of parts such as piston pins, bearings, etc.	Check oil level. Expansion valve open too wide; adjust. Thermo-bulb incorrectly placed or loose; check and relocate or fasten. Determine location of cause. Repair compressor.
Water supply pressure too low	Water pump suction line restricted Pressure-reducing valve in fire flushing line improperly adjusted	Check for closed valves, check strainer and clean. Check and readjust.
Water supply pressure too high	Pressure-reducing valve improperly adjusted Water valves open too wide.	Check and adjust. Check and close to proper pressure.
Water overboard temperature too low	Excessive water flow through condenser	Correlate with discharge pressure and check water regulating valve operation, adjust if necessary. (See "Water supply pressure too high.")
Water overboard temperature too high	Restricted water flow through condenser	Correlate with discharge pressure. Check water-regulating valve and adjust, if necessary. (See "Water supply pressure too low.")
Liquid line refrigerant temperature too warm	High condensing temperature	Check condenser for water quantity.
Liquid line refrigerant temperature too cold	Shortage of refrigerant Excessive oil in circulation	Test for shortage, charge with refrigerant, test for R-12 leakage. See "Oil leaves crankcase."
Sight flow indicator shows bubbles in refrigerant	Shortage of refrigerant	Test for shortage, charge with refrigerant, test for R-12 leakage.
Ice-making tank temperature too high	Automatic controls not functioning Brine solution too weak and freezing	Check electrical circuit for open switches, blown fuses, burnt solenoid coil, and repair or replace. Check adjustment of control switch. Check salinity of brine for proper density. Add stronger solution.

Trouble-Diagnosis Chart Continued		
Symptom or difficulty	Condition may be due to	Correction
Ice-making tank temperature too high (Continued)	Expansion valve not feeding sufficient refrigerant	Check for improper adjustment, or moisture at valve orifice. Adjust or clean. Put dehydrator in operation if moisture is in evidence.
Ice-making tank temperature too low	Automatic controls not functioning Hand expansion valve leaking	Check solenoid valve switch setting and adjust if necessary. Check position of valve for tight closing. Check for dirt or corrosion at seat and pin. Clean, repair, or replace.
Compartment temperature too high	Automatic controls not functioning Excessive frost on cooling coils Expansion valve not feeding sufficient refrigerant Airflow restricted on forced air coolers Excessive infiltration of uncooled air	Check solenoid valve switch or thermostat setting, electrical circuit, fuses, and solenoid coil. Repair or replace. If there is a forced air cooler, check to see that fan is operating. Defrost. Check for improper adjustment, or moisture at valve orifice. Adjust or clean. Put dehydrator in operation if moisture is present. Check filters, duct work obstructions, and fan operation. Clean and repair as required. Check unwarranted traffic in and out of compartment. Take steps to limit traffic as to personnel and entrance periods. Check compartment openings and door gaskets. Repair or replace.
	Introduction of warm and/or moist product	Temporary. If within the capacity of equipment, temperature will eventually return to normal. Start an additional compressor if system is arranged for isolating loads carried by more than one unit in operation.

Compartment temperature too low	Automatic controls not functioning Hand expansion valve leaking	Check solenoid valve switch or thermostat setting, electrical circuit, fuses, and solenoid coils. Repair or replace. Check position of valve for tight closing. Check for dirt, or corrosion at seat and pin. Clean, repair, or replace.
Liquid refrigerant cycling through the cooling coil with wide variation in superheat at thermal element location	Excessive oil circulating through system Moisture or ice at thermal element contact with	Check other symptoms for a like condition. (See "Oil leaves crankcase" and "Oil does not return to crankcase.") Remove, dry, and properly insulate.

Trouble-Diagnosis Chart Continued

Symptom or difficulty	Condition may be due to	Correction
Liquid refrigerant cycling through the cooling coil with wide variation in superheat at thermal element location (Continued)	suction line affecting true operation Expansion valve defective Thermal element located in such a position as to be affected by airflow Expansion valve too large or has improper thermo-static charge Moisture in expansion valve port or working parts	Check thermal element for response. Repair or replace. Remove and relocate; insulate. See technical manual furnished with equipment for selected size and type. Install proper valve. Check heat valve body slowly taking care not to damage power element and gaskets. Heat will temporarily free valve parts and resume automatic operation. If moisture is present disassemble valve, clean and replace. Put dehy-drator into service.
Liquid refrigerant carrying through the coil and far beyond the thermal element location with little superheat at this point	Expansion valve open too wide Thermal element making poor contact with suction piping Thermal element improperly located or insulated. Expansion valve leaking	Adjust to close. Remove, clean both surfaces, and insulate. Remove, locate properly, and insulate. When compressor shuts down, check by listening at valve for a hissing sound. Check for dirt or corrosion of seat. Clean, repair, or replace.
Liquid refrigerant carrying partially through the coil with considerable superheat at thermal element location	Moisture in expansion valve port or working parts Liquid line strainer clogged or dirty Expansion valve improperly adjusted Shortage of refrigerant Expansion valve thermal element improperly located Expansion valve too small Refrigerant gas in liquid line	See same condition and correction as above. Remove, clean, and replace. Check superheat and adjust. Check storage, test for leaks and charge. Check and relocate. See technical manual furnished with equipment, and install proper size and type. Check for excessive pressure loss in liquid line. Open valves or restrictions affecting loss. Check sub-cooler, if installed, for proper operation.

Trouble-Diagnosis Chart Continued		
Symptom or difficulty	Condition may be due to	Correction
Liquid refrigerant carrying partially through the coil with considerable superheat at thermal element location- (Continued)	Pressure drop through cooling coils excessive Expansion valve power element has lost charge of refrigerant Expansion valve equalizer line closed or restricted Expansion valve thermal element being affected by refrigerant from another cooling coil circuit	Check for restrictions, oil traps or valves partially closed. Drain oil or open restrictions as applicable. Remove thermal element and hand-warm to body temperature. If not responsive, replace power assembly or valve. Check, and open or replace. Check location of thermal element. Remove and properly locate.
Compressor will not start	Overload tripped, fuses blown Switch out No charge of gas in system operated by low-pressure control switch Solenoid valves closed No flow of circulating water through condenser to actuate water-failure switch	Reset overload, replace fuses, and examine for cause of condition. Throw in switch. With no gas in system there is insufficient pressure to throw in low-pressure control. Recharge system with refrigerant; check and repair leaks. Examine coil, switch, etc.; if defective or out of adjustment, replace or adjust. Provide condenser circulating water.
Compressor runs continuously	Shortage of refrigerant Discharge or suction valves leak badly Head gasket blown between cylinders Improper functioning of low-pressure control switch Overloaded compressor Stuck-open or leaky relief valve	Test for shortage of refrigerant; if insufficient, add proper amount. Test system for leaks. Test valves; if leaking, repair or replace. Replace gasket. Adjust or replace switch. Start an additional compressor if system is arranged for isolating loads carried by more than one unit in operation. Overhaul relief valve.
Compressor short cycles on high pressure cutout	High pressure cutout incorrectly set.	Check setting of high pressure cutout; switch should throw out at about 150 pounds head pressure.

Trouble-Diagnosis Chart Continued		
Symptom or difficulty	Condition may be due to	Correction
Compressor short cycles on low-pressure control switch	Low-pressure control incorrectly set. (See "Low suction pressure.")	Check setting and adjust.
Water valve chatters	Water pressure too high	Reduce water pressure by adjusting water pressure-reducing valve or throttling stop valve.
Water runs continuously when compressor *is* shut off	Water-regulating valve open too wide Dirt under seat of water-regulating valve Valve mechanism stuck Pump motor controller contact stuck shut	Readjust valve to give correct head pressures corresponding to water inlet temperature and condensing pressure. Remove valve from lines, disassemble, and examine; replace defective parts, clean and reassemble. If valve then does not function properly, replace. Remove and disassemble. Clean valve seats and valve pins, lubricate, adjust packing, etc. Adjust
Head gasket leaks	Head bolts stretched, or washers crushed Oil or refrigerant slugging	Examine gaskets; replace if necessary. Tighten head bolts. Replace washers. Check operating conditions for flooding of refrigerant back to compressor. Correct.
Oil seepage at shaft seal connection is excessive	Failure of shaft seal	Test, repair, or replace crankshaft seal.
Oil seepage at refrigerant system piping and compressor connections	Leakage of refrigerant	Test; remake connections or provide replacement gaskets, as required.

REFRIGERATION AND AIR CONDITIONING TERMINOLOGY AND TROUBLESHOOTING

TABLE OF CONTENTS

		Page
A.	TERMINOLOGY	
	Absolute Pressure ... Bimetallic Element	1
	Boiling Point ... Conduction	2
	Conductor (Heat or Thermal) ... Equalizer	3
	Evaporation ... Humidistat	4
	Humidity ... Saturated Liquid	5
	Saturated Vapor ... Wet-Bulb Depression	6
B.	TROUBLESHOOTING	7

REFRIGERATION AND AIR CONDITIONING

TERMINOLOGY AND TROUBLESHOOTING

A. TERMINOLOGY

Many of the terms used in connection with refrigeration and air conditioning have quite definite and specialized meanings. In order to understand any written material in the field of refrigeration and air conditioning, it is essential to have a thorough knowledge of correct terminology. Some important terms used in connection with refrigeration and air conditioning are defined in the following list.

ABSOLUTE PRESSURE.—Pressure measured from absolute zero rather than from normal atmospheric pressure; the sum of atmospheric pressure plus gage pressure.

ABSOLUTE TEMPERATURE.—Temperature measured from absolute zero (-459.67° F, or -273.15°'C).

ABSORBENT.—A material that has the ability to extract certain substances from a liquid or a gas with which it is in contact, causing physical changes, chemical changes, or both during the absorption process.

ACCUMULATOR.—A shell placed in a suction line for separating liquid refrigerant entrained in suction gas; serves as a storage chamber for low side liquid refrigerant; also known as a surge drum or surge header.

ADIABATIC PROCESS.—Any thermodynamic process that is accomplished without the transfer of heat to or from the system while the process is occurring.

ADSORBENT.—A material that has the ability to cause molecules of gases, liquids, and solids to adhere to its internal surfaces without causing any chemical or physical change.

AIR CONDITIONING.—The process of treating air to simultaneously control its temperature, humidity, cleanliness, and distribution to meet the requirements of the conditioned space.

AIR CONDITIONING UNIT.—An assembly of equipment for the control of (at least) the temperature, humidity, and cleanliness of the air within a conditioned space.

AIR DIFFUSER.—A device arranged to promote the mixing of the air leaving the duct with the room air.

AMBIENT AIR TEMPERATURE.—The temperature of the air surrounding an object; in a system using an air-cooled condenser, the temperature of the air entering the condenser.

ANEMOMETER.—An instrument for measuring the velocity of air flow.

ATMOSPHERIC PRESSURE.—Pressure exerted by the weight of the atmosphere; standard atmospheric pressure is 14.696 psia or 29.921 inches of mercury at sea level.

BACK PRESSURE.—Same as suction pressure.

BAFFLE.—A partition to direct the flow of a fluid.

BAROMETER.—An instrument for measuring atmospheric pressure.

BAROMETRIC PRESSURE.—The actual atmospheric pressure existing at any given moment; at certain times, barometric pressure is not identical with standard atmospheric pressure.

BIMETALLIC ELEMENT.—A device formed from two different metals having different

TERMINOLOGY AND TROUBLESHOOTING

coefficients of thermal expansion; used in temperature indicating and controlling instruments.

BOILING POINT.—Temperature at which a liquid boils at a given pressure.

BORE.—Inside diameter of a cylinder.

BRINE.—Any liquid cooled by the refrigerant and used for the transmission of heat without change of state.

BRITISH THERMAL UNIT.—The amount of heat required to produce a temperature rise of 1° F in 1 pound of water. Abbreviated Btu.

CENTIGRADE.—A thermometric system in which the freezing point of water is 0° C and the boiling point of water is 100° C, at standard atmospheric pressure.

CENTRAL FAN SYSTEM.—A mechanical, indirect system of air conditioning in which the air is treated by equipment outside the area served and is conveyed to and from the area by means of a fan and a distributing duct system.

CENTRIFUGAL MACHINE.—A compressor employing centrifugal force for compression.

CHANGE OF AIR.—The introduction of new, cleansed, or recirculated air to conditioned spaces, measured in the number of complete air changes in a specified time.

CHANGE OF STATE.—The change from one phase (solid, liquid, or gas) to another.

CHARGE.—The amount of refrigerant in a system; also the act of putting refrigerant into a system.

CHILL.—To refrigerate meats, water, etc., moderately, without freezing.

COEFFICIENT OF EXPANSION.—The change in length per unit length per degree of change in temperature of a material; or the change in volume per unit volume per degree of change in temperature of a material.

COEFFICIENT OF PERFORMANCE.—The ratio of the refrigeration produced to the work supplied, with refrigeration and work being expressed in the same units.

COIL.—Any cooling or heating element made of pipe or tubing.

COMFORT CHART.—A chart showing effective temperature, with dry-bulb temperature and humidity, by which the effects of various conditions on human comfort may be determined.

COMFORT COOLING.—Refrigeration for comfort, as opposed to refrigeration for manufacture or storage.

COMFORT ZONE.—The range of effective temperatures over which the majority of adults feel comfortable.

COMPRESSION, MULTI-STAGE. — Compression in two or more stages, as when the discharge of one compressor is connected to the suction of another.

COMPRESOR, HERMETIC.—A compressor in which the electric motor and the compressor are enclosed within a sealed housing.

COMPRESSOR, "V" AND "W".—High speed, single-acting, multi-cylinder compressor with straight-line piston movement in the various cylinders; the cylinders are in the "V" position or the "W" position with respect to the shaft axis.

CONDENSATE.—The liquid formed by the condensation of a vapor. In steam heating, water condensed from steam; in air conditioning, water removed from air by condensation on the cooling coil of a refrigeration system.

CONDENSATION.—The process by which a vapor changes to a liquid when heat is removed from the vapor.

CONDENSER.—A vessel or an arrangement of pipe or tubing in which the compressed refrigerant vapor is liquefied by the removal of heat.

CONDENSING UNIT.—A specific refrigerating machine combination for a given refrigerant; the unit consists of one or more power-driven compressors, condensers, liquid receivers (when required), and the necessary accessories.

CONDUCTION.—The method of heat transfer by which heat is transferred from molecule to

REFRIGERATION AND AIR CONDITIONING

molecule within a homogeneous substance or between two substances that are in physical contact with each other.

CONDUCTOR (HEAT OR THERMAL).—A material that readily transmits heat by conduction; the opposite of an insulator.

CONTROL.—Any device for the regulation of a machine in normal operation. May be manual or automatic; if automatic, it is responsive to changes in temperature, pressure, liquid level, time, or other variables.

CONVECTION.—The movement of a mass of fluid (liquid or gas) caused by differences in density in different parts of the fluid; the differences in density are caused by differences in temperature. As the fluid moves, it carries with it its contained heat energy, which is then transferred from one part of the fluid to another and from the fluid to the surroundings.

COOLER, OIL.—A heat exchanger used for cooling oil in a lubrication system.

COOLING TOWER.—A device for lowering the temperature of water by evaporative cooling, as the water is showered through a space in which outside air is circulated.

COOLING WATER.—Water used in a condenser to cool and condense a refrigerant.

COPPER PLATING.—The depositing of a film of copper on the surface of another metal (such as iron or steel) by electrochemical action; in refrigeration, copper plating usually occurs on compressor walls, pistons, discharge valves, shafts, and seals.

COUNTERFLOW.—In a heat exchanger, opposite direction of flow of the cooling liquid and the cooled liquid (or of the heating liquid and the heated liquid).

CRYOGENICS.—The branch of physics that relates to the production and the effects of very low temperatures.

CYCLE.—The complete course of operation of a refrigerant, from starting point back to starting point, in a closed refrigeration system; also, a general term for any repeated process in any system.

DEGREE.—Unit of temperature.

DEGREE OF SUPERHEAT.—The amount by which the temperature of a superheated vapor exceeds the temperature of the saturated vapor at the same pressure.

DEHUMIDIFIER.—An air cooler or washer used for lowering the moisture content of the air passing through it.

DEHUMIDIFY.—To reduce, by any process, the quantity of water vapor within a given space.

DEHYDRATE.—To remove water (in any form) from some other substance.

DENSITY.—Mass per unit volume or weight per unit volume.

DESICCANT.—Any absorbent or adsorbent, liquid or solid, that removes water or water vapor from a material. In a refrigeration circuit, the desiccant should be insoluble in the refrigerant and refrigerant oils.

DEWPOINT.—The temperature at which water vapor begins to condense in any given sample of air; dewpoint depends upon humidity, temperature, and pressure.

DISTRIBUTOR.—A device for guiding the flow of liquid into parallel paths in an evaporator.

DRIER.—A device containing a desiccant placed in a refrigerant circuit for the purpose of collecting and holding within the desiccant all water in the system above the amount that can be tolerated in the circulating refrigerant.

ELECTROLYSIS.—Chemical decomposition caused by action of an electric current in a solution.

ENTHALPY.—A term used to mean TOTAL HEAT or HEAT CONTENT.

EQUALIZER.—Piping arrangement on an enclosed compressor to equalize refrigerant gas pressure in the crankcase and suction; device for dividing the liquid refrigerant between parallel low-side coils; a piping arrangement to divide the lubricating oil between the crankcases of compressors operating in parallel; the method by which refrigerant pressure is

TERMINOLOGY AND TROUBLESHOOTING

transmitted to the diaphragm or bellows of a thermostatic expansion valve.

EVAPORATION.—The change of state from the liquid phase to the vapor phase.

EVAPORATOR.—The unit in a refrigeration system in which the refrigerant is vaporized to produce refrigeration.

EXFILTRATION.—The flow of air outward from a space through walls, leaks, etc.

EXPANSION VALVE SUPERHEAT.—The difference between the temperature of the thermal bulb and the temperature corresponding to the pressure at the coil outlet or at the equalizer connection (where provided).

FAHRENHEIT.—Thermometric scale in which 32° F denotes the freezing point of water and 212° F denotes the boiling temperature of water under standard atmospheric pressure at sea level.

FIN.—An extended surface used on tubes in some heat exchangers to increase the heat transfer area.

FLASH CHAMBER.—A separation tank placed between the expansion valve and the evaporator in a refrigeration system to separate and bypass any flash gas formed in the expansion valve.

FLASH GAS.—The gas resulting from the instantaneous evaporation of refrigerant in a pressure-reducing device, to cool the refrigerant to the evaporating temperature corresponding to the reduced pressure.

FLUID.—The general term that includes liquids and gases (or vapors).

FOAMING.—The formation of a foam or froth on an oil-refrigerant mixture; caused by a reduction in pressure with consequent rapid boiling out of the refrigerant.

FREEZING.—The change of state from the liquid phase to the solid phase.

GAGE PRESSURE.—Absolute pressure minus atmospheric pressure.

GAS.—A substance in the gaseous state; a highly superheated vapor that satisfies the perfect gas laws, within acceptable limits of accuracy. See VAPOR.

GAS, INERT.—A gas that does not readily enter into or cause chemical reactions.

GAS, NONCONDENSABLE.—A gas in a refrigeration system which does not condense at the temperature and partial pressure existing in the condenser, thereby exerting a higher head pressure on the system.

GRILLE.—A lattice or grating for an intake opening or a delivery opening.

HEAD PRESSURE.—The operating pressure measured in the discharge line at the compressor outlet.

HEAT.—A basic form of energy, which is transferred by virtue of a temperature difference.

HEAT OF CONDENSATION.—The latent heat given up by a substance as it changes from a gas to a liquid.

HEAT OF FUSION.—The latent heat absorbed when a substance changes from a solid state to a liquid state.

HEAT OF VAPORIZATION.—The latent heat absorbed by a substance as it changes from a liquid to a vapor.

HEAT PUMP.—Refrigeration equipment; used for year-round air conditioning. In summer used to cool and condition the air in a space; in winter used to warm and condition the air.

HOT-GAS DEFROSTING.—The use of high pressure or condenser gas in the low side or condenser gas in the evaporator to effect the removal of frost.

HUMIDIFY.—To increase the percentage of water vapor within a given space.

HUMIDISTAT.—A control instrument or device, actuated by changes in humidity within the conditioned areas, which automatically regulates the relative humidity of the area.

REFRIGERATION AND AIR CONDITIONING

HUMIDITY.—The water vapor within a given space.

HUMIDITY, SPECIFIC.—The weight of water vapor mixed with 1 pound of dry air, expressed as the number of grains of moisture per pound of dry air.

HYDROLYSIS.—The splitting up of compounds by reaction with water. For example, the reaction of R-12 with water which results in the formation of acid materials.

INDUSTRIAL AIR CONDITIONING.—Air conditioning used for purposes other than comfort.

JACKET WATER.—The water used to cool the cylinder head and cylinder walls of a water-cooled compressor.

LATENT HEAT.—Heat transfer that is NOT reflected in a temperature change but IS reflected in a changing physical state of the substance involved.

LIQUEFACTION.—The change of state from a gas to a liquid. (The term liquefaction is usually used instead of condensation when referring to substances which are in a gaseous state at ordinary pressures and temperatures.)

LIQUID LINE.—The tube or pipe through which liquid refrigerant is carried from the condenser or receiver to the pressure-reducing device.

LIQUID RECEIVER.—A vessel permanently connected to the high side of a system for the storage of liquefied refrigerant.

LOAD.—The amount of heat imposed upon a refrigeration system in any specified period of time, or the required rate of heat removal; usually expressed in Btu per hour.

LOW SIDE.—The parts of the refrigeration system that are at or below the evaporating temperature.

MANOMETER.—A U-tube, or a single tube and reservoir arrangement, used with a suitable fluid to measure pressure differences.

MELTING.—The change of state from a solid to a liquid.

OZONE.—Triatomic oxygen (O_3). Sometimes used in cold storage or air conditioning installations as an odor eliminator. Can be toxic in certain concentrations.

PLENUM CHAMBER.—An air compartment maintained under pressure for receiving air before distribution to the conditioned spaces.

PNEUMATIC.—Operated by air pressure.

PREHEATING.—In air conditioning, to heat the air in advance of other processes.

PRESSURE.—Force per unit area.

PRESSURE DROP.—Loss of pressure, as from one end of a refrigerant line to the other, because of friction.

PRESSURE EQUALIZING.—Allowing the high side and the low side of the refrigeration system to become equal or nearly equal in pressure during idle periods, to prevent excessive starting loads on the compressor.

PRESSURE REGULATOR, SUCTION.—An automatic valve designed to limit the suction pressure to prevent motor overload.

PSYCHROMETER.—An instrument for measuring relative humidities by means of wet-bulb and dry-bulb temperatures.

PSYCHROMETRIC CHART.—A graphical representation of the properties of water vapor and air mixtures.

PURGING.—The act of blowing out gas from a refrigeration system, usually for the purpose of removing air or other noncondensable gases.

REFRIGERATION TON.—The removal of heat at a rate of 288,000 Btu in 24 hours or 12,000 Btu in 1 hour.

RETURN AIR.—The air returned from a space being conditioned.

SATURATED LIQUID.—A liquid which is at saturation pressure and saturation temperature; in other words, a liquid which is at its boiling point for any given pressure.

TERMINOLOGY AND TROUBLESHOOTING

SATURATED VAPOR.—A vapor which is at saturation pressure and saturation temperature. A saturated vapor cannot be superheated as long as it is in contact with the liquid from which it is being generated.

SATURATION PRESSURE and SATURATION TEMPERATURE.—The pressure and temperature at which a liquid and the vapor it is generating can exist in equilibrium contact with each other. The boiling point of any liquid depends upon pressure and temperature; a liquid boils when it is at the saturation temperature for any particular saturation pressure.

SELF-CONTAINED UNIT.—A refrigeration unit that can be removed from the premises without disconnecting any refrigerant-containing part.

SENSIBLE HEAT.—Heat transfer that is reflected in a change of temperature.

SILICA GEL.—A form of silicon dioxide which absorbs moisture readily; used as a drying agent.

SPECIFIC GRAVITY.—The density of a substance compared to the density of a standard material such as water.

SPECIFIC VOLUME.—The space occupied by unit amount of a substance at a specified pressure and temperature; often measured in cubic feet per pound.

SUBCOOLED LIQUID.—A liquid that is at a temperature below its boiling point for any given pressure.

SUBCOOLING.—The process of cooling a liquid to a temperature below its saturation temperature for any given saturation pressure.

SUPERHEATING.—The process of adding heat to a vapor in order to raise its temperature above saturation temperature. It is impossible to superheat a saturated vapor as long as it is in contact with the liquid from which it is being generated; hence the vapor must be led away from the liquid before it can be superheated.

TEMPERATURE.—A measure of the concentration of heat (thermal energy) in a body or substance.

THERMODYNAMICS.—The branch of physics that deals with heat and its transformations to and from other forms of energy.

THERMOSTAT.—A temperature-sensing automatic control device.

TOXIC.—Having temporary or permanent poisonous effects.

TUBE, CAPILLARY.—In refrigeration, a tube of small internal diameter used as a liquid refrigerant flow control or expansion device between the high side and the low side of the refrigeration system.

UNLOADER.—A device in or on the compressor for equalizing high-side and low-side pressures for a brief time during starting and for controlling compressor capacity by rendering one or more cylinders ineffective.

VACUUM.—Pressure that is less than atmospheric pressure.

VALVE, KING.—A stop valve between the receiver and the expansion valve, normally close to the receiver.

VAPOR.—A gaseous substance, particularly one that is at or near saturation temperature and pressure.

VENTILATION.—The process of supplying or removing air by natural or mechanical means, to or from a space; such air may or may not have been conditioned.

VITAL HEAT.—The heat generated by fruits and vegetables in storage; caused by ripening.

VOLATILE LIQUID.—A liquid that evaporates (vaporizes) readily at atmospheric pressure and room temperature.

WATER (OR BRINE) COOLER.—A factory-made assembly or elements in which the water or brine and the refrigerant are in heat transfer relationship causing the refrigerant to evaporate and absorb heat from the water or brine.

WATER VAPOR.—In air conditioning, the water in the atmosphere.

WET-BULB DEPRESSION.—The difference between the dry-bulb temperature and the wet-bulb temperature.

REFRIGERATION AND AIR CONDITIONING

B. TROUBLESHOOTING

The two trouble charts that follow may be used as a guide for locating and correcting malfunctions in refrigeration systems. The first chart deals with troubles that may be encountered in vapor compression systems. The second chart deals with troubles that may be encountered in absorption-type (lithium bromide) systems. If the points and procedures outlined in these charts are closely adhered to, a great deal of time can be saved in troubleshooting.

To use these charts, the first thing to do is to isolate the trouble. Then check all possible causes. And finally, make the indicated corrections. In general, the correction of a malfunction is a process of elimination. The easiest corrections should be made first; then, if necessary, the more difficult corrections should be made.

TERMINOLOGY AND TROUBLESHOOTING

Trouble	Possible Cause	Corrective Measure
High condensing pressure.	Air on non-condensable gas in system.	Purge air from condenser.
	Inlet water warm.	Increase quantity of condensing water.
	Insufficient water flowing through condenser.	Increase quantity of water.
	Condenser tubes clogged or scaled.	Clean condenser water tubes.
	Too much liquid in receiver, condenser tubes submerged in liquid refrigerant.	Draw off liquid into service cylinder.
Low condensing pressure.	Too much water flowing through condenser.	Reduce quantity of water.
	Water too cold.	Reduce quantity of water.
	Liquid refrigerant flooding back from evaporator.	Change expansion valve adjustment, examine fastening of thermal bulb.
	Leaky discharge valve.	Remove head, examine valves. Replace any found defective.
High suction pressure.	Overfeeding of expansion valve.	Regulate expansion valve, check bulb attachment.
	Leaky suction valve.	Remove head, examine valve and replace if worn.
Low suction pressure.	Restricted liquid line and expansion valve or suction screens.	Pump down, remove, examine and clean screens.
	Insufficient refrigerant in system.	Check for refrigerant storage.
	Too much oil circulating in system.	Check for too much oil in circulation. Remove oil.
	Improper adjustment of expansion valves.	Adjust valve to give more flow.
	Expansion valve power element dead or weak.	Replace expansion valve power element.

Trouble Chart for Vapor Compression Refrigeration Systems.

REFRIGERATION AND AIR CONDITIONING

Trouble	Possible Cause	Corrective Measure
Compressor short cycles on low pressure control.	Low refrigerant charge.	Locate and repair leaks. Charge refrigerant.
	Thermal expansion valve not feeding properly.	Adjust, repair or replace thermal expansion valve.
	(a) Dirty strainers.	(a) Clean strainers.
	(b) Moisture frozen in orifice or orifice plugged with dirt.	(b) Remove moisture or dirt (Use system dehydrator).
	(c) Power element dead or weak.	(c) Replace power element.
	Water flow through evaporators restricted or stopped. Evaporator coils plugged, dirty, or clogged with frost.	Remove restriction. Check water flow. Clean coils or tubes.
	Defective low pressure control switch.	Repair or replace low pressure control switch.
Compressor runs continuously.	Shortage of refrigerant.	Repair leak and recharge system.
	Leaking discharge valves.	Replace discharge valves.
Compressor short cycles on high pressure control switch.	Insufficient water flowing through condenser, clogged condenser.	Determine if water has been turned off. Check for scaled or fouled condenser.
	Defective high pressure control switch.	Repair or replace high pressure control switch.
Compressor will not run.	Seized compressor.	Repair or replace compressor.
	Cut-in point of low pressure control switch too high.	Set L.P. control switch to cut-in at correct pressure.
	High pressure control switch does not cut-in.	Check discharge pressure and reset H.P. control switch.
	1. Defective switch.	1. Repair or replace switch.
	2. Electric power cut off.	2. Check power supply.
	3. Service or disconnect switch open.	3. Close switches.

Trouble Chart for Vapor Compression Refrigeration Systems—Continued.

TERMINOLOGY AND TROUBLESHOOTING

Trouble	Possible Cause	Corrective Measure
Compressor will not run. (Cont'd)	4. Fuses blown.	4. Test fuses and renew if necessary.
	5. Over-load relays tripped.	5. Re-set relays and find cause of overload.
	6. Low voltage.	6. Check voltage (should be within 10 percent of nameplate rating).
	7. Electrical motor in trouble.	7. Repair or replace motor.
	8. Trouble in starting switch or control circuit.	8. Close switch manually to test power supply. If OK check control circuit including temperature and pressure controls.
	9. Compressor motor stopped by oil pressure differential switch.	9. Check oil level in crankcase. Check oil pump pressure.
Sudden loss of oil from crankcase.	Liquid refrigerant slugging back to compressor crank case.	Adjust or replace expansion valve.
Capacity reduction system fails to unload cylinders.	Hand operating stem of capacity control valve not turned to automatic position.	Set hand operating stem to automatic position.
Compressor continues to operate at full or partial load.	Pressure regulating valve not opening.	Adjust or repair pressure regulating valve.
Capacity reduction system fails to load cylinders.	Broken or leaking oil tube between pump and power element.	Repair leak.
Compressor continues to operate unloaded.	Pressure regulating valve not closing.	Adjust or repair pressure regulating valve.

Trouble Chart for Vapor Compression Refrigeration Systems—Continued.

REFRIGERATION AND AIR CONDITIONING

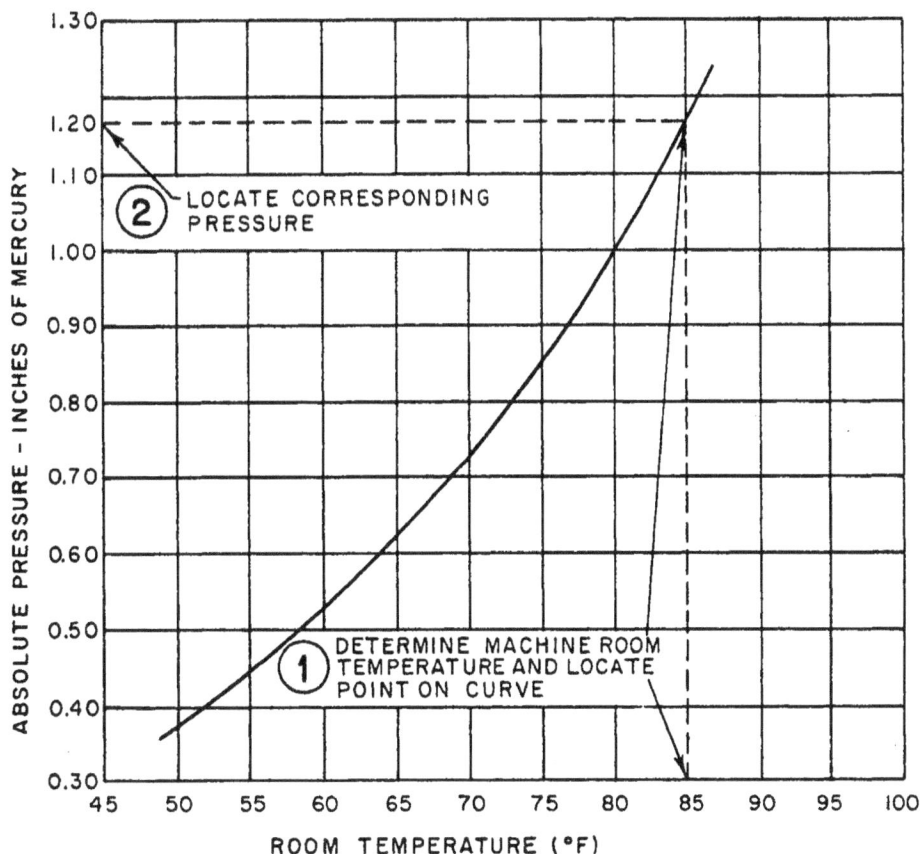

Figure 1.—Pressure temperature curve for lithium-bromide machine.

TROUBLE CHART FOR ABSORPTION TYPE (LITHIUM-BROMIDE) REFRIGERATION SYSTEM		

TROUBLE: SOLUTION SOLIDIFIED AT START-UP

	CAUSE	CHECK	CORRECTION
1.	Dilution cycle too short.	- dilution cycle time delay relay.	-Reset time delay relay to 10 minutes.
2.	Steam valve did not close during dilution cycle.	- operation of steam valve and steam EP relay.	-Repair faulty operation. Steam EP relay should close when stop button is pushed and control air pressure at steam valve should go to 0 PSIG.
3.	Cooling load lost during dilution cycle.	- Shut down procedure.	Make certain that the cooling load remains on during the dilution cycle.

TERMINOLOGY AND TROUBLESHOOTING

TROUBLE CHART FOR ABSORPTION TYPE (LITHIUM-BROMIDE) REFRIGERATION SYSTEM—Continued.

TROUBLE: SOLUTION SOLIDIFIED AT START-UP—Continued

CAUSE	CHECK	CORRECTION
4. Condenser sea water too cold.	- 3 way mixing valve and sea water thermostat.	-Maintain a constant inlet sea water temperature of 85°F.
5. Air in machine.	- absolute pressure indicator before starting.	-Turn "Not Purged-Purged" switch to "Not Purged" until machine vacuum corresponds to that given in Fig. 12-1. Find reason for air entering machine.
6. Machine shut down on safety.	-All safety switches and settings. The following safeties will do this: 1. Low temp. cutout. 2. High temp. cutout. 3. Chilled water pump overload. 4. Absorber - generator pump overload. 5. Refrigerant pump overload. 6. Chilled water failure switch.	-Correct reason for safety cutout or reason for pump overload. -Correct reason for loss of chilled water flow.

TROUBLE: OVER CONCENTRATION OF SOLUTION IN ABSORBER

	CAUSE	CHECK	CORRECTION
1.	High solution temperature in absorber	- solution temperature at generator pump and condensing water temperature leaving absorber. If difference is greater than 10°F, poor heat transfer is indicated.	Add octyl alcohol. If this does not correct the trouble, clean the absorber tubes and check condensing water flow through the absorber.
2.	Plugged spray nozzles in absorber	- discharge pressure of the absorber pump. This should be approximately 11" Hg. Vac.	Inspect and clean spray header and nozzles.

REFRIGERATION AND AIR CONDITIONING

TROUBLE CHART FOR ABSORPTION TYPE (LITHIUM-BROMIDE)
REFRIGERATION SYSTEM—Continued.

TROUBLE: OVER CONCENTRATION OF SOLUTION IN ABSORBER—Continued

CAUSE	CHECK	CORRECTION
3. Low condensing sea water flow	- condensing water rise across absorber. At full load this should be 10°F or lower.	Clean inlet sea water strainer. Reset condenser bypass valve.
4. Air in machine	- refrigerant vapor pressure to absorber vapor pressure. Measure temperature at discharge of refrigerant pump and read corresponding vapor pressure on equilibrium diagram. Should be 2° or 3°F.	Reset purge pressure stat to allow more purge operation.
5. Insufficient purging	- purge cycle. With purge pump in operation the purge pump cycle should be about 1 - 1/2 hours. - specific gravity and temperature of purge solution. - pump impeller and jet evacuator for wear - purge system for leaks	Adjust drip tube. Purge valve not opening. This should be about 70° or less with a specific gravity of 1.57 or more to give a purge vapor pressure of less than .18" Hg. If worn - replace Turn off purge pump at the panel board. Blank off the carbon filter tube. Raise pressure in purge system to 25 PSIG and leak test. Correct any leaks

TROUBLE: POOR EVAPORATOR PERFORMANCE

CAUSE	CHECK	CORRECTION
1. Fouled heat transfer surface on chilled water coil	- at full load, check spread between evaporator temperature (at discharge of refrigerant pump) and	Clean tubes - chilled water side. Check division plate gasket in water box, if

TERMINOLOGY AND TROUBLESHOOTING

TROUBLE CHART FOR ABSORPTION TYPE (LITHIUM-BROMIDE) REFRIGERATION SYSTEM—Continued.

TROUBLE: Poor Evaporator Performance—Continued.

CAUSE	CHECK	CORRECTION
	leaving chilled water temperature. Spread should not be greater than 3°F.	out of position, reposition or replace.
2. Incorrect refrigerant pump discharge pressure	- pump pressure; should be approximately 4 PSIG.	Inspect evaporator spray nozzles. Clean if necessary.
	- Refrigerant charge.	Add refrigerant at full load until overflow temperature begins to drop.
	- refrigerant pump impeller.	If worn, replace.
	- pump rotation, should be counter-clockwise as viewed from the pump end.	If incorrect reverse motor rotation.

TROUBLE: WEAK SOLUTION IN ABSORBER, UNABLE TO CONCENTRATE WITH STEAM VALVE WIDE OPEN AT FULL LOAD. —Continued.

CAUSE	CHECK	CORRECTION
1. Vapor condensate above 110°F	- condensing water approach, leaving condenser water temperature to vapor condensate temperature should not be greater than 8°F.	Clean condenser tubes.
	- condensing sea water flow	Clean inlet sea water strainer - adjust condenser bypass valve.
	- refrigerant overflow temperature	If below 45°F, remove refrigerant until temperature begins to rise.
	- calibration of vapor condensate thermometer	recalibrate
2. Strong solution Temperature below 205°F.	- steam pressure	Raise steam pressure to 18 PSIG at generator inlet.
	- steam strainer	Clean strainer
	- steam traps	Open bypass valve, if any change is noted in solution temperature, repair traps.

REFRIGERATION AND AIR CONDITIONING

TROUBLE CHART FOR ABSORPTION TYPE (LITHIUM-BROMIDE) REFRIGERATION SYSTEM—Continued.

TROUBLE: SOLIDIFICATION DURING OPERATION—Continued

CAUSE	CHECK	CORRECTION
3. Low solution flow to generator	- calibration of strong solution thermometer	Recalibrate
	- generator pump discharge pressure. Should be 4 PSIG, approximately.	Inspect valves for restrictions. Inspect generator spray nozzles. Clean or replace.

TROUBLE: SOLIDIFICATION DURING OPERATION

CAUSE	CHECK	CORRECTION
1. See over concentration of solution in absorber.		
2. See poor evaporator performance.		Desolidify machine
3. Sudden drop in entering condensing sea water temperature.	- 3-way pneumatic mixing valve (4) and condensing water temperature control.	Correct reason for malfunction of valve or control.
4. Sudden rise in steam pressure above 18 PSIG.	- control air pressure to steam control pilot and steam regulating valve bypass (12).	Reduce control air pressure to 15 PSIG and make certain valve is closed.

TROUBLE: LOST SOLUTION LEVEL IN ABSORBER

CAUSE	CHECK	CORRECTION
1. Heat exchanger strong solution valve restricted	- valve closed or collapsed diaphragm	Open valve. Replace diaphragm.

TROUBLE: PURGE WILL NOT OPERATE

CAUSE	CHECK	CORRECTION
1. Off on safety	- solution level in purge tank	Drain solution from tank. Clean probes.
2. Malfunction of purge pump.	- purge pump starter - purge level control - purge pressurestat - purge pump motor	Repair or replace if necessary.

TROUBLE: LOSS OF VACUUM DURING SHUT DOWN PERIOD

CAUSE	CHECK	CORRECTION
1. Valve open.	- all of these valves	Close valves and pull vacuum on machine.

TERMINOLOGY AND TROUBLESHOOTING

TROUBLE CHART FOR ABSORPTION TYPE (LITHIUM-BROMIDE)
REFRIGERATION SYSTEM—Continued.

TROUBLE: LOSS OF VACUUM DURING SHUT-DOWN PERIOD. —Continued.

	CAUSE	CHECK	CORRECTION
2.	Pneumatic purge valve stuck open.	- purge valve operation air pressure to valve diaphragm	Repair if necessary. Open air bleed or correct reason for purge EP relay not closing and bleeding air.
3.	Seal leak	- water level in seal water tank, should be above suction and connection of seal water pump.	Replace leaking seal
4.	Check valve in seal water make up line did not seat	- ball check and check valve seat.	Replace ball check or repair valve seat.
5.	Leak in machine proper	- leak test machine.	Repair all leaks

TROUBLE: LOSS OF VACUUM DURING OPERATION

	CAUSE	CHECK	CORRECTION
1.	Seal leak	- all pump seals	Replace faulty seal.
2.	Malfunction of purge pump	- purge pump starter - purge pump motor	Repair if necessary Replace if burned out.

TROUBLE: REFRIGERANT OVERFLOW TEMPERATURE ALWAYS COLD MUST REMOVE REFRIGERANT PERIODICALLY

	CAUSE	CHECK	CORRECTION
1.	Tube leak.	- leak test across all tube bundles.	-Repair any leaks.
2.	Purge cooling coil.	- level in purge tank for an extended period while purge pump is off.	-Repair leaky coil if level in tank rises during test.

TROUBLE: COPPER PLATING

	CAUSE	CHECK	CORRECTION
1.	Air leakage into machine.	- leak test.	-Repair any leaks.
2.	Did not break vacuum with nitrogen and provide continuous bleed during repair work.	- procedure for breaking vacuum with nitrogen.	

REFRIGERATION AND AIR CONDITIONING

TROUBLE CHART FOR ABSORPTION TYPE (LITHIUM-BROMIDE) REFRIGERATION SYSTEM—Continued.

TROUBLE: MACHINE SHUT DOWN ON SAFETY

CAUSE	CHECK	CORRECTION
1. Power failure and control failure.	- fuses and power supply.	-Replace blown fuses and restore power.
2. Shutdown on low temperature cutout switch.	- switch setting.	-Set at 36°F.
	- chilled water temperature and steam valve.	-Recalibrate control and adjust steam valve.
3. Shutdown on chilled water failure switch.	- switch setting	-Set at 360 GPM minimum.
	- chilled water pump operation.	-Start pump.
	- chilled water flow.	-Open chilled water line valves.
4. Sea water pump, chilled water pump, refrigerant pump, or absorber-generator pump motor trips out on overload.	- heater elements.	-Install correct size.
	- amperage draw of motor.	-Find reason for overload if present.
	- power supply to all phases.	-Should be 440-3-60AC.
	- ambient temperature around starter too high.	-Provide air circulation or move starter.
	- pump head against pump curves.	-Correct reason for abnormal pump head.
	- binding due to impeller or bearing wear.	-Change impeller or bearings.
	- solidification in absorber-generator pump.	-Desolidify.

HEATING AND ENVIRONMENTAL CONTROL

CONTENTS

		Page
I.	Introduction	1
II.	Definitions	1
III.	Fuels	3
IV.	Central Heating Units	6
V.	Fuel-Burning Procedures and Automatic Firing Equipment	9
VI.	Refractory	11
VII.	Heating Systems	11
VIII.	Domestic Hot Water Jack Stoves (Coal Stoves)	23
IX.	Hazardous Installations	23

HEATING AND ENVIRONMENTAL CONTROL

I. Introduction

The function of a heating system is to provide for human comfort. The variables to be controlled are temperature, air motion, and relative humidity. Temperature must be maintained uniformly throughout the heated area. Field experience indicates a variation from 6 to 10 degrees F from floor to ceiling. The adequacy of the heating device and the tightness of the structure or room determine the degree of personal comfort within the dwelling.

Coal, wood, oil, gas, and electricity are the main sources of heat energy. Heating systems commonly used are steam, hot water, and hot air. The housing inspector should have a knowledge of the various heating fuels and systems to be able to determine their adequacy and safety in operation. To cover fully all aspects of the heating system, the entire area and physical components of the system must be considered.

II. Definitions

A **Anti-flooding Control** — A safety control that shuts off fuel and ignition when excessive fuel accumulates in the appliance.

B **Appliance:**
1 **High-heat** — a unit that operates with flue entrance temperature of combustion products above 1,500°F.
2 **Medium heat** — same as high-heat, except above 600°F.
3 **Low heat** — same as high heat, except below 600°F.

C **Boiler:**
1 **High pressure** – a boiler furnishing pressure at 15 psi or more.
2 **Low pressure** — (hot water or steam) — a boiler furnishing steam at a pressure less than 15 psi or hot water not more than 30 psi.

D **Burner** — A device that provides the mixing of fuel, air, and ignition in a combustion chamber.

E **Chimney** — A vertical shaft containing one or more passageways.
1 **Factory-built chimney** — a tested and accredited flue for venting gas appliances, incinerators and solid or liquid fuel-burning appliances.
2 **Masonry chimney** — a field-constructed chimney built of masonry and lined with terra cotta flue or firebrick.
3 **Metal chimney** — a field-constructed chimney of metal.
4 **Chimney Connector** — A pipe or breeching that connects the heating appliance to the chimney.

F **Clearance** — The distance separating the appliance, chimney connector, plenum, and flue from the nearest surface of combustible material.

G **Central Heating System** — A boiler or furnace, flue connected, installed as an integral part of the structure and designed to supply heat adequately for the structure.

H **Controls:**
1 **High-low limit control** — an automatic control that responds to liquid level changes and pressure or temperature changes and that limits operation of the appliance to be controlled.

2. **Primary safety control** — the automatic safety control intended to prevent abnormal discharge of fuel at the burner in case of ignition failure or flame failure.

3. **Combustion safety control** — a primary safety control that responds to flame properties, sensing the presence of flame and causing fuel to be shut off in event of flame failure.

I **Convector** — A convector is a radiator that supplies a maximum amount of heat by convection, using many closely-spaced metal fins fitted onto pipes that carry hot water or steam and thereby heat the circulating air.

J **Conversion** — a boiler or furnace, flue connected, originally designed for solid fuel but converted for liquid or gas fuel.

K **Damper** — a valve for regulating draft. Generally located on the exhaust side of the combustion chamber, usually in the chimney connector.

L **Draft Hood** — a device placed in and made a part of the vent connector (chimney connector or smoke pipe) from an appliance, or in the appliance itself, that is designed to (a) ensure the ready escape of the products of combustion in the event of no draft, back-draft, or stoppage beyond the draft hood; (b) prevent backdraft from entering the appliance; (c) neutralize the effect of stack action of the chimney flue upon appliance operation.

M **Draft Regulator** — a device that functions to maintain a desired draft in oil-fired appliances by automatically reducing the chimney draft to the desired value. Sometimes this device is referred to, in the field, as air-balance, air-stat, or flue velocity control.

N **Fuel Oil** — a liquid mixture or compound derived from petroleum that does not emit flammable vapor below a temperature of 125°F.

O **Heat** — the warming of a building, apartment, or room by a stove, furnace, or electricity.

P **Heating Plant** — the furnace, boiler, or the other heating devices used to generate steam, hot water, or hot air, which then is circulated through a distribution system. It uses coal, gas, oil, or wood as its source of heat.

Q **Limit Control** — a thermostatic device installed in the duct system to shut off the supply of heat at a predetermined temperature of the circulated air.

R **Oil Burner** — a device for burning oil in heating appliances such as boilers, furnaces, water heaters, and ranges. A burner of this type may be a pressure-atomizing gun type, a horizontal or vertical rotary type, or a mechanical or natural draft-vaporizing type.

S **Oil Stove** — a flue-connected, self-contained, self-supporting oil-burning range or room heater equipped with an integral tank not exceeding 10 gallons; it may be designed to be connected to a separate oil supply tank.

T **Plenum Chamber** — an air compartment to which one or more distributing air ducts are connected.

U **Pump, Automatic Oil** — a device that automatically pumps oil from the supply tank and delivers it in specific quantities to an oil-burning appliance. The pump or device is designed to stop pumping automatically in case of a breakage of the oil supply line.

V **Radiant Heat** — a method of heating a building by means of electric coils, hot water, or steam pipes installed in the floors, walls, or ceilings.

W **Register** — a grille-covered opening in a floor or wall through which hot or cold air can be introduced into a room. It may or may not be arranged to permit closing of the grille.

X **Room Heater** — a self-contained, free-standing heating appliance intended for installation in the space being heated and not intended for duct connection (space heater).

Y **Smoke Detector** — a device installed in the plenum chamber or in the main supply air duct of an air-conditioning system to shut off the blower automatically and close a fire damper in the presence of smoke.

Z **Tank** — a separate tank connected, directly or by pump, to an oil-burning appliance.

AA **Thimble** — a term applied to a metal or terra cotta lining for a chimney or furnace pipe.

BB **Valve — Main Shut-off Valve** — a manually operated valve in an oil line for the purpose of turning on or off the oil supply to the burner.

CC **Vent System** — the gas vent or chimney and vent connector, if used, assembled to form a continuous, unobstructed passageway from the gas appliance to the outside atmosphere for the purpose of removing vent gases.

III. Fuels

A Coal

Classification and composition — the four types of coal are: anthracite, bituminous, sub-bituminous, and lignitic.

Coal is prepared in many sizes and combinations of sizes. The combustible portions of the coal are fixed carbons, volatile matter (hydrocarbons), and small amounts of sulfur.

In combination with these are non-combustible elements composed of moisture and impurities that form ash. The various types differ in heat content. The heat content is determined by analysis and is expressed in British Thermal Units (BTU) per pound. The type and size of coal used are determined by the availability and by the equipment in which it is burned.

The type and size of coal must be proper for the particular heating unit; that is, the furnace grate and flue size must be designed for the particular type of coal. Excessive coal gas can be generated through improper firing as a result of improper fuel or improper furnace design, or both.

The owner should be questioned about his procedure for adding coal to his furnace. It should be explained that a period of time must be allowed to pass before damping to prevent the release of excessive coal gas. This should also be done before damping for the night or other periods when full draft is not required.

Improper coal furnace operation can result in an extremely hazardous and unhealthful occupancy — the inspector should be able to offer helpful operational procedures. Ventilation of the area surrounding the furnace is very important in order to prevent heat buildup and to supply air for combustion.

B Fuel Oil

Fuel oils are derived from petroleum, which consists primarily of compounds of hydrogen and carbon (hydrocarbons) and smaller amounts of nitrogen and sulfur.

Classification of fuel oils Domestic fuel oils are controlled by rigid specifications. Six grades of fuel oil are generally used in heating systems; the lighter two grades are used primarily for domestic heating.

These grades are:

1. **Grade Number 1** — A volatile, distillate oil for use in burners that prepare fuel for burning solely by vaporization (oil-fired space heaters).

2. **Grade Number 2** — A moderate-weight, volatile, distillate oil used for burners that prepare oil for burning by a combination of vaporization and atomization. This grade of oil is commonly used in domestic heating furnaces.

3. **Grade Number 3** — A low-viscosity, distillate oil used in burners wherein fuel and air are prepared for burning solely by atomization.

4. **Grade Number 4** — A medium-viscosity oil used in burners without preheating. (Small industrial or apartment house applications.)

5. **Grade Number 5** — A medium-viscosity oil used in burners with preheaters that require an oil of lower viscosity than Grade Number 6. (Industrial or apartment house application.)

6. **Grade Number 6** — A high-viscosity oil for use in burners with preheating facilities adequate for handling oil of high viscosity. (Industrial applications.)

7. **Heat content** — Heating values of oil vary from approximately 152,000 BTU per gallon for Number 6 oil to 136,000 BTU per gallon for Number 1.

Oil is more widely used today than coal and provides a more automatic source of heat and comfort. It also requires more complicated systems and controls.

If the oil supply is used within the basement or cellar area, certain basic regulations must be followed (see Figure 1). No more than two 275-gallon tanks may be installed above ground in the lowest story of any one building. The tank shall not be closer than 7 feet horizontally to any boiler, furnace, stove, or exposed flame. Fuel oil lines should be embedded in a concrete or cement floor or protected against damage if they run across the floor. Bach tank must have a shutoff valve that will stop the flow from each tank if a leak develops in the line to or in the burner itself.

The tank or tanks must be vented to the outside, and a gauge showing the quantity of oil in the tank or tanks must be tight and operative. Tanks must be off the floor and on a stable base to prevent settlement or movement that may rupture the connections.

A buried outside tank installation is shown in Figure 2.

C Gas

Commercial gas fuels are colorless gases. Some have a characteristic pungent odor, while others are odorless and cannot be detected by smell. Although gas fuels are easily handled in heating equipment, their presence in air in appreciable quantities becomes a serious health hazard. Gases diffuse readily in the air, making explosive mixtures possible. (A proportion of combustible gas and air that is ignited burns with such a high velocity that an explosive force is created.) Because of these characteristics of gas fuels, precautions must be taken to prevent leaks, and care must be exercised when gas-fired equipment is lit.

Classification of gas - Gas is broadly classified as natural or manufactured.

1. **Manufactured Gas** — This gas as distributed is usually a combination of certain proportions of gases produced by two or more processes as obtained from coke, coal, and petroleum. Its BTU value per cubic foot is generally closely regulated, and costs are determined on a guaran-

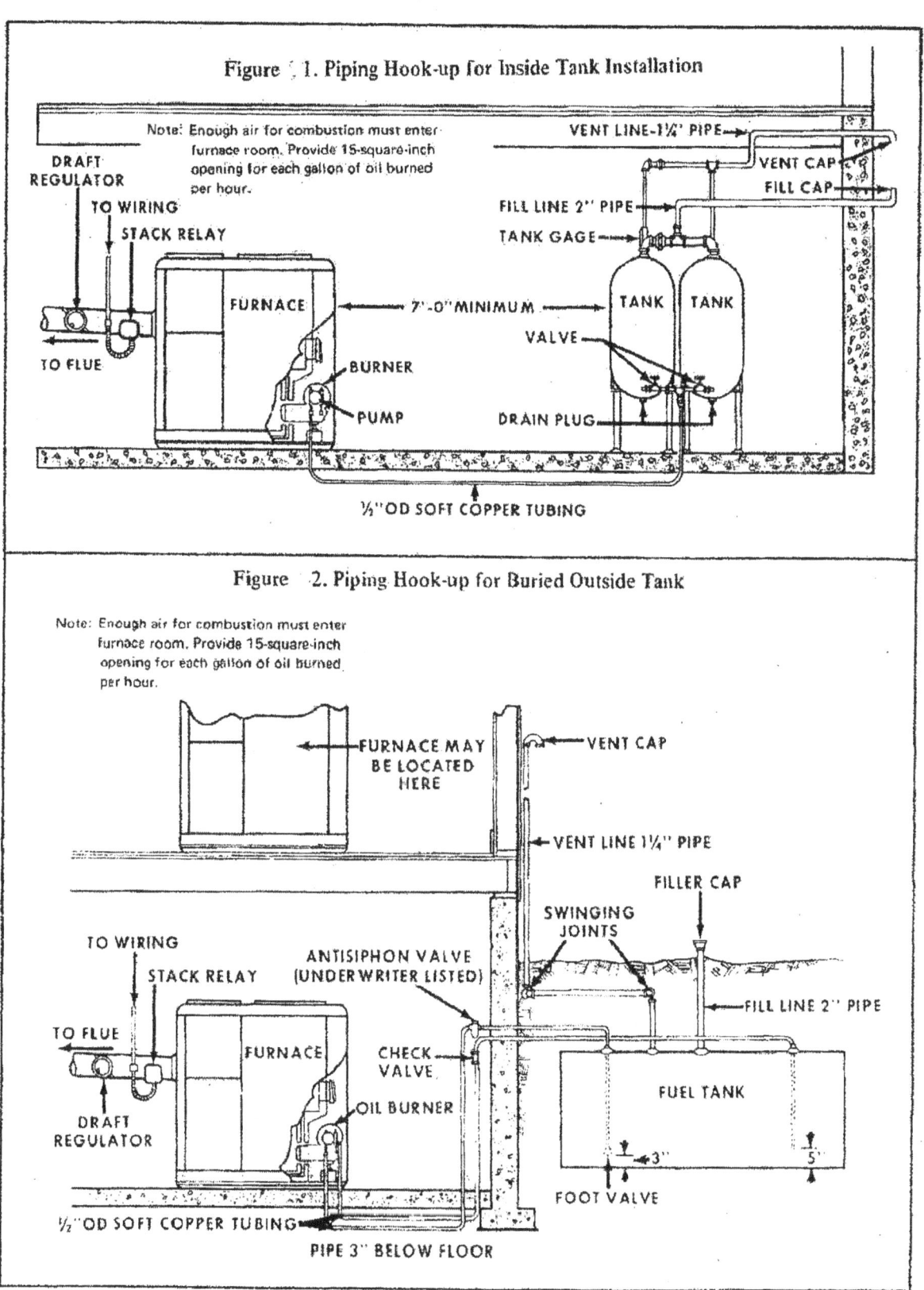

Figure 1. Piping Hook-up for Inside Tank Installation

Figure 2. Piping Hook-up for Buried Outside Tank

teed BTU basis, usually 520 to 540 per cubic foot.

2. **Natural Gas** — This gas is a mixture of several combustible and inert gases. It is one of the richest gases and is obtained from wells ordinarily located in petroleum-producing areas. The heat content may vary from 700 to 1,300 BTU's per cubic foot with a generally accepted average figure of 1,000 BTU's per cubic foot. Natural gases are distributed through pipe lines to point of utilization and are often mixed with manufactured gas to maintain a guaranteed BTU content.

3. **Liquified Petroleum Gas** — Principal products of liquified petroleum gas are butane and propane. Butane and propane are derived from natural gas or petroleum refinery gas and are chemically classified as hydrocarbon gases.

Specifically, butane and propane are on the borderline between a liquid and a gaseous state. At ordinary atmospheric pressure butane is a gas above 33°F and propane a gas at -42°F. These gases are mixed to produce commercial gas suitable for various climatic conditions. Butane and propane are heavier than air. The heat content of butane is 3,274 BTU's per cubic foot while that of propane is 2,519.

The gas burner should be equipped with an automatic cutoff in case the flame fails. Shutoff valves should be located within 1 foot of the burner connection and on the output side of the meter.

CAUTION — Liquified petroleum gas is heavier than air; therefore, the gas will accumulate at the bottom of confined areas. If a leak should develop, care should be taken to ventilate the appliance before lighting.

D Electricity

Electricity is gaining popularity in many regions, particularly where costs are competitive with other sources of heat energy. With an electric system, the housing inspector should rely mainly on the electrical inspector for proper installation. There are a few items, however, to be concerned with to ensure safe use of the equipment. Check to see that the units are accredited testing agency approved and installed according to the manufacturer's specifications. Most convector-type units are required to be installed at least 2 inches above the floor level, not only to ensure that proper convection currents are established through the unit, but also to allow sufficient air insulation from any combustible flooring material. The housing inspector should check for curtains that extend too close to the unit or loose, long pile rugs that are too close. A distance of 6 inches on the floor and 12 inches on the walls should separate rug or curtains from the appliance.

Radiant heating plastered into the ceiling or wall is technical in nature and not a part of the housing inspector's competence. He should, however, be knowledgeable about the system used. These systems are relatively new. If wires are bared in the plastering they should be treated as open and exposed wiring.

IV. Central Heating Units

The boiler should be placed in a separate room whenever possible; in new construction this is usually required. In most housing inspections, however, we are dealing with existing conditions; therefore, we must adapt the situation as closely as possible to acceptable safety standards. In many old buildings the furnace is located in the center of the cellar or basement, and this location does not lend itself for practical conversion to a boiler room.

A Boiler Location
Consider the physical requirements for a boiler room.

1 Ventilation — More circulating air is required for the boiler room than for a habitable room, in order to reduce the heat buildup caused by the boiler or furnace as well as to supply oxygen for combustion.

2 Fire Protection Rating — As specified by various codes (fire code, building code, and insurance underwriters) the fire regulations must be strictly adhered to in areas surrounding the boiler or furnace. This minimum dimension from which a boiler or furnace is to be spaced from a wall or ceiling is shown in Figure 3.

Many times the enclosure of the furnace or boiler creates a problem of providing adequate air supply and ventilation for the room. Where codes and local authority permit, it may be more practical to place the furnace or boiler in an open area. The ceiling above the furnace should be fire protected to a distance of 3 feet beyond all furnace or boiler appurtenances and this area should be free of all storage material. The furnace or boiler should be set on a firm foundation of concrete if located in the cellar or basement. If the codes permit furnace installations on the first floor, then the building code must be consulted for proper setting and location.

B Heating Boilers
Boilers may be classified according to several kinds of characteristics. The material may be cast iron or steel. Their construction may be section, portable, fire-tube, water-tube, or special. Domestic heating boilers are generally of low-pressure type with a maximum working pressure of 15 pounds per square inch for steam and 30 pounds per square inch for hot water.

All boilers have a combustion chamber for burning fuel. Automatic fuel-firing devices help supply the fuel and control the combustion. Handfiring is accomplished by the provision of a grate, ash pit, and controllable drafts to admit air under the fuel bed and over it through slots in the firing door. A check draft is required at the smoke pipe connection to control chimney draft. The gas passes from the combustion chamber to the flue, passages (smoke pipe) designed for maximum possible transfer of heat from the gas. Provisions must be made for cleaning flue passages.

The term boiler is applied to the single heat source that can supply either steam or hot-water (boiler is often called a heater).

Cast iron boilers are generally classified as:
1 Square or rectangular boilers with vertical sections.
2 Round, square, or rectangular boilers with horizontal pancake sections.

Cast iron boilers are usually shipped in sections and assembled at the site.

C Steel Boilers
Most steel boilers are assembled units with welded steel construction and are called portable boilers. Larger boilers are installed in refractory brick settings built on the site. Above the combustion chamber a group of tubes is suspended, usually horizontally, between two headers. If flue gases pass through the tubes and water surrounds them, the boiler is designated as the fire-tube type. When water flows through the tubes, it is termed water-tube. Fire-tube is the predominant type.

D Heating Furnaces
Heating furnaces are the heat sources used when air is the heat-carrying medium. When air circulates because of the different densities of the heated and cooled air, the furnace is a gravity type. A fan may be included for the air circulation; this type is called a mechanical warm-air furnace. Furnaces may be of cast iron or steel and burn various types of fuel.

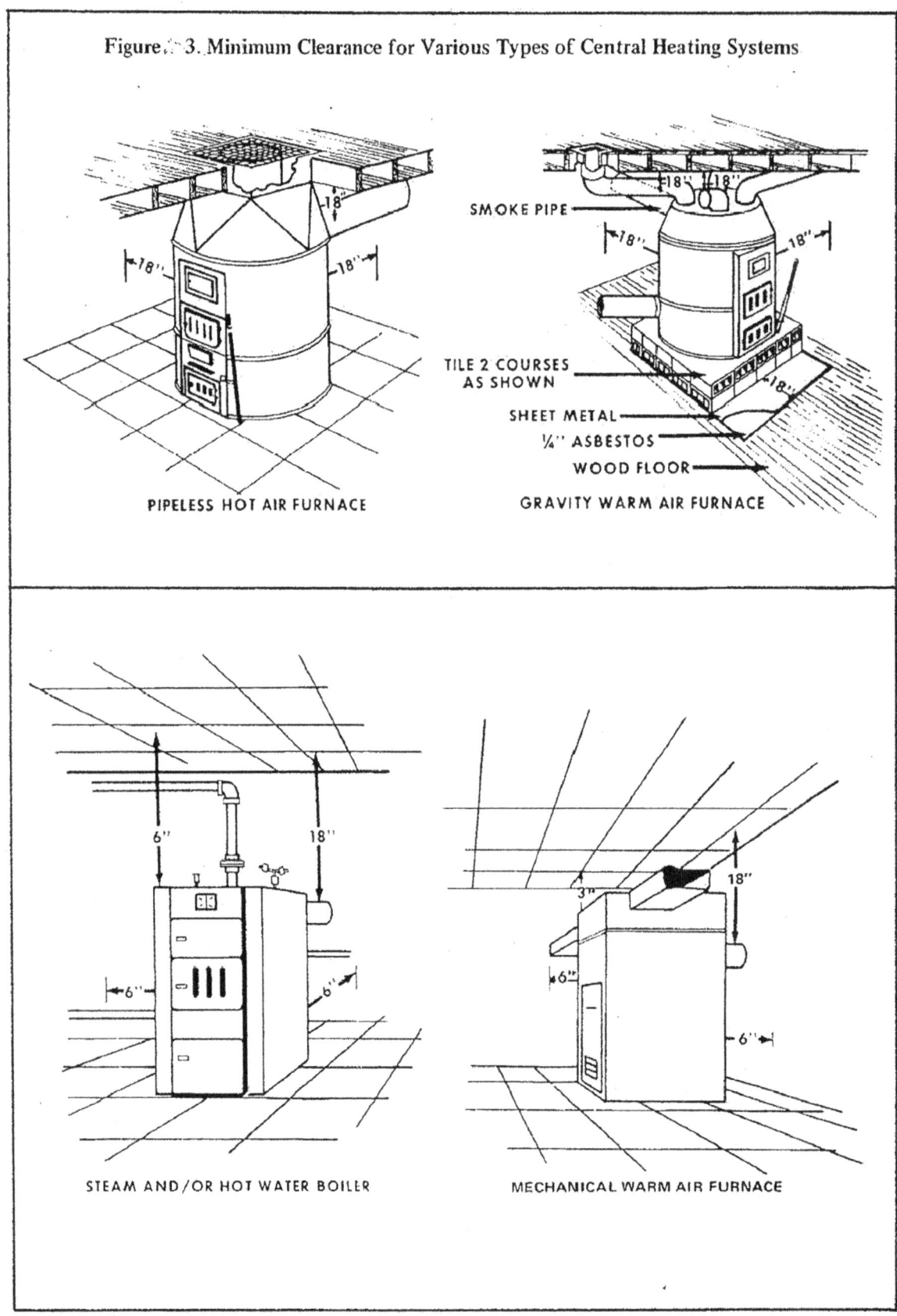

Figure 3. Minimum Clearance for Various Types of Central Heating Systems

V. Fuel-Burning Procedures and Automatic Firing Equipment

A Coal — Many localities throughout the nation still use coal as a heating fuel.

1. **Hand Stoking** - In many older furnaces, the coal is stoked or fed into the fire box by hand.

2. **Automatic Stokers** - The single-retort, underfeed-type bituminous coal stoker is the most commonly used domestic-type steam or hot water boiler (see Figure 4). The stoker consists of a coal hopper, a screw for conveying coal from hopper to retort, a fan that supplies air for combustion, a transmission for driving coalfeed and fan, and an electric motor for supplying power. The air for combustion is admitted to the fuel through tuyeres at the top of the retort. The stoker feeds coal to the furnace intermittently in accordance with the temperature or pressure demands.

B Oil Burners — Oil burners are broadly designated as distillate, domestic, and commercial or industrial. Distillate burners are usually found in oil-fired space heaters. Domestic oil burners are usually power driven and are used in domestic heating plants. Commercial or industrial burners are used in larger central-heating plants for steam or power generation.

1. **Domestic Oil Burners** — These vaporize and atomize the oil, and deliver a predetermined quantity of oil and air to the combustion chambers. Domestic oil burners operate automatically to maintain a desired temperature.

   a. **Gun-type burners** — These burners atomize the oil either by oil pressure or by low-pressure air forced through a nozzle.

The oil system pressure atomizing burner (see Figure 5) consists of a strainer, pump, pressure-regulating valve, shutoff valve, and atomizing nozzle. The air system consists of a power-drive fan and an air tube that surrounds the nozzle and electrode assembly. The fan and oil pump are generally connected directly to the motor. Oil pressures normally used are about 100 pounds per square inch, but pressures con-

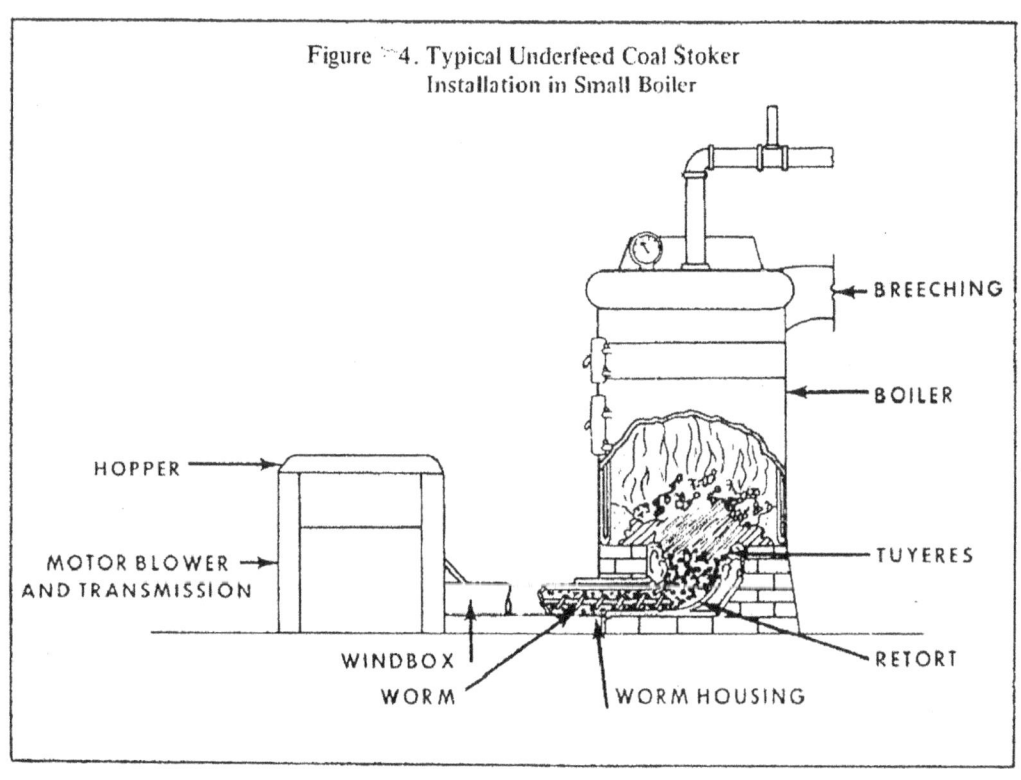

Figure 4. Typical Underfeed Coal Stoker Installation in Small Boiler

siderably in excess of this are sometimes used.

The form and parts of low-pressure air-atomizing burners (see Figure 5), are similar to high-pressure atomizing burners except for addition of a small air pump, and a different way of delivering air and oil to the nozzle or orifice.

b **Vertical rotary burners** - The atomizing-type burner, sometimes known as a radiant or suspended-flame burner, atomizes oil by throwing it from the circumference of a rapidly rotating motor-driven cup. The burner is installed so that the driving parts are protected from the heat of the flame by a hearth of refractory material at about the grate elevation. Oil is fed by pump or gravity, while the draft is mechanical or a combination of natural and mechanical.

c **Horizontal rotary burners** These were originally designed for commercial and industrial use but are available in sizes suitable for domestic use. In this burner, oil is atomized by being thrown in a

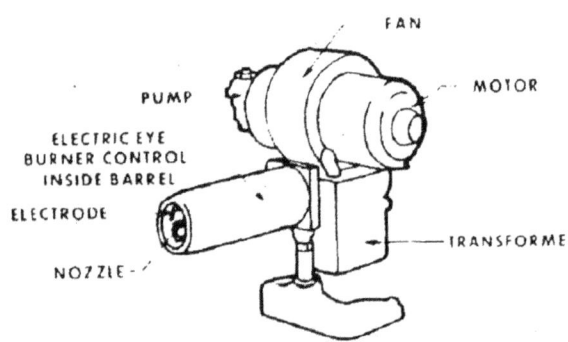

Figure 5. Cut-Away of Typical High-Pressure Gun-Burner

conical spray from a rapidly rotating cup. Horizontal rotary burners employ electric-gas or gas-pilot ignition and operate with a wide range of fuels, primarily with Numbers 1 and 2 fuel oil. Primary safety controls for burner operation are necessary. An anti-flooding device must be a part of the system so that, if ignition in the burner should fail, the oil will not continue to flow. Likewise, a stack control is necessary to shut off the burner if the stack temperatures become excessive. A reset button on the older stack control units releases if excessive (predetermined) temperatures are exceeded and thus cuts off all power to the burner. This button must be reset before starting can be attempted. The newer models now use electric eye-type control on the burner itself.

2 **Ignition** — On the basis of the method employed to ignite fuels, burners are divided into five groups as follows:

a **Electric** — A high-voltage electric spark is made in the path of an oil and air mixture and this causes ignition. This electric spark may be continuous or may be in operation only long enough to ignite the oil. Electric ignition is almost universally used. Electrodes are located near the nozzles (see Figure 5) but not in the path of the oil spray.

b **Gas pilot** — A small gas pilot light that burns continuously is frequently used. Gas pilots usually have expanding gas valves that automatically increase flame size when motor circuit starts. After a fixed interval, the flame reverts to normal size.

c. **Electric gas** — An electric spark ignites a gas jet, which in turn ignites the oil air mixture.

d **Oil pilot** — A small oil flame is used.

e **Manual** — A burning wick or torch is placed in the combustion space through peepholes and thus ignites the charge. Operator should stand to one side of the fire door to guard against injury from chance explosion.

VI. Refractory

The refractory lining or material should be an insulating fireproof brick-like substance. Never use ordinary firebrick. The insulating brick should be set on end so as to build a 2 inch-thick wall in the pot. Size and shape of the refractory pot vary from furnace to furnace (see Figure 6 for various shapes). The shape can be either round or square, whichever is more convenient to build. It is important to use a special cement having properties similar to that of the insulating refractory-type brick.

VII. Heating Systems

A Steam Heating Systems - Steam heating systems are classified according to the pipe arrangement, accessories used, method of returning the con-densate to the boiler, method of expelling air from the system, or the type of control employed. The successful operation of a steam heating system consists of generating steam in sufficient quantity to equalize building heat loss at maximum efficiency, expelling entrapped air, and returning all condensate to the boiler rapidly. Steam cannot enter a space filled with air or water at pressure equal to the steam pressure. It is important, therefore, to eliminate air and to remove water from the distribution system. All hot pipe lines exposed to contact by residents must be properly insulated or guarded.

Steam heating systems are classified according to the method of returning the condensate to the boiler.

1 Gravity One-pipe Air-vent System — The gravity one-pipe air-vent system is one of the earliest types used. The condensate is returned to the boiler by gravity. This system is generally found in one-building-type heating systems. The steam is supplied by the boiler and carried through a single system or pipe to radiators as shown in Figure 7. Return of the condensate is dependent on hydrostatic head. Therefore, the end of the steam main, where it attaches to the boiler, must be full of water (termed a wet return) for a distance above the boiler line to create a pressure drop balance between the boiler and the steam main.

Radiators are equipped with an inlet valve and with an air valve (see Figure 8). The air valve permits venting of air from the radiator and its displacement by steam. Condensate is drained from the radiator through the same pipe that supplies steam.

2 Two-pipe Steam Vapor System with Return Trap — The two-pipe vapor system with boiler return trap and air eliminator is an improvement of the one-pipe system. The return connection of the radiator has a thermostatic trap that permits flow of condensate and air only from the radiator and prevents steam from leaving the radiator. Since the return main is at atmospheric pressure or less, a boiler return trap is installed to equalize condensate return pressure with boiler pressure.

B **Hot Water Heating Systems** — All hot water heating systems are similar in design and operating principle.

1 One-pipe Gravity System —The one-pipe gravity hot water heating system is the most elementary of the gravity systems and is shown in Figure 9. Water is heated at the lowest point in the system. It rises through a single main because of a difference in density between hot and cold water. The supply rise or radiator branch takes off from the top of the main to supply water to the radiators. After the water gives up heat in the radiator it goes back to the same main through return piping from the radiator. This cooler return water mixes with water in the supply main and causes the water to cool a little. As a result, the next radiator on the system has a lower emission rate and must be larger.

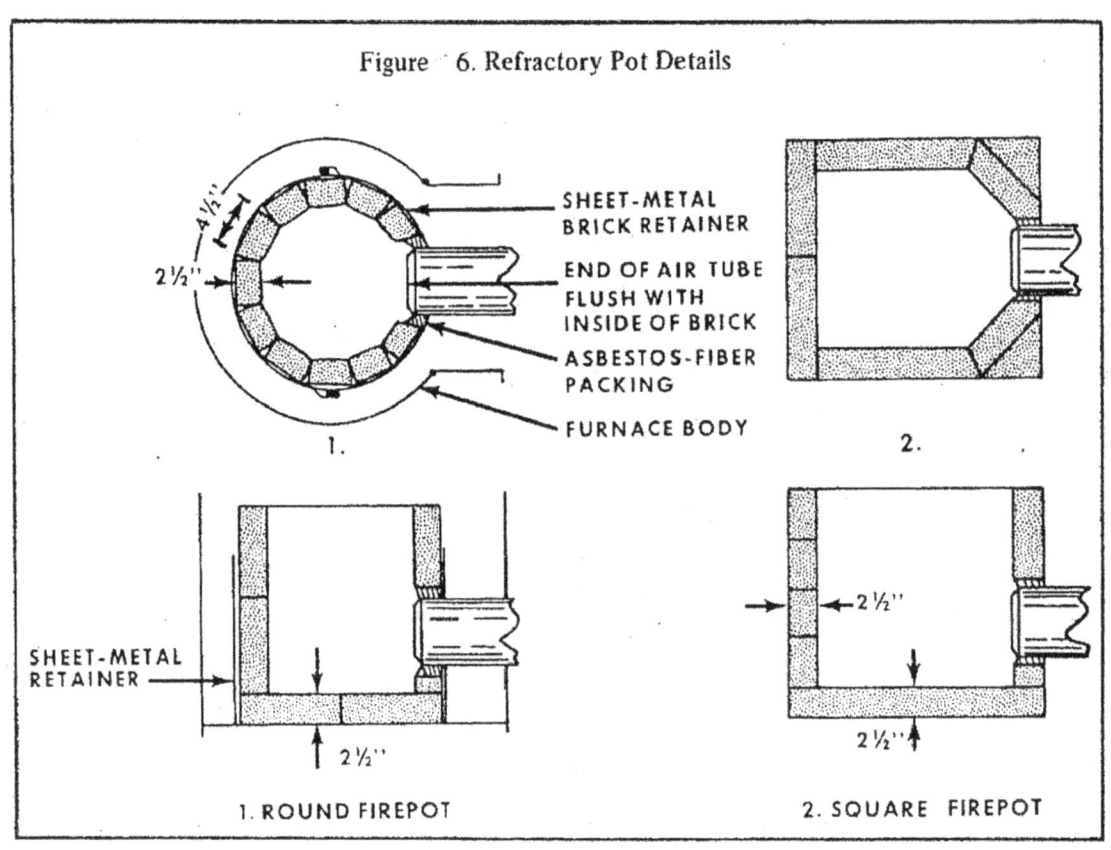

Figure 6. Refractory Pot Details

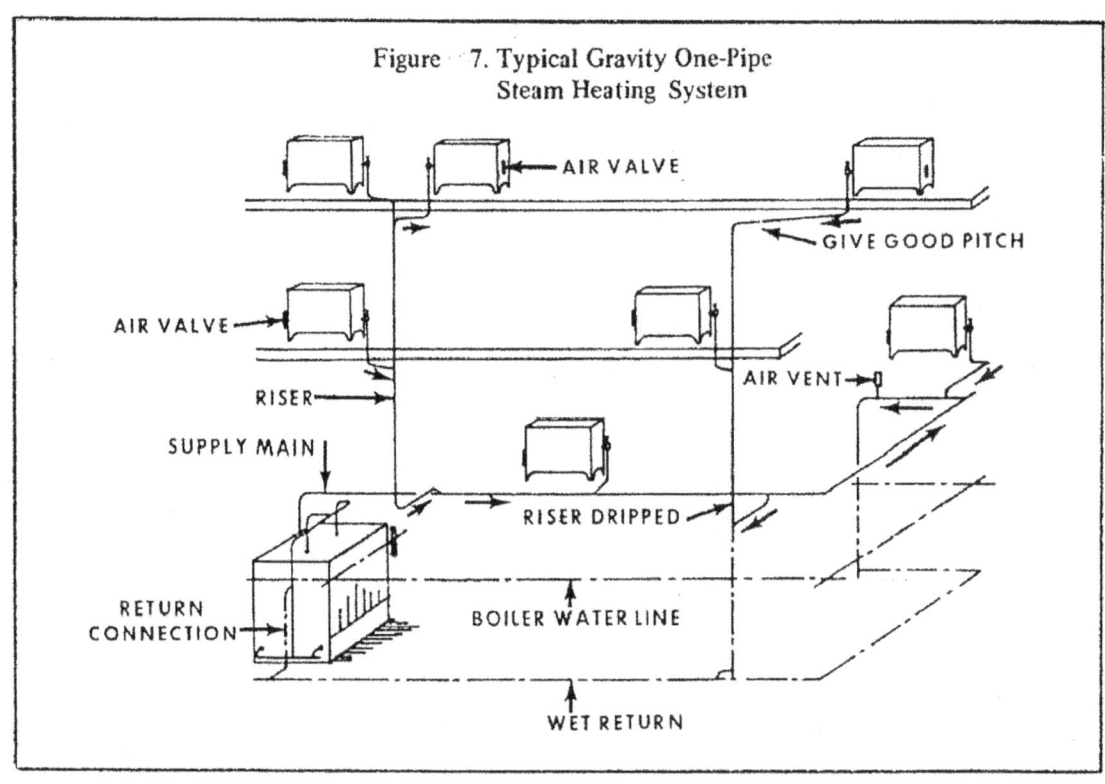

Figure 7. Typical Gravity One-Pipe Steam Heating System

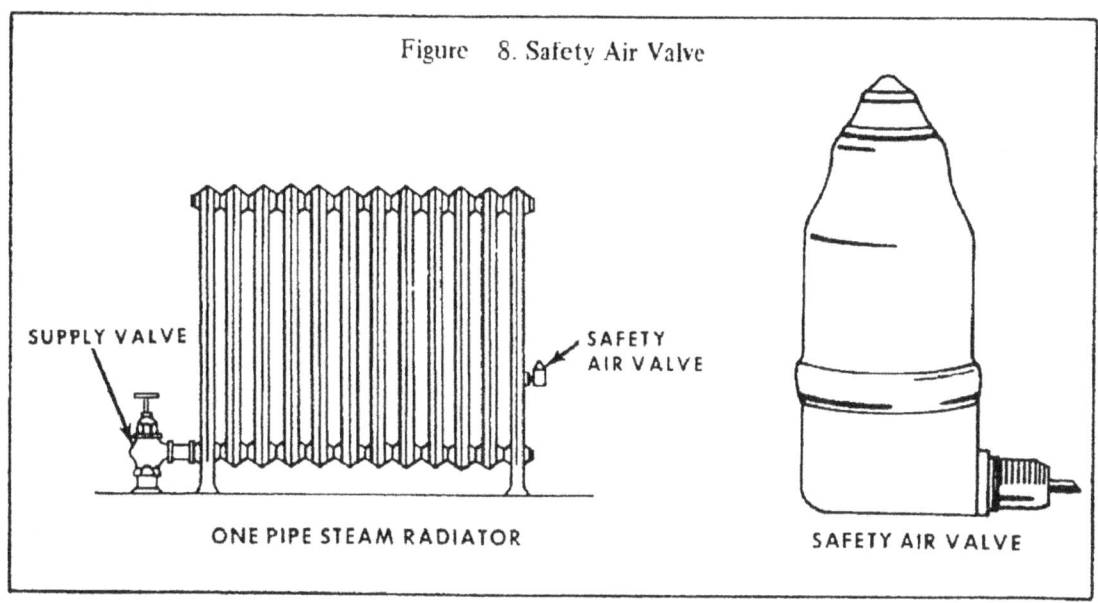

Figure 8. Safety Air Valve

Note in Figure 9 that the high points of the hot water system are vented and the low points are drained. In this case, the radiators are the high points and the heater is the low point.

2 **One-pipe Forced-feed System** — If a pump or circulator is introduced in the main near the heater of the one-pipe system, we have a forced system that can be used for much larger

applications than the gravity type. This system can operate at higher water temperatures than the gravity system. The faster moving higher temperature water makes a more responsive system with a smaller temperature drop through each radiator. Higher operating temperatures and lower temperature drops permit the use of smaller radiators for the same heating load.

3 **Two-pipe Gravity Systems** — One-pipe gravity systems may become a two-pipe system if the return radiator branch connects to a second main that returns water to the heater (see Figure 10). Water temperature is practically the same in all the radiators.

4 **Two-pipe Forced-circulation System** — This system is similar to a one-pipe forced-circulation system except that the same piping arrangement is found in the two-pipe gravity flow system.

5 **Expansion Tanks** — When water is heated it tends to expand. Therefore, in a hot water system an expansion tank is necessary. The expansion tank, either of open or closed type, must be of sufficient size to permit a change in water volume within the heating system. If the expansion tank is of the open type it must be placed at least 3 feet above the highest point of the system. It will require a vent and an overflow. The open tank is usually in an attic, where it needs protection from freezing.

The enclosed expansion tank is found in modern installations. An air cushion in the tank compresses and expands according to the change of volume and pressure in the system. Closed tanks are usually at the low point in the system and close to the heater. They can, however, be placed at almost any location within the heating system.

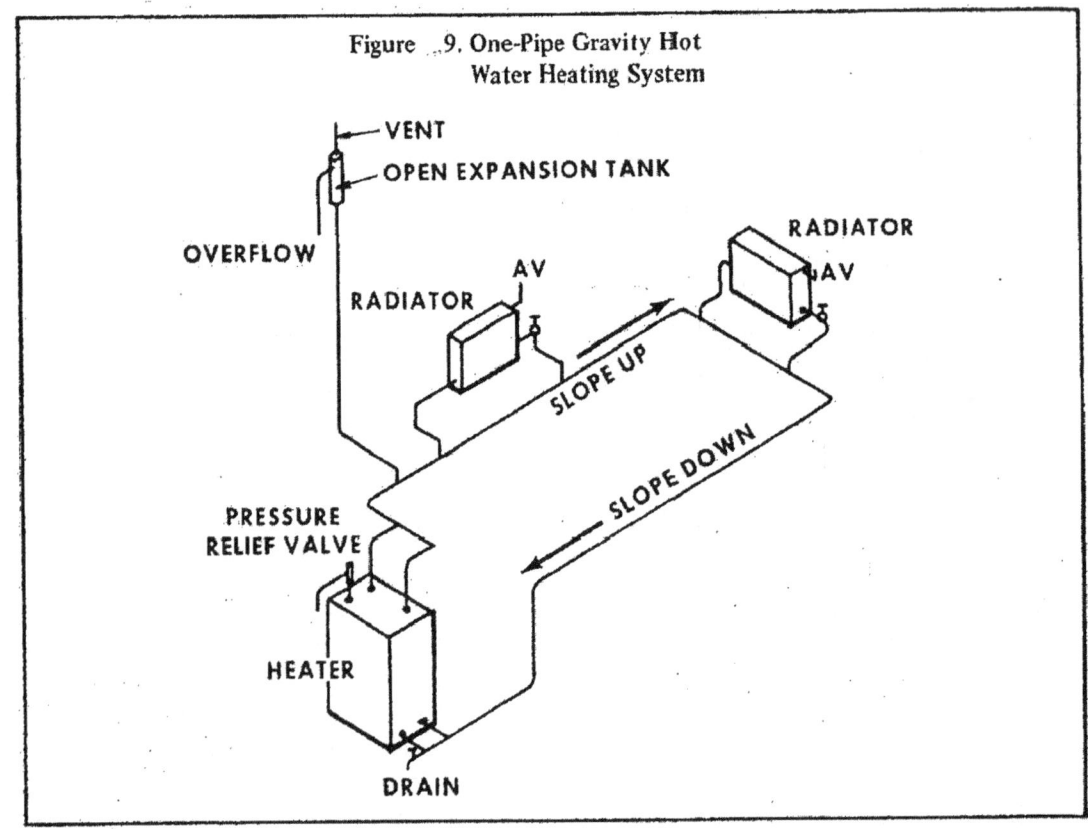

Figure 9. One-Pipe Gravity Hot Water Heating System

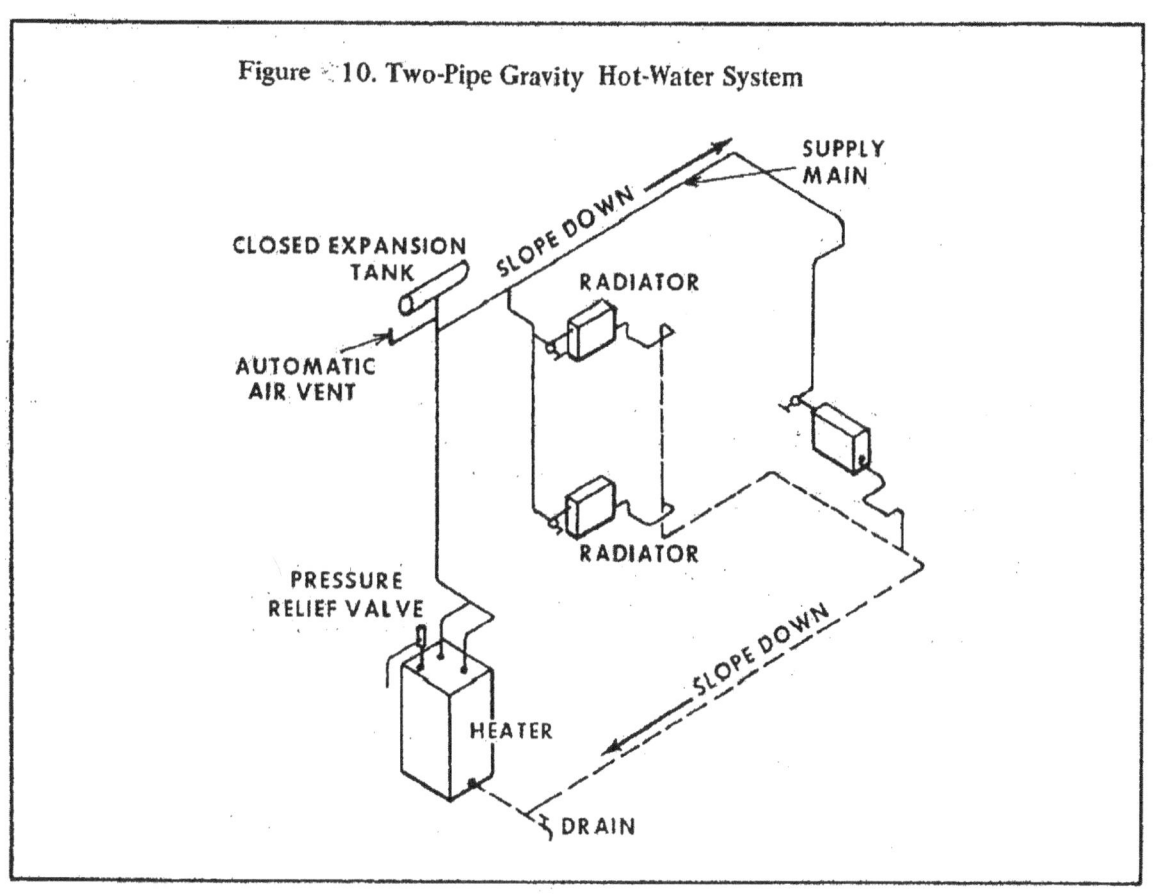

Figure 10. Two-Pipe Gravity Hot-Water System

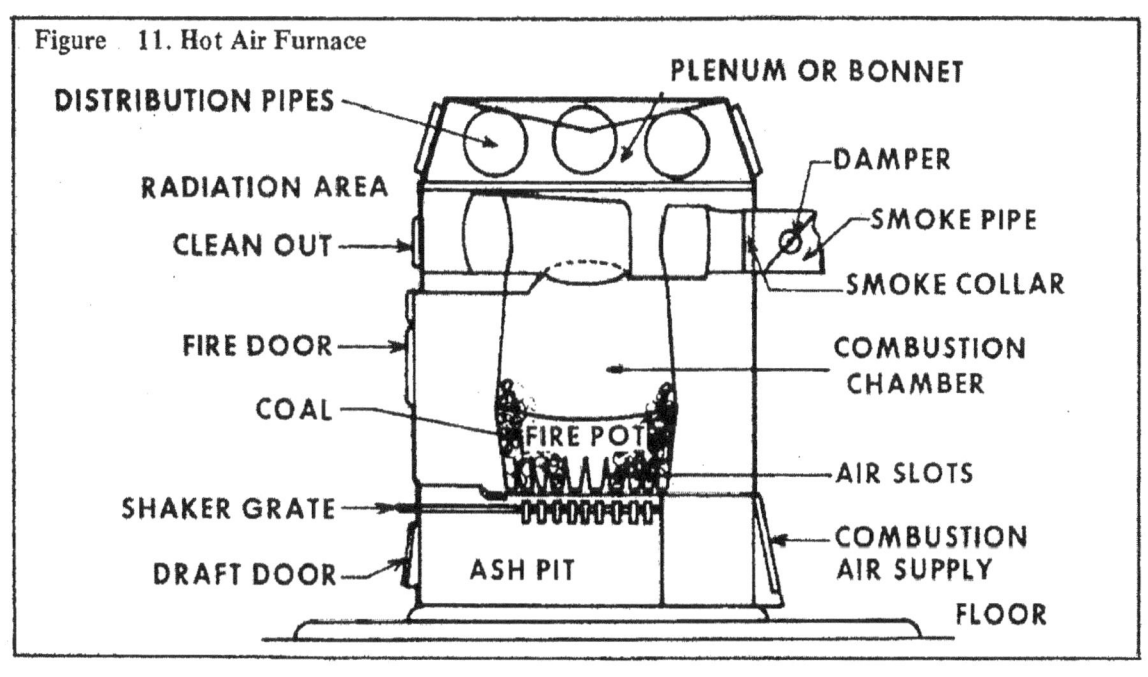

Figure 11. Hot Air Furnace

COAL NOTES

1. Approximately 12 pounds of air is required for complete combustion of 1 pound of hard coal.

2. Approximately 5 pounds of hard coal is consumed per hour for each square foot of grate area.

3. Approximately 12 inches of fire bed will heat most efficiently.

4. Anthracite coal burns more slowly than soft coal, is cleaner to handle-hence more widely used.

5. Large-size coal does not compact-hence the air spaces are too great and allows gases to escape into the flue unburned. Small size coal compacts too much and inhibits airflow through the coal to allow for good combustion. Mixing of coal size is recommended, i.e., stove and chestnut.

6. Fires burn best when the weather is clear and cold, because of reduced atmospheric pressure on the air in the flue—hence greater draft velocity. During periods of heavy atmosphere or rainy weather the temperature of flue gases must exceed normal temperatures to overcome the heavier atmospheric weight.

7. During extreme cold weather, coal should be added to a fire once in approximately 8 hours; moderate weather-12 hours.

C Hot Air Heating Systems

1 Gravity-Warm-Air Heating Systems — These operate because of the difference in specific gravity of warm air and cold air. Warm air is lighter than cold air and rises if cold air is available to replace it (see Figure 11).

a Operation — Satisfactory operation of a gravity-warm-air heating system depends on three factors. They are: (1) size of warm air and cold ducts, (2) heat loss of the building, (3) heat available from the furnace.

b Heat distribution — The most common source of trouble in these systems is insufficient pipe area usually in the return or cold air duct. The total cross-section area of the cold duct or ducts must be at least equal to the total cross-section area of all warm ducts.

c Pipeless furnaces — The pipeless hot-air furnace is the simplest type of hot-air furnace and is suitable for small homes where all rooms can be grouped about a single large register (see Figure 3). Other pipeless gravity furnaces are often installed at floor level. These are really oversized jacketed space heaters. The most common difficulty experienced with this type of furnace is supplying a return air opening of sufficient size on the floor.

2 Forced-Warm-Air Heating Systems — The mechanical warm-air furnace is the most modern type of warm-air equipment (see Figure 12). It is the safest type because it operates at low temperatures. The principle of a forced-warm-air heating system is very similar to that of the gravity system, except that a fan or blower is added to increase air movement. Because of the assistance of the fan or blower, the pitch of the ducts or leaders can be disregarded and it is therefore practical to deliver heated air in the most convenient places.

a Operation — In a forced-air system, operation of the fan or blower must be controlled by air temperature in a bonnet or by a blower control furnacestat. The blower control starts the fan or blower when the temperature reaches a certain point and turns the fan or blower off when the temperature drops to a predetermined point.

b Heat distribution — Dampers in the various warm-air ducts control distribution

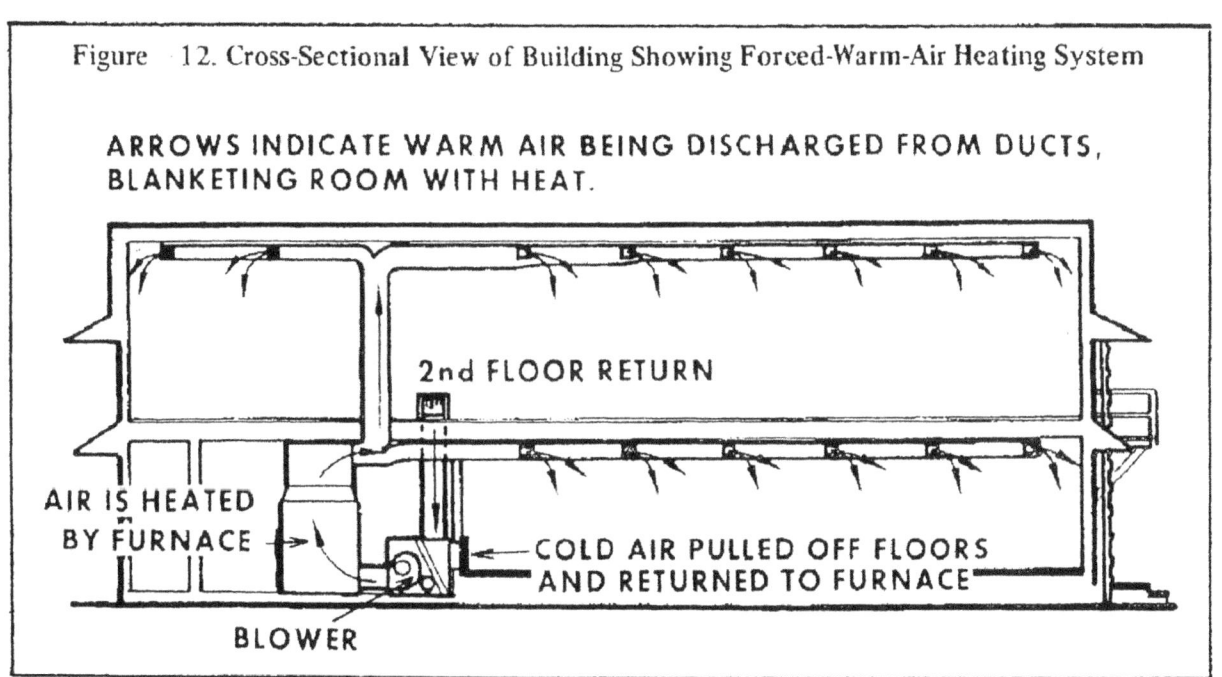

Figure 12. Cross-Sectional View of Building Showing Forced-Warm-Air Heating System

of warm air either at the branch takeoff or at the warm-air outlet.

Humidifiers are often mounted in the supply bonnet in order to regulate the humidity within the residence.

D Space Heaters — Space unit heaters are the least desirable from the viewpoint of fire safety and housing inspection. All space unit heaters must be vented to the flue.

1 **Coal-Fired Space Heaters (Cannon stove)** — This is illustrated in Figure 13 and is made entirely of cast iron. In operation, coal on the grates receives primary air for combustion through the grates from the ash-door draft intake. Combustible gases driven from the coal by heat burn in the barrel of the stove, where they received additional or secondary air through the feed door. Side and top of the stove absorb the heat of combustion and radiate it to the surrounding space.

2 **Oil-Fired Space Heaters** — Oil-fired space heaters have atmospheric vaporizing-type burners. The burners require a light grade of fuel oil that vaporizes easily and is comparatively low in temperature. In addition, the oil must be such that it leaves only a small amount of carbon residue and ash within the heater. Oil-fired space heaters are basically of two types:

a **Perforated-sleeve burner** — The perforated-sleeve burner (see Figure 14) consists essentially of a metal base formed of two or more angular fuel-vaporizing bowl burners (see Figure 15) and is widely used in space heaters and some water heaters.

The burner consists essentially of a bowl, 8 to 13 inches in diameter, with perforations in the side that admit air for combustion. The upper part of the bowl has a flame ring or collar. When several space heaters are installed in a building, an oil supply from an

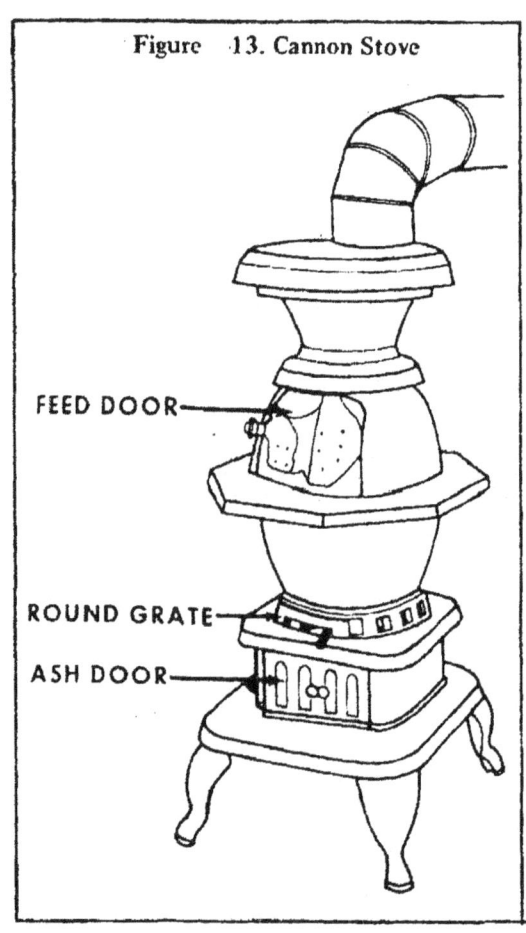

Figure 13. Cannon Stove

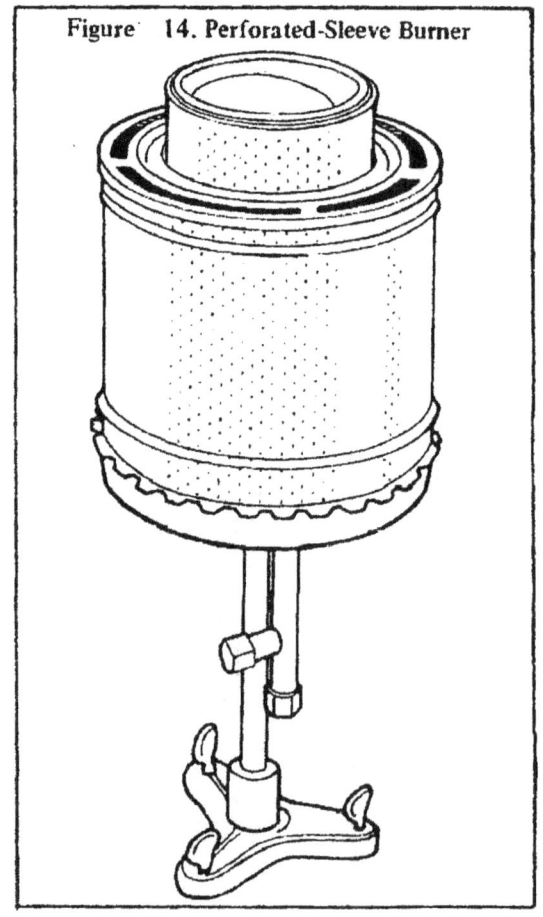

Figure 14. Perforated-Sleeve Burner

outside tank to all heaters is often desirable. Figure 16 shows the condition of a burner flame with different rates of fuel flow and indicates the ideal flame height.

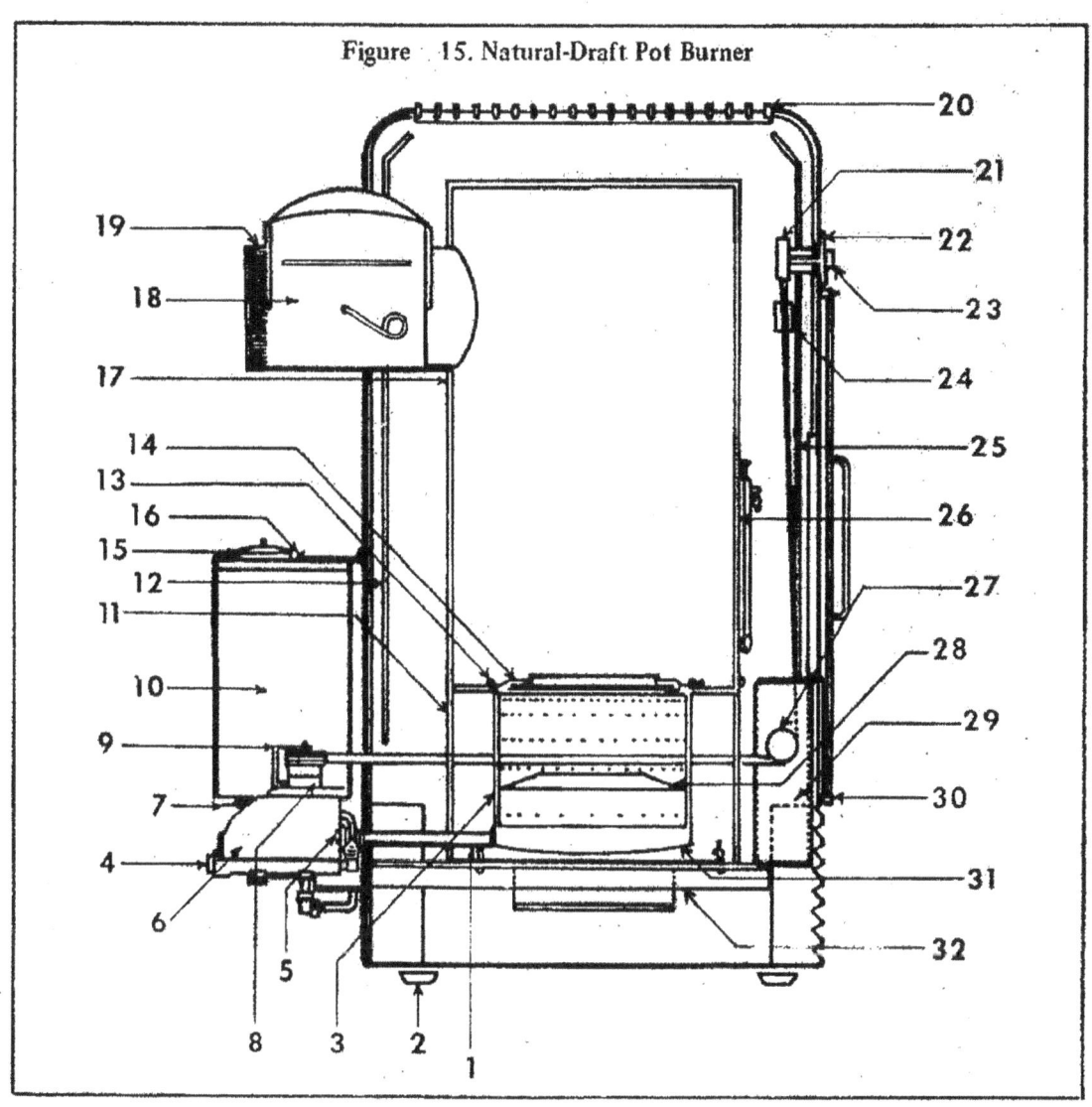

Figure 15. Natural-Draft Pot Burner

1. Burner-pot pipe.
2. Leg Leveler.
3. Pilot-ring clip.
4. Strainer unit.
5. Burner-pot drain plug.
6. Constant-level valve.
7. Tank valve
8. Control drum (to fit 6).
9. Control pulley bracket
10. Fuel tank.
11. Lower heat unit.
12. Heat shield (rear).
13. Burner-ring clamp.
14. Burner-top ring.
15. Fuel tank cap.
16. Tank fuel gauge.
17. Heat unit.
18. Cold draft regulator.
19. Flue connections, 6-inch diameter.
20. Top grille.
21. Dial control drum.
22. Escutcheon plate.
23. Dial control knob.
24. Pulley assembly (short).
25. Heat shield (front).
26. Heat-unit door.
27. Pulley assembly (long).
28. Pilot ring.
29. Humidifier.
30. Trim bar.
31. Burner pot.
32. Heat-unit support.

3 **Gas-Fired Space Heaters**—There are three types of gas-fired space heaters: natural, manufactured, and liquified petroleum gas. Space heaters using natural, manufactured, or liquified petroleum gases have a similar construction. All gas-fired space heaters must be vented to prevent a dangerous buildup of poisonous gases.

Each unit console consists of an enamel steel cabinet with top and bottom circulating grilles or openings, gas burners, heating element, gas pilot, and gas valve (see Figure 17). The heating element or combustion chamber is usually cast iron.

CAUTION: All gas-fired space heaters and their connections must be of the type approved by the American Gas Association (AGA). They must be installed in accordance with the recommendations of that organization or the local code.

a **Venting** — Use of proper venting materials and correct installation of venting for gas-fired space heaters is necessary to minimize harmful effects of condensation and to ensure that combustion products are carried off. (Approximately 12 gallons of water are produced in the burning of 1,000 cubic feet of natural gas. The inner surface of the vent must therefore be heated above the dewpoint of the combustion products to prevent water from forming in the flue.) A horizontal vent must be given an upward pitch of at least 1 inch per foot of horizontal distance.

When the smoke pipe extends through floors or walls the metal pipe must be insu-

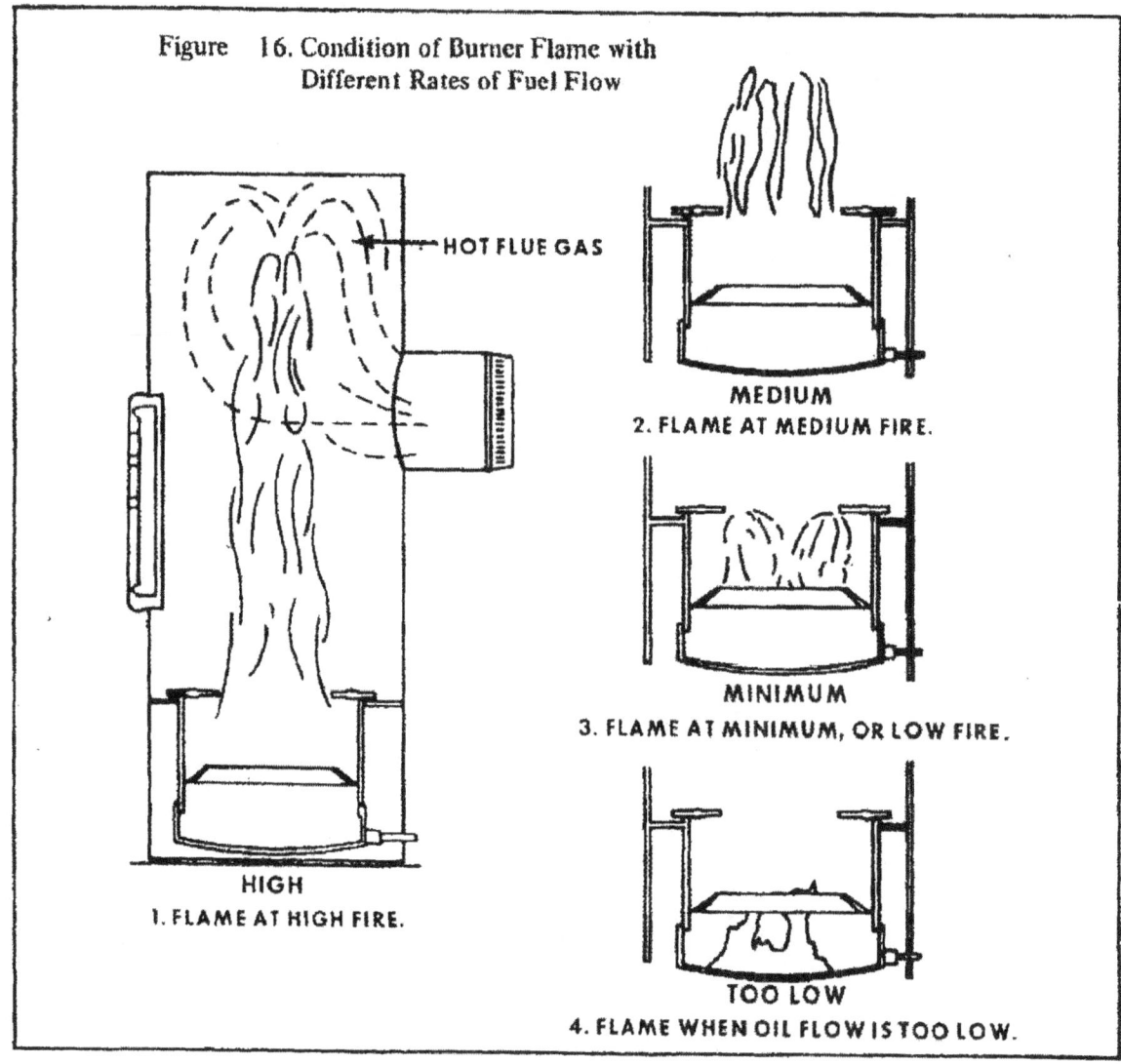

Figure 16. Condition of Burner Flame with Different Rates of Fuel Flow

1. FLAME AT HIGH FIRE.
2. FLAME AT MEDIUM FIRE.
3. FLAME AT MINIMUM, OR LOW FIRE.
4. FLAME WHEN OIL FLOW IS TOO LOW.

lated from the floor or wall system by an air space (see Figure 18). Avoid sharp bends. A 90° vent elbow has a resistance to flow equivalent to a straight section of pipe having a length of 10 times the elbow diameter. Be sure vent is of a rigid construction and resistant to corrosion by flue gas products. Several types of venting material are available such as B-vent and several other ceramic-type materials. A chimney lined with fire-brick type of terra cotta must be relined with an acceptable vent material if it is to be used for venting gas-fired appliances.

Use the same size vent pipe throughout its length. Never make a vent smaller than heater outlet except when two or more vents converge from separate heaters. To determine the size of vents beyond the point of convergence, add one-half the area of each vent to the area of the largest heater's vent.

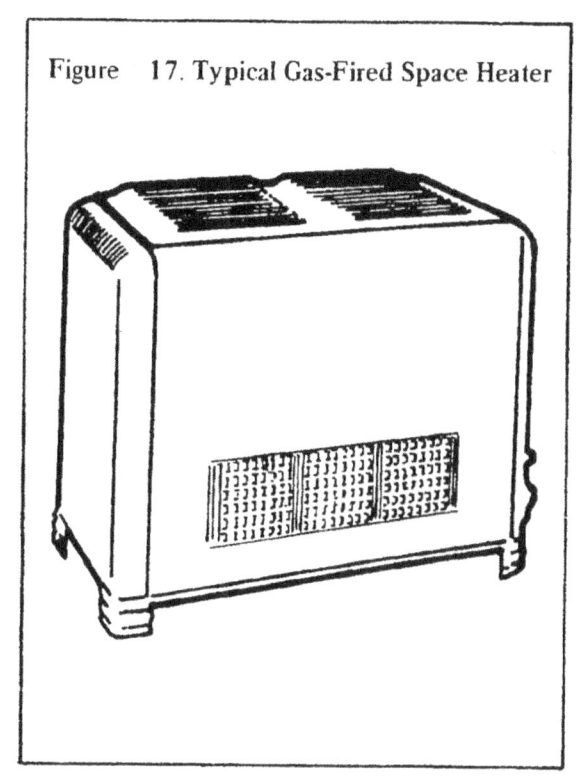

Figure 17. Typical Gas-Fired Space Heater

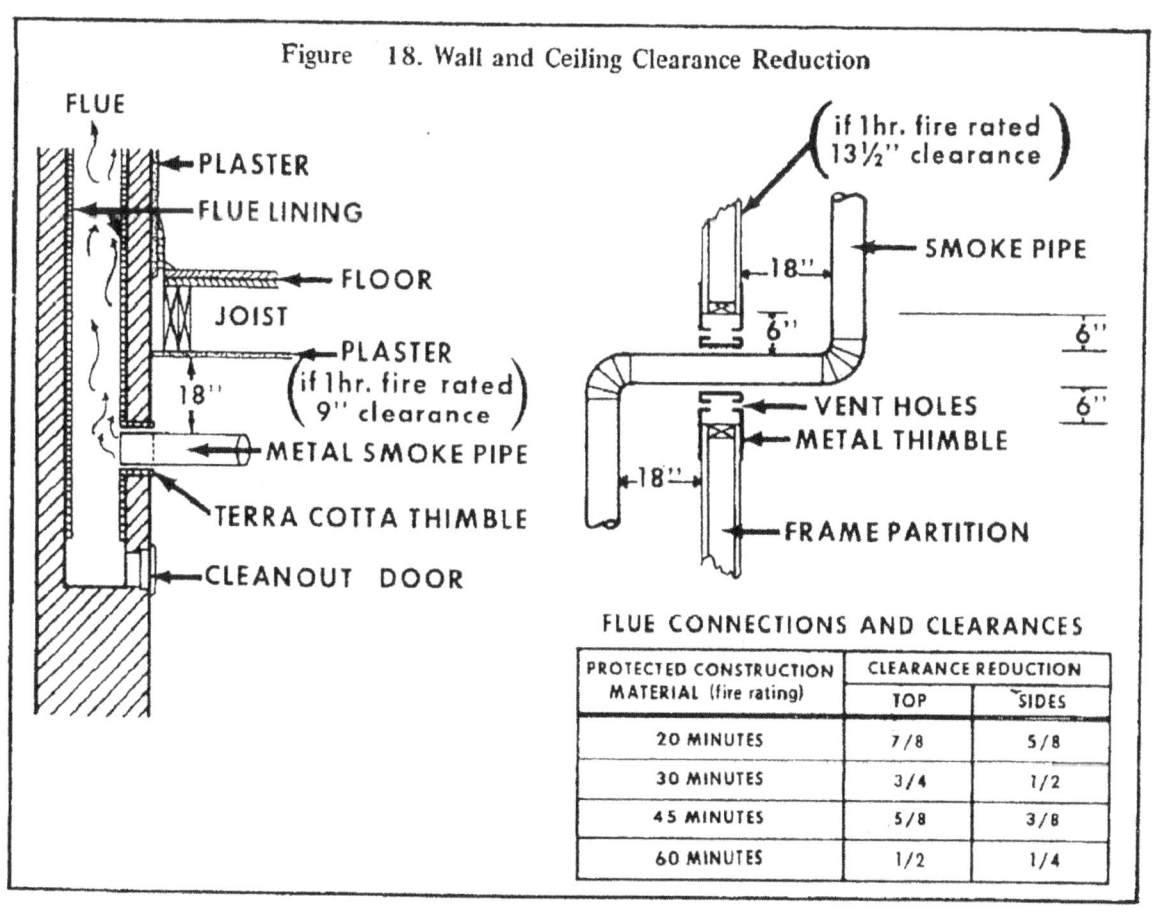

Figure 18. Wall and Ceiling Clearance Reduction

FLUE CONNECTIONS AND CLEARANCES

PROTECTED CONSTRUCTION MATERIAL (fire rating)	CLEARANCE REDUCTION	
	TOP	SIDES
20 MINUTES	7/8	5/8
30 MINUTES	3/4	1/2
45 MINUTES	5/8	3/8
60 MINUTES	1/2	1/4

Install vents with male ends of inner liner down to ensure condensate is kept within pipes on a cold start. The vertical length of each vent or stack should be at least 2 feet greater than the length between horizontal connection and stack.

Run vent at least 3 feet above any projection of the building within 20 feet to place it above a possible pressure zone due to wind currents (see Figure 19). End it with a weather cap designed to prevent entrance of rain and snow.

Gas-fired space heaters as well as gas furnaces and hot water heaters must be equipped with a backdraft diverter (see Figure ,20) designed to protect heaters against downdrafts and excessive updrafts. Use only draft diverters of the type approved by the AGA.

The combustion chamber or firebox must be insulated from the floor, usually with an airspace of 15 to 18 inches, or the firebox is sometimes insulated within the unit and thus allows for lesser clearance for combustibles.

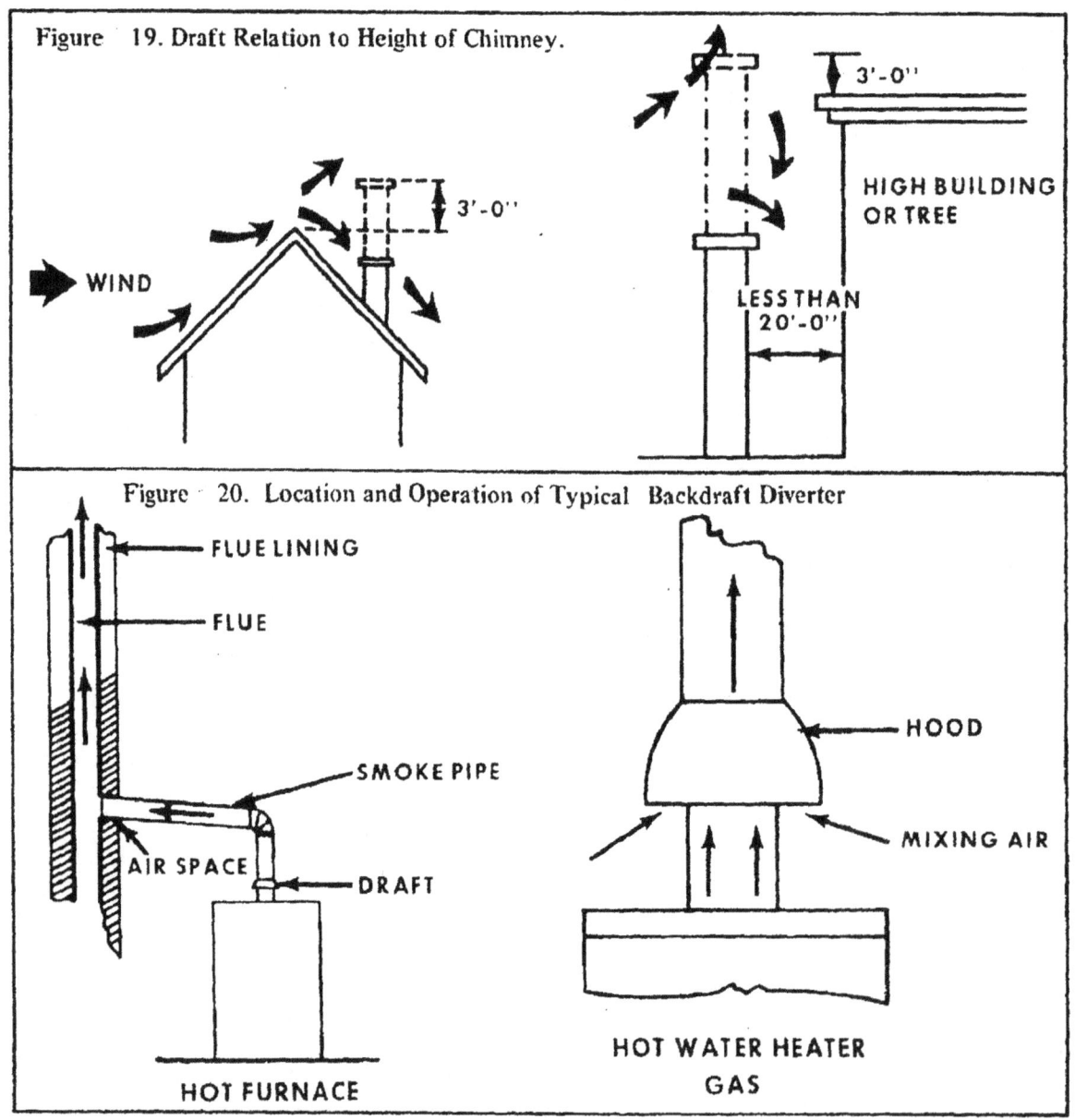

Figure 19. Draft Relation to Height of Chimney.

Figure 20. Location and Operation of Typical Backdraft Diverter

Where coal space heaters are located, a floor protection should be provided. This would be a metal-covered asbestos board or a similar durable insulation material. One reason for the floor protection would be to allow cooling off of hot coals and ashes if they drop out while ashes are being removed from the ash chamber. Walls and ceilings of a non-combustible construction exposed to furnace radiation should be installed, and the following clearances are recommended: Space heaters — A top or ceiling clearance of 36 inches, a wall clearance of 18 inches, and a smoke pipe clearance of 18 inches, (see Figure 18).

VIII. Domestic Hot Water Jack Stoves (Coal Stoves)

Domestic hot water jack stoves (coal stoves) equipped with water jackets to supply hot water for domestic use are to be treated as coal-fired furnaces or boilers previously discussed. Note that flue connections should not exceed two to the same flue unless the draft and size are sufficient to accommodate both exhausting requirements. One flue with one smoke pipe is the rule; however, housing inspectors may find a jack stove and main furnace connected to the same flue. Where these conditions are encountered and no complaint about malfunctioning of this system is found, it can be assumed that the system is operating satisfactorily. Where more than two units, other than gas, are attached to a single flue, the building agency should be notified, since this can be considered an improper installation. Gas, oil, and electric hot water heating units for domestic hot water should be treated the same as previously discussed for central heating units.

IX. Hazardous Installations

A **Generalities** — The housing inspector should be on the alert for unvented open burning flame heaters, such as manually operated gas logs. Coil-type wall-mounted hot-water heaters that do not have safety relief valves are not permitted. Kerosene (portable) units for cooking or heating should be prohibited. Generally, open-flame portable units are not allowed under fire safety regulations.

In oil heating units, other than integral tank units, the oil filling and vent must be located on the exterior of the building. Filling of oil within buildings is prohibited.

Electric wiring to heating units must be installed as indicated in the electrical section. Cutoff switches should be close to the entry but outside of the boiler room. The inspector should be able to appraise the heating installation and determine its adequacy. Any installation that indicates haphazard location, workmanship, or operation, whether it be building, zoning, plumbing, electrical, or housing, will dictate further inspection.

B **Chimneys (see Figure 21 and 22)** - Chimneys, as all inspectors know, are an integral part of the building. The chimney is a point of building safety and should be understood by the housing inspector. The chimney, if of masonry, must be tight and sound; flues should be terra cotta lined, and where no linings are installed, the brick should be tight to permit proper draft and elimination of combustion gases.

Chimneys that act as flues for gas-fired equipment must be lined with either B-vent or terra cotta.

To the inspector, on exterior inspection, "banana peel" on the portion of the chimney above the roof will indicate trouble and a need for rebuilding. Exterior deterioration of the chimney will, if let go too long, gradually permit erosion from within the flues and eventually block the flue opening.

Rusted flashing at the roof level will also contribute to the chimney's deterioration. Effervescence on the inside wall of the chimney below the roof and on the outside of the chimney, if exposed, will show salt accumulations — a tell-tale sign of water penetration and flue gas escape and a sign of chimney deterioration. In the spring and fall, during rain seasons, if terra cotta chimneys leak, the joint will be indicated by dark areas permitting actual counting of the number of flues inside the masonry chimney. When this condition occurs, it usually requires 2 or 3 months to dry out. Upon drying out, the mortar joints are discolored (brown), and so after a few years of this type of deterioration the joints can be distinguished wet or dry. The above-listed conditions usually develop during coal operation and become more pronounced usually 2 to 5 years after conversion to oil or gas.

An unlined chimney can be checked for deterioration below the roof line by checking the residue deposited at the base of the chimney, usually accessible through a cleanout (door or plug) or breaching. Red granular or fine powder showing through coal soot or oil soot will generally indicate, if in quantity (a handful), that deterioration is excessive and repairs are needed.

Gas units attached to unlined chimneys will be devoid of soot, but will usually show similar tell-tale brick powder and deterioration as previously mentioned. Manufactured gas has a greater tendency to dehydrate and decompose brick in chimney flues than natural gas. For gas installations in older homes, utility companies usually specify chimney requirements before installation, and so older chimneys may require the installation of terra cotta liners, lead-lined copper liners, or transite pipe. Oil burner operation using a low air ratio and high oil consumption is usually indicated by black carbon deposits around the top of the chimney. Prolonged operation in this burner setting results in long carbon water deposits down the chimney for 4 to 6 feet or more and should indicate to the inspector a possibility of poor burner maintenance. This will accent his need to be more thorough on the ensuing inspection. This type of condition can result from other related causes, such as improper chimney height or exterior obstructions such as trees or buildings that will cause downdrafts or insufficient draft or contribute to a faulty heating operation.
Rust spots and soot-mold usually occur on galvanized smoke pipe deterioration.

C Fireplace — Careful attention should be given to the construction of the fireplace. Improperly built fireplaces are a serious safety and fire hazard (see Figure 22). The most common causes of fireplace fires are thin walls, combustible materials such as studding or trim against sides and back of the fireplace, wood mantels, and unsafe hearths.

Fireplace walls should be not less than 8 inches thick, and if built of stone or hollow masonry units, not less than 12 inches thick. The faces of all walls exposed to fire should be lined with firebrick or other suitable fire-resistive material. When the lining consists of 4 inches of firebrick, such lining thickness may be included in the required minimum thickness of the wall.

The fireplace hearth should be constructed of brick, stone, tile, or similar incombustible material and should be supported on a fireproof slab or on a brick arch. The hearth should extend at least 20 inches beyond the chimney breast and not less than 12 inches beyond each side of the fireplace opening

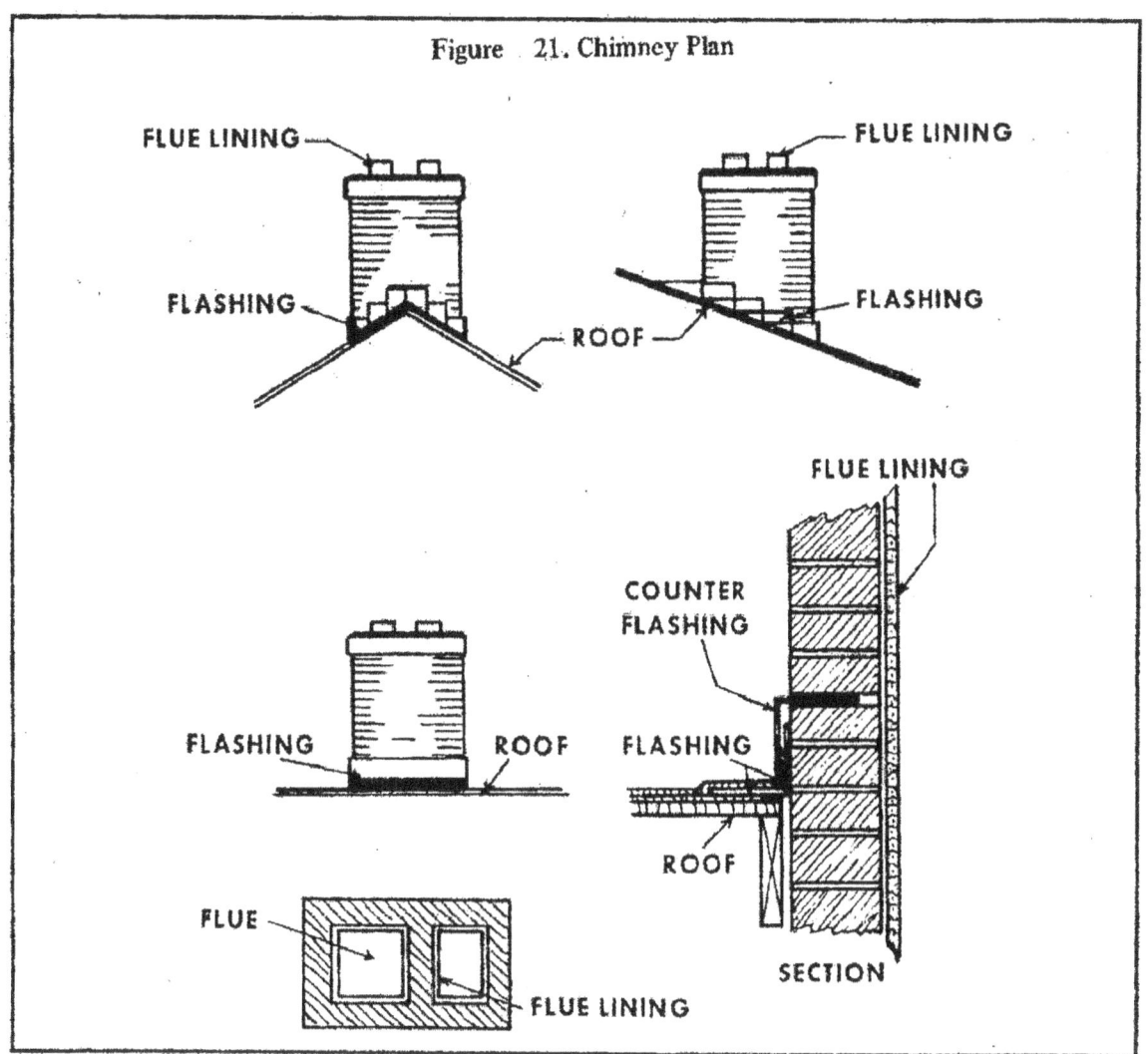

Figure 21. Chimney Plan

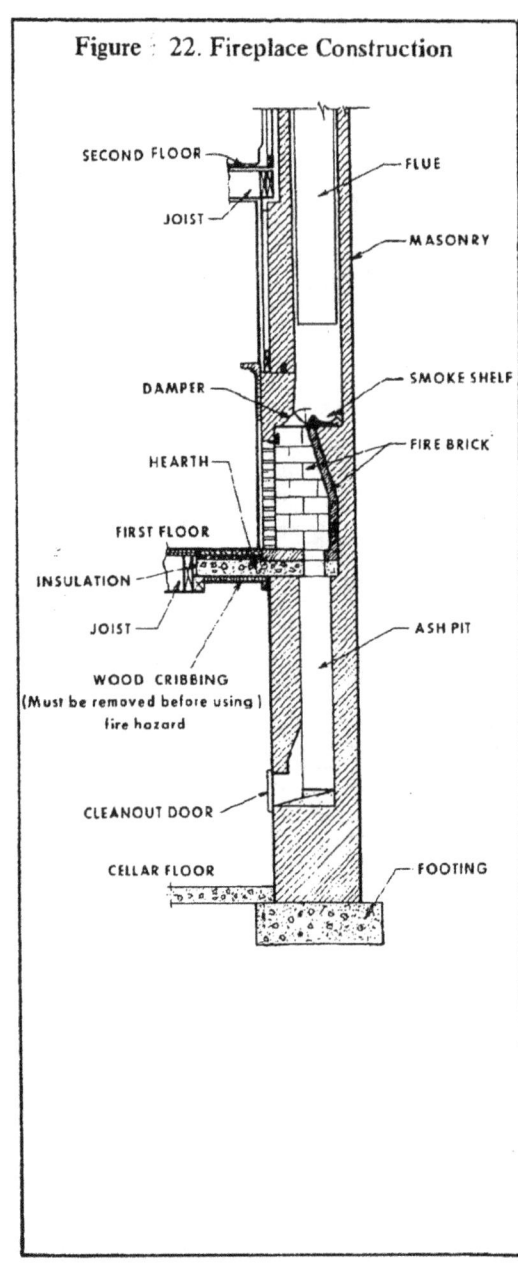

Figure 22. Fireplace Construction

along the chimney breast. The combined thickness of the hearth and its supporting construction should be not less than 6 inches at any point.

It is important that all wooden beams, joists, and studs are set off from the fireplace and chimney so that there is not less than 2 inches of clearance between the wood members and the sidewalls of the fireplace or chimney and not less than 4 inches of clearance between wood members and the back wall of the fireplace.

The housing inspector is a very important person in maintaining sound, safe, and healthful community growth. This should be a challenge to every inspector to provide himself with the necessary tools for better and more efficient housing inspection. He must develop the extra senses so necessary in spotting and correcting faults. He must know when to refer and to whom the referral is to be made; he must be continually seeking knowledge, which may be found by consulting with technicians, tradesmen, and professionals. No finer satisfaction can be realized than to know and feel that the security, safety, and comfort of each and every family within your community has a better and more healthful life because of that extra bit of knowledge you have imparted. "An inspector who stops learning today is uneducated tomorrow."

www.ingramcontent.com/pod-product-compliance
Lightning Source LLC
Chambersburg PA
CBHW081809300426
44116CB00014B/2293